Young PATRIOTS

THE REMARKABLE STORY OF TWO MEN, THEIR IMPOSSIBLE PLAN, AND THE REVOLUTION THAT CREATED THE CONSTITUTION

CHARLES CERAMI

SOURCEBOOKS, INC.®
NAPERVILLE, ILLINOIS

Published by Sourcebooks, Inc.
P.O. Box 4410, Naperville, Illinois 60567-4410
(630) 961-3900
FAX: (630) 961-2168
www.sourcebooks.com

Library of Congress Cataloging-in-Publication Data

Cerami, Charles A.
  The young patriots : the remarkable story of two men, their impossible
plan, and the revolution that created the Constitution / Charles A. Cerami.
       p. cm.
  Includes index and bibliographical references.
  (alk. paper)
  1. United States--Politics and government--1783-1789. 2. United States.
Constitution. 3. Hamilton, Alexander, 1757-1804. 4. Madison, James,
1751-1836. 5. Statesmen--United States--Biography. 6.
Revolutionaries--United States--Biography. 7. Constitutional
history--United States. I. Title.

E303.C38 2005
973.4'092'2--dc22

                                                                2005003154

Printed and bound in the United States of America
QW   10 9 8 7 6 5 4 3 2 1

For Victoria and Huck,
with confidence that the
Young Patriots would approve.

TABLE OF CONTENTS

AUTHOR TO READER

One night, I hoisted an old family copy of a massive 1,246 page volume called *Constitution of the United States of America*, published by the U.S. Government Printing Office in 1938. Because I have owned or borrowed numerous books on the subject, I had not opened this one for at least twenty years. But now it seemed like an old friend, and for all its weight, I opened it in the rather careless way that one flips a bedside book. I had barely turned the first few pages when I realized that I was near the end of the Constitution itself. In that massive volume, the key document occupies only seventeen pages, and only thirty-four if the Bill of Rights and other amendments are added. The other 1,212 pages refer to interpretations written over the generations. I realized once again how sublimely simple are the few pages that guide our nation, perhaps the greatest social and political document created by man.

But how did this happen, I wondered. The creation of the Constitution was masterminded by James Madison, a young man in his thirties who still lived sparingly on an allowance from his father. It was written by Gouverneur Morris, a wealthier young man who had the nerve to be a playboy despite his wooden leg. He had long been known for cleverness, but not for the sagacity that came forth every time he took the floor during the Constitutional Convention. And its fate had depended on an even younger politician who shattered one meeting with a speech that almost declared, "We cannot trust the American people." Alexander Hamilton left Philadelphia after that, then returned because George Washington pleaded with him to do so.

Madison and Hamilton are the odd couple of American history. Their relationship featured a series of bitter ends and reunions. The Constitution would never have been created without the one nor ratified without the other.

As for Washington himself, he too was deeply displeased with the American people for having seemed to show themselves incapable of self-government. He had to be prodded to attend the Convention. Now he was presiding over it, but mainly keeping order—saying few words, thanking James Madison for allowing him to "peep behind the curtain," and later writing to his old friend Lafayette that "the reception of this is not for me to decide, nor shall I say anything for or against it."

If peeping behind the curtain and finding the source of the magic could entice Washington, it struck me as a worthy aim. I wanted to discover how these men who were so full of doubt—hoping for a document that might give the nation ten good years, at best—could have taken the risk of creating laws that were feared, but that would last over two centuries. In the course of tiresome, maddeningly hot days, a new realization of what this country could be seized them—a rare turn at a time when the United States was secondary in the minds of most Americans. Nearly all of the country's four million people were attached primarily to their own states.

The city of Philadelphia itself played a role. Its size, beauty, and elegance reminded the fifty-five men who attended these meetings of what the whole nation could aspire to become. More than the refinement of streets and squares, they saw here humane principles that were not only ahead of *their* time, but in some aspects of human relations and treatment of lawbreakers, were also ahead of *our* time. Newly reminded of what America could mean to the entire world, these delegates steeled themselves to establish a permanent union of the thirteen disparate states, even knowing that they would win more blame than praise. Some could not stand the terrible pressure of making compromises they abhorred. Others could not face going back and admitting that they had agreed to arrangements their neighbors would detest. But four out of every five delegates came to see that this bitter battle over ideas would determine the life or death of a country and a system that had already become a beacon of hope for so many of the world's people.

In the end, it was youth who saw America as indispensable and would not let it die. Some of the leaders were barely thirty years old. And the two oldest men there happened to ally themselves with these younger delegates, for Benjamin Franklin and Roger Sherman had the most flexible minds of all. They would consider any compromise, so long as it moved toward agreement. And it was Franklin who, just as when he discovered the true nature of lightning, knew that he might be witnessing another principle that would outlast the moment. Chiding the doubters to "overlook their own infallibility," he gave that deliciously pragmatic reason for signing: "Because I expect no better, and I am not sure that it is not the best."

Charles A. Cerami
Washington, D.C.

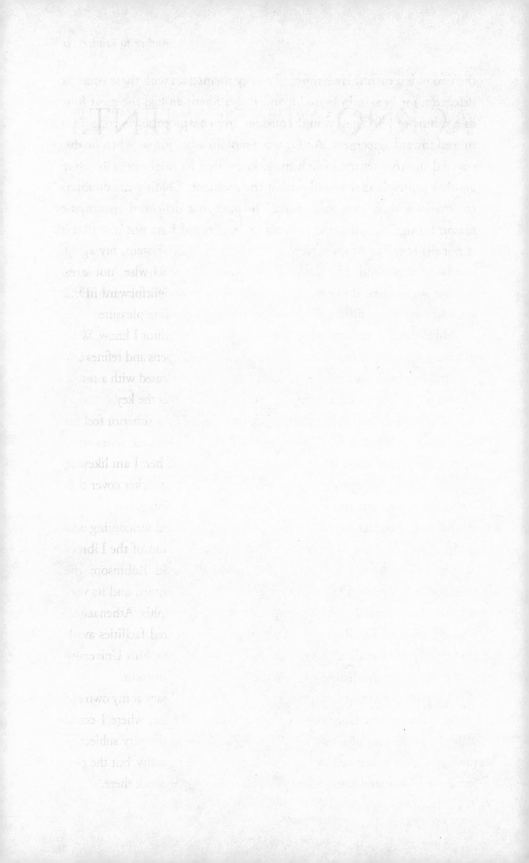

ACKNOWLEDGMENTS

My first words of thanks are reserved for Bob Silverstein, my agent and longtime friend. His counsel always strikes me as wise, not only because we so often think alike, but because he is straightforward in the few cases where we differ. Working with him is a genuine pleasure.

Hillel Black is, to begin with, the hardest working editor I know. With this energy he combines a sensitivity for words that sharpens and refines any page that has been touched by his pencil. When I am pleased with a result, I am often obliged to acknowledge that Hillel's touch was the key.

Michelle Schoob's enlightened copyediting showed a superior feel for what I was trying to accomplish, and her handling of source notes went beyond the call of duty. It was a pleasure to work with her. I am likewise grateful to Derek Wegmann for his skillful creation of a jacket cover that captures the conflicts and exaltation of the Young Patriots.

Among the great number of libraries where I found welcoming and helpful hands, I want to mention the Rare Books section of the Library of Congress, where I had fine guidance from David Robinson; the remarkable American Philosophical Society of Philadelphia, and its very helpful chief librarian, Roy Goodman; the Philadelphia Athenaeum, whose president, Dr. Roger W. Moss, made its treasured facilities available to me; and the Eisenhower Library at the Johns Hopkins University in Baltimore, an invaluable addition to a respected institution.

A special word must be reserved for the Lauinger Library at my own old school, Georgetown University's school of foreign service, where I could walk the better part of a mile while seeing volumes on the very subject of my research on either side of me. Not only the sheer quantity, but the perfect arrangement and care of the shelves make it a joy to work there.

I am grateful to Ms. Ellen Clark of the Society of the Cincinnati for helping to clarify George Washington's baffling relationship with the group.

And my thanks also go to Mr. Dustin Smith, librarian of the Masonic Temple, Alexandria, Virginia, for taking time to verify points that figure in this book and particularly James Madison's connections with Freemasonry.

My daughter, Victoria Huckenpahler, is both an expert copy reader and a favorite in-house critic. The reading job we do together is inevitably brightened by looking forward to our well-planned lunchtime breaks.

My dearest friend, Mary Ann Gale, is unbelievably patient while hearing my complaints about the infinite number of elusive and sometimes contradictory facts that have to be sought and sifted. She has developed exactly the right touch for minimizing these problems without making light of them. I wonder how any book can be completed without the presence of an expert in "damage control."

Chapter One

LESS THAN A NATION

B y 1786, five years after George Washington's victory over the British, the American people had lost their way. They were flushed with early success, but desperately unsure of how to hold the Union together.

The memory of how the revolutionaries, with the aid of the French fleet, had trapped Cornwallis quickened the heart. The feeling of liberty still seemed a miracle. In the treaty of peace, the British, keenly anxious to detach their old colonies from the French and perhaps even to win some of them back, had been astonishingly generous. They gave the Americans all the land they asked for, which was double what they actually expected. Instead of the Adirondacks and Appalachians as boundaries, all the lands that stretched to the Mississippi River were theirs, and that great river was to be America's western boundary. "If we are not a happy people, it will be our own fault," said John Jay, just after his abrupt decision to go to London on a solo diplomatic mission helped to hasten these decisions.

Meanwhile, the French, manipulated by the sly suggestions Benjamin Franklin had made years earlier, tried to retain America's favor with grants of cash that King Louis's treasury could scarcely afford.

Along with these favorable omens, a heavy influx of immigrants was heartening. At the middle of the century, before any thought of independence, the total population from Georgia to Maine is believed to have been slightly over one million white inhabitants. Despite the war, this number had almost quadrupled to nearly four million by the mid 1780s. Arrivals at the rate of over a half-million per decade showed no sign of abating. But the pattern of growth was mixed with troubling talk about the near-collapse of the old Articles of Confederation, which were supposed to keep the states together.

While numerous distinguished Americans were wondering how to strengthen those Articles, two much younger men were the unlikely team that dreamed of creating a new American Revolution. Averaging little more than thirty years of age between them, James Madison and Alexander Hamilton were ahead of all others in seeing that this old pseudo-government had to be destroyed in order to allow a true nation to develop.

The Articles had been drawn up in 1777 to enable the thirteen colonies to fight a war together, but the Congress they created was intentionally made weak because the determination to keep any federal government from taking full control and blotting out "states' rights" was an emotionally charged issue. Many reveled in the term "sovereign state," even though historians have questioned whether the word "sovereignty" ever really applied to states that did not control their own foreign affairs. During the Revolutionary War and for several years after that, it was the Continental Congress that loosely directed the foreign policy and commerce of the United States, once having as many as twelve American commercial agents in Europe.

Even before independence was declared, this Congress, on March 3, 1776, sent one of its members, Silas Deane, to France to scout for ways to secure financial advantages and perhaps even military assistance. Knowing that the English would be opposed to such signs of independence, Deane made attempts to be secretive that were often clumsy and humorous: he gave himself the name Jones as a disguise, wrote letters in invisible ink, and declared that he would use only the French language whenever English people were near. France's foreign minister, Count de

Vergennes, had such a low opinion of Deane's French that he said, "This Deane must be the most silent man in France, for I defy him to say six consecutive words in French."

The comic-opera approach, however, turned out to be quite effective as it attracted the attention of France's playwright, Pierre Augustin de Beaumarchais, creator of *The Barber of Seville* and *The Marriage of Figaro*. This genius, who was also a leading inventor and pioneer watchmaker, was a power at court. He made sure that Vergennes saw the wisdom of helping to humiliate Great Britain by detaching her finest colonies, and this laid the groundwork for Benjamin Franklin's much more adroit theatrical touches in dealing with the French. Franklin discarded his wig, substituted a fur cap, and made himself seem the embodiment of Jean-Jacques Rousseau's ideal simplicity. In Franklin's own words, "Figure me in your mind...very plainly dressed, wearing my thin, gray, straight hair, that peeps out under my only coiffure, a fine fur cap, which comes down my forehead almost to my spectacles. Think how this must appear among the powdered heads of Paris!" While taking blasé Paris by storm, Franklin brilliantly maneuvered the willing Vergennes into arranging the cash advances and military assistance that made America's liberation possible.

It was not long after his arrival that the practical side of Franklin's performance was made apparent by a shipment of 8,750 pairs of shoes, 3,600 blankets, 164 brass cannon, 37,000 light muskets, 11,000 grenades, 4,000 tents, and more.

On February 6, 1778, Franklin and two assistants signed a treaty of amity and commerce with France—the first official recognition of the new nation by a foreign government. Meanwhile, the British prime minister, Lord North, tardily trying to salvage England's empire, startled Parliament by announcing that he would consider concessions to the rebellious Americans, and he had these conciliation bills approved on March 9, 1778. Edward Gibbon, the great English historian who was then a member of Parliament, summed up the situation when he said, "The two greatest countries of Europe are fairly running a race for the favor of America." The French won, for they had already offered the

Americans everything Britain held out—plus total independence. It could also be said that France lost, for just as the great finance minister, Anne Robert Jacques Turgot, warned Louis XVI, the costs of supporting the American cause would mean ruin for the French treasury.

Vergennes once said, "Relations between nations should never be governed by gratitude." But the French never stopped looking for American gratitude, though they seldom got it from the Continental Congress, because the latter was aware that French help was given as part of their anti-British strategy. The American people, however, ignored the smattering of complaints about having aligned themselves with monarchy. Instead, they rejoiced over the national status they acquired through their first formal alliance with a foreign power.

Yet, throughout the war and the five years that followed, each American state clung to the feeling that it was virtually a small independent nation. That is what "freedom" meant to most Americans—being free to stay as they were, with just enough cohesion among states to scare off any foreign threats. But now far more complaints than cooperation existed between the states; deadly in-fighting that felt more like old European behavior than modern American ways. Some saw a looming possibility that the "United States" might no longer deserve that name, even that they might have to break into two or three separate groups.

Historians have differed about just how bad conditions had become within each of the thirteen states at that moment in the mid 1780s. In Virginia and states to the south, crime was rising as population soared. More violence was added by masters' abuse of slaves and by the desperation of slaves who escaped or were freed with nowhere to go. New England experienced less violence, for there were not as many slaves and the influence of patriarchal families created more stability and authority.

But countrywide, it could be said that the general uneasiness over disorder and crime was offset by a sense of expansion and glimpses of increasing prosperity. America's rate of growth was a phenomenon never seen before, although some questioned whether a collection of thirteen partner states could experience a successful future while they constantly disagreed and refused to support a properly functioning treasury. However well individual states were doing, a great many thinking Americans believed the country—as a union—was about to tear itself apart.

George Washington was one of the country's most disappointed citizens. By nature a businessman (a developer), he knew that a prime way of increasing the value of property was to open the states to easier access by building roads or canals that linked them with population centers or supply sources. Before the war, he had a dream of constructing a better road into the more than thirty thousand acres of western lands that he had patiently accumulated over several years. With the fighting over, he quickly turned back to this dormant idea, for as a private citizen he had the right to invest and deal. Thomas Jefferson contributed the enticing idea of opening several rivers to greater traffic—the Potomac, of course, but also the James, and perhaps even the Hudson—telling his friend James Madison, "General Washington has the Potomac much at heart. I am of the opinion he would accept the direction [of such a plan] as long as the money should be employed on the Potomac. The popularity of his name would carry it through the assembly." Getting Washington's support was a favorite way to invigorate any plan.

But things that seemed simple, such as moving manageable amounts of earth, turned out to be like moving mountains. What was really immovable was the very thing Washington feared: the small-mindedness of local leaders who wanted to hold fast to their little piece of the continent. And Washington's attempts to get backing by the Congress foundered, even over costs that would have been relatively trifling. He was depressed not just over the failure of a project, but also because he saw for the first time how little the praise that had been heaped on him was really worth. Disgustedly, he wrote to a group of individuals who had proposed to work with him on land development: "From the present juvenile state of the country, the abundance of land, the scarcity of laborers, and the want of resources, I say from these and many other circumstances it appears to me that this is too early a day for accomplishing such great undertakings."

Even when the beloved Marquis de Lafayette came to visit America and brought back the vision of old times by saying, "Yes, my Dear General, before the month of June is over, you will see a vessel coming up the Potomac, and out of that vessel will your friend jump," Washington feared he would be pulled away by a forced trip to his western lands, where he was losing money because tenants refused to pay rent.

The reunion with Lafayette worked out splendidly because the Marquis was as magically personable as ever; kissing the General on both cheeks, kissing Martha's hands, tossing the grandchildren in the air. Everywhere he went in America, he was received as the greatest friend of all, and each person, high and low, felt that this delightful nobleman's love for them gave a new affirmation of how great they were.

But when Washington wrote to "My dear Marquis" on December 8, 1784, he could not express the joyous emotions that marked Lafayette's visit. "In the moment of our separation upon the road as I travelled and every hour since, I felt all that love, respect, and attachment for you...I often asked myself as our carriages distanced, whether that was the last sight I ever should have of you. And though I wished to say no, my fears answered yes." That was the mood into which this secretly tenderhearted man of only fifty-two years had fallen.

Europeans, meanwhile, hardly noticed what a divided world America had become. They had a different and glamorous impression. And because they saw a glowing general picture, rather than the transitory flaws, their perception had a certain validity.

The people of Europe heard reports of how any individual could become rich in America. Studies have shown that sudden wealth was not as common as people believed. Long-established families actually prospered most because they owned gold and other solid assets they could use to buy the bargains that were created by war and the property left by the fleeing Tories. But popular tales in Europe described a new form of human being that Americans called the "self-made man," and these stories spread from person to person.

In a more serious way, European companies were delighted with orders they received from the growing American market and probably had no idea that the same Americans who traded so actively with them were engaging in sharp practices to steal business from their American neighbors. The states were in constant competition, but they all appeared as suppliers and customers to the Europeans. Even foreign bankers, especially the British and Dutch, were often eager to lend to some of the states (which behaved better with these moneymen than they did among themselves). Perhaps, too, the foreigners saw more clearly than the locals, who were too close for clarity, that every month brought reports of great numbers of new people sailing to America. And the surprise was that most of the new arrivals found work. The rate of absorption and assimilation seemed, from a distance, to be beyond anything ever known before.

When that many newcomers appear, nature's logic normally decrees that they will start to produce—or die. In much of the world, such an influx would indeed have meant death. But in America, the active and willing ones quickly found places to work. The jobs were lowly, but they taught basic facts about what was expected of an employee. Within months, some of these newcomers were teaching simple skills to the latest arrivals, passing on what they had learned so that people at all levels were earning enough to become modest customers, encouraging nearby shopkeepers to expand their space and carry more goods.

New and typically American commercial methods were evolving. European merchants usually put high prices on their wares and held them until customers met those demands. In contrast, American merchants gladly parted with their inventory at lower mark-ups and simply ordered more. This affected the customer's side of the equation. Tempted by the goods and the prices, they became the forerunners of The American Shopper—acquiring a habit that would enlarge to world-changing proportions.

Incredibly, Americans were expanding business even though they had no real currency of their own and had to make do with a variety of foreign coins and a mass of nearly worthless paper money. By the mid 1780s, they were buying far more goods than they had acquired just ten years earlier, beginning to surpass Europeans in home conveniences.

Only about two hundred thousand residents were classified as urban at this time, not much more than 5 percent of the population. But for those city dwellers, the wish for comfort brought improved heating devices, while ice cutting and the first simple iceboxes began to change food-buying habits. City folk were also purchasing carpets and colorful prints for the walls. Although the much greater mass of country people still lived on sand-covered floors surrounded by bare walls, some heard about the city ways and began to copy them in simple form. Buying chairs became a craze; in both rural and city areas, a remarkable number, plain or fancy, were widely used because they combined comfort and decoration.

Many families that once made such comforts themselves were now acquiring furniture and basic housewares ready-made. Clothing too, which had mostly been made by family members, was now often bought in finished form, thus inspiring bright entrepreneurs to hire workers who produced such products in growing numbers. Other alert merchants soon began to purchase them in wholesale quantities, then hitch up horses and wagons to take them for sale through the countryside.

Some of the newcomers who had the courage to be self-employed but not enough capital to start a shop became peddlers. Their rolling carts, as well as all their pockets, were filled with knives, scissors, needles, thread, thimbles, balls to amuse children, and games to amuse their parents. They worked wherever they found people gathered and for as long as there was daylight.

Ten-hour workdays that continued into the candle-lit nighttime left few leisure hours. But now that many of their belongings were bought ready-made, more people could find the time to read at home. Even where literacy was primitive, just good enough to pick out a word at a time, country stores began to carry a few books—a simple reader, a primer of arithmetic, a book of home recipes, a religious volume—in addition to the mandatory almanac.

There were enough well-to-do people to import European and Oriental goods, which sometimes had wondrous repercussions. The Ellicotts, a great Maryland family who introduced new industries near Baltimore with laborsaving devices, imported every major new book published abroad and often loaned volumes to a black tobacco farmer named Benjamin Banneker. This man of genius startled George Washington when he became the assistant surveyor of the new capital city of Washington, D.C., in 1790, having learned from Gibson's *Treatise of Practical Surveying*, judged to be the best book on the subject. The untutored black man also taught himself astronomy from two borrowed books, and one of his intuited theories concerned the existence of the planets beyond the solar system circling the stars—one hundred fifty years before extra-solar planets were confirmed by modern science. A number of other American intellectuals also purchased as many foreign books as they could afford. Thomas Jefferson's spending on works purchased abroad helped plunge him into lifelong debt.

The brisk American buying of many other imports helped make Europeans think of Americans as gloriously rich. The extent of this perception can be judged from the fact that in 1802, just a few years later, Robert Livingston, President Jefferson's somewhat unruly ambassador in Paris, tried to pique Napoleon Bonaparte's interest in a deal for Louisiana by suggesting that France might win favored access to the American market for her "wines, cheeses, silks, and other delicacies." Livingston had no authority to propose new American trade policies, but the fact that Napoleon and his brilliant foreign minister Talleyrand took an interest in the idea indicates how well established the American importation of such products had become.

But the booming industry—eclipsing all others—was travel. "Americans always seem to be going somewhere!" visiting Europeans invariably remarked. A Boston journalist wrote, ungrammatically, "There is more travelling in the United States than in any part of the world." Whereas, in the old country, most people had never been beyond the peal of the parish bell, the readiness of Americans to go from one place to another—for business, for pleasure, or for a permanent change of residence—astonished all who witnessed it. Americans seemed desperately anxious to use all their glorious space, and the expansion this brought demanded a more coherent political life.

People could be seen walking, riding on horseback, traveling in wagons or on stagecoaches—and quickly adapting to each new form of transport as canals and the first steamboats appeared, in advance of the early railroads.

Even the standard mode of travel, the stagecoach, began to improve in speed, reliability, comfort, and especially in the creation of expanding transportation lines. It was still an adventure, requiring agility to climb up to the seat and fortitude to sit on a plain board for many hours. The rough roads caused jouncing that often crushed a man's hat against the ceiling. And male travelers were not infrequently asked to help with emergency repairs. But each year brought improvements—easier ways to climb aboard, better seats, and most of all, speed and reliability—which were being demanded by a growing army of commercial travelers. It took four to six days to travel by stagecoach from Boston to New York in 1786, but this was the very year a determined drive to improve transportation methods began. More reliable vehicles, better supervision of drivers, and more frequent changes of horses would reduce the time to a day and a half in the next few decades.

This tendency to "get a move on" was so pervasive that many Americans changed residences more frequently. Settlers thought in terms of moving to new plots of land with larger farms that promised richer output. City dwellers, too, regarded frequent changes of address as a regular part of family life. In New York City, where most leases expired on the first of May each year, the date became known as "moving day," when the change to new apartments or new shops would create chaos in the streets. As described by an observant English woman of that day, Frances Trollope, the population seemed to be "flying from the plague, with rich furniture and ragged furniture; carts, wagons, and drays; ropes, canvas, and straw; packers, porters, and draymen" all jumbled together in the streets.

It was entirely understandable that these bustling colonies—each a separate entity—should have had to settle for the loose connections of the Confederation in 1777, when a minimum amount of cohesion in wartime was better than none at all. It has been much less clear why the founders who arrived at the victory of 1781 did not band together to make the term "confederation and perpetual union" something more than an empty phrase. Instead, just as the founders persisted in overlooking the terrible blot of slavery, they ignored the clear problem that states were demonizing each other rather than cooperating. Some states actually subsidized businessmen who waged unfair competition to control lucrative trade. The leaders were all men of property, for the state constitutions made this a requirement for holding public office. Lower property qualifications were applied even for the simple right to vote. Several states were printing their own worthless paper money, causing wild inflation, and their growing cities were falling into increasing disorder. The citizens looked up to the men they knew as leaders, and they doubtless hoped for more order and cooperation. But they were disinclined to pay a great deal more in taxes to make that come true. Hardly anyone welcomed the idea of paying taxes the state would send on to the confederate treasury.

Thoughts about a major move to make the United States into a real nation, to make its government adapt to change just as its many successful businessmen were doing, did exist. But such ideas were mainly in the minds of a small cluster of young men who were holding rather obscure meetings and talking excitedly about changes they hoped to see.

This new breed of political planners looked to James Madison as one of its prime leaders for several years, and more recently the name of Alexander Hamilton appeared. The groups they met with were small, so the two men were not yet celebrated national figures. But their few followers saw them as persons who might gain wider attention for their ambitious ideas. And by this time, the two men themselves were beginning to see how involved they were in each other's ideas. Both were anxious to do great things for mankind, but perhaps by different methods. Especially to Hamilton, this was a puzzle, because for the first time he saw a person whom he felt somehow forced to obey. Not even George Washington produced this feeling of compliance within him, and he wondered whether he should follow the impulse or fight it.

One thing Madison and Hamilton had in common was one superior aspect of leadership; a willingness to propose new ideas. And both men were memorable. No one met either man without thinking each was most unusual—Hamilton the Apollo, Madison the brain. Observant persons, after talking with either of them at length, were known to say,

"That is a most remarkable young man." But they were opposites in every other way—in shape, voice, quickness, frankness, interests, style, method of working, and, most of all, in how they had been educated and prepared for life.

Chapter Two

❖

YOUNG HOPEFULS

M any Americans raised on rural estates became as literate and polished as the displaced young Englishmen they were. A memoir that James Madison wrote about his own earliest days shows an extreme version of this accomplishment. He began with the time, at age eight, when he was taken seventy miles from his Virginia home to a school run by Donald Robertson, who charged notably high fees for training the sons of well-to-do persons.

Although Madison's father was a respected leader in Virginia's Orange County, his estate did not allow for great extravagances. But the elder Madison was proud of his delicate boy who showed a wonderfully quick grasp of everything around him and even a rare amount of good judgment seldom seen in a child. In any accident or encounter that posed a sudden problem, James would often startle his elders by suggesting a good solution. His father was not brilliant, but he was a solid man, clear-headed enough to know that this kind of mind deserved special nurturing.

At Robertson's school, James studied Latin, Greek, French, algebra, geometry, geography, and "miscellaneous literature" for five years. After that he studied at home with a highly qualified teacher who convinced his father that William and Mary College was not the place for James, as it "had become rowdy and debauched." The Madison finances were plundered once more so James could go to Princeton to study with the dynamic Dr. John Witherspoon, a Scot who was building a great reputation as an educator. James became one of the select hundred young men who lived and studied in a single building known as Nassau Hall.

Fine scholar that he was, James was a normal freshman in one respect: his first letter to his father complained that, "Everything costs more than it should, so it is important to realize that my funds might run out sooner than expected." After which he added a practical Madisonian afterthought: "I hope the recent drought has not hurt the crops enough to reduce your income."

Although financial subjects bored him, he knew their importance and forced himself to take an interest. At age fifteen, he ended a long letter to a close young friend, William (Billey) Bradford, "We have a very great scarcity of circulating cash in this colony which has reduced the price of provisions and other commodities more than half. I do not meddle with Politicks, but this Calamity lies so near the heart of every friend of the country that I could not but mention it."

This immersion in practical affairs did not prevent him from taking a lusty interest in the ferocious combat of student societies whose competition sounded close to warfare. Madison was the cofounder of a group called Whigs, indicating a liberal turn of mind. And because he was quite skillful in composing comic poetry, which he did not mind denigrating as "collegiate doggerel," he used this form of ammunition to fire at a conservative group known as Tories. In the summer of 1771, he wrote a verse that was bluntly titled "A Poem Against the Tories."

Of late our muses keen satire drew
and humorous thoughts in vollies flew
Because we took our foes for men
Who might deserve a decent pen.
A gross mistake, with brutes we fight,
and goblins from the realms of night

With lice collected from the beds
Where Spring and Craig lay down their heads.
Sometimes a goat steps on the pump
Which animates old Warford's trunk.

Come noble Whigs, disdain these sons
of screech owls, monkeys, and baboons…
Until this tribe of dunces find
the baseness of their grovelling mind
and skulk within their dens together
where each one's stench will kill his brother.

Spring and Craig were fellow students who were Tories. Archibald Craig later practiced medicine in Albany, New York. John Warford, another Tory, became a Presbyterian minister in Amhel, New Jersey, and later in Salem, New York.

Madison's Whig society was even more inviting because the charming and charismatic Henry Lee, the future Light-Horse Harry of cavalry fame, joined it during his riotous Princeton career. Harry somehow had time for every form of difficult study and every type of merrymaking, always avoiding the ultimate discipline of expulsion. Something Harry wrote later makes it probable that Madison had a part in Harry's nearest brush with disaster. The young men all had telescopes for study purposes, but Dr. Witherspoon found these ingeniously placed on the top floor sleeping quarters. Looking through them, the headmaster saw that they all focused on the distant bedroom of an attractive young woman. "No one was expelled," Harry wrote, "because nearly the whole of my class…is involved. Just a very long sermon on the event."

When two brilliant years at Princeton were behind Madison, he was allowed to spend an extra six months there to top off his learning. Then, as he wrote to his friend Billey Bradford, "I was on the point of determining what profession I would choose and absolutely fixing my choice, which had long been wavering between law and trade! As your sentiments coincided with those of my other friends, I have begun the study of law."

The sentiments Madison referred to included a March 1774 letter from Bradford pointing out that the law could produce a great deal of money. It quoted Samuel Butler:

For what's the worth of anything
But as much money as 'twill bring.

When America's break with England threatened, Madison wrote to Billey Bradford that "I am afraid an insurrection (among the slaves) may and will be promoted by Britain. It is prudent such attempts should be concealed to prevent infection—concealed as well as suppressed." Madison had grown up thinking of slavery as a normal part of life. It was also understandable that he talked about preventing the spread of a slave uprising, for such things could produce deaths on both sides. But Madison quickly grew to despise slavery. Later, he was deeply conflicted by the fact that he was still living on funds partly created by the work of his father's slaves, even though he passionately detested the system and was hoping to see Virginia abandon its status as a slave state. He thought of leaving Virginia and moving to a state that had the fewest slaves. At several points in his career, however, he faced situations in which he compromised with the institution he hated.

Madison had once joined with a group of young men who planned to draw up and publicize a great document filled with all possible arguments for outlawing slavery. But the idea was abandoned because Madison's characteristic calculations told him that they would inevitably lose, thereby helping preserve the institution of slavery. They opted instead to chip away at slavery's hold, state by state, but with little success.

His training soon qualified him to practice law, but after just two weeks spent visiting the law office of a friend, Edmund Randolph, Madison decided against the grubby business of representing clients whose routine affairs held little interest for him. He was fascinated with public law—the study of rights and wrongs on the highest level, which could only be put to practical use by "meddling in Politicks." As the county executive, his father appointed James to several committees, where he was always the youngest member. The several years of seasoning in Virginia's lively state politics included terms in the state legislature, where he began to take firm stands on issues and to gather political friends and enemies.

In 1777, while in his mid twenties and serving in the Virginia House of Delegates, he had lost a bid for reelection because of "the whiskey issue." Madison refused to comply with the custom of setting up barrels of free whiskey for the voters, and they decided to turn against him for his parsimony. As John C. Payne, Madison's brother-in-law, stiffly explained in a note to a friend many years later:

> Previous to the Revolution, the election of county representatives was, as in England, septennial, and it was the usage for candidates to recommend themselves to the voters, not only by personal solic-itation, but by the corrupting influence of spirituous liquors and other treats, having a like tendency. Regarding this as equally incon-sistent with the purity of moral and republican principles, and anx-ious to promote the proper reform, he trusted to the new views of the subject which he hoped would prevail with the people...The consequence was that the election went against him.

It is amusing to find that Madison and Thomas Jefferson, who were fast becoming close friends, were more light-hearted in recalling this experience and joked about the fact that Madison at least had the biggest vote "among the non-alcoholic contingent." But although he lost his seat as a delegate, state leaders who thought highly of him quickly arranged for Madison to be named to the Governor's Council—a nonelective office with considerable influence on practical legislation. He was too young to merit a charge of cronyism, but this did show how different life could be for one who was to the manor born.

These were the years that gave rise to Madison's conviction that a much stronger federal government was needed in order to keep the thir-teen states together as a union. He never thought of himself as a revolu-tionary, but he had already fixed his mind on ways to overthrow a government and create a new one.

He was unknown outside of Virginia and still dependent on his father for support when he moved up to the national level, shyly taking a seat in the Continental Congress in Philadelphia. (This congress is occasionally referred to as the Confederate Congress, but will be called the Continental Congress in this book to avoid confusion with the southern Confederate legislature during the Civil War.) He did not rise to speak for six months. A fellow delegate of no great merit, Thomas Rodney of Delaware, wrote demeaningly of Madison in his diary. But two much wiser observers showed the kind of interest that made Franco–American ties almost as enduring as the "special relationship" with Britain: Louis Otto, who was France's legation secretary, called Madison "a man one must study for a long time in order to make a fair appraisal of him." And the French minister, Chevalier de Luzerne, carefully observed this unprepossessing young man and wondered if he might turn out to be "the man of the soundest judgment in Congress."

Madison was small in stature, "with pale skin like parchment," and a soft, quiet voice—some said squeaky—that was not made for great oratory. The first time he spoke before hundreds of persons, a listener said he rose "as if with a view of expressing some thought that had casually occurred to him, with his hat in his hand and with his notes in his hat; and the warmest excitement of debate was visible in him only by a more or less rapid back-and-forward seesaw motion of his body."

In fairness, Madison's small size, pallor, and frailty have been exaggerated in the way that every prominent person's features are caricatured. He was either five feet, five inches or five feet, six inches tall (accounts differ), which means he was just one or two inches shorter than the average American of his day. But the world would hear that he was called "The Great Little Madison" by his loving wife and would never let go of the image. Madison responded by living to the thenphenomenal age of eighty-five, so his famous ill health seems to have agreed with him.

Although he would make some very effective addresses during his career, he never became an orator. Yet, time after time, when more exciting speakers with a dominating presence finished, Madison's gently uttered remarks made listeners settle in their chairs with a look of antic-ipation and then approval.

Realizing his own limitations, Madison relied on intense preparation to take the place of spontaneity. Critics have pointed to this trait as a weakness. But it can also be seen as a great strength to have known so clearly the ways to make best use of his unusual turn of mind. He is said to have carried separate little notebooks listing the "Vices of the Political System of the United States," the separate traits of "Ancient and Modern Confederacies," and every conceivable example of governmental suc-cesses and failures. The failures should be emphasized, for the study of these did most to bring him success. Those were just the background facts to which he added a battery of his own highly original preparations for the discussion that he expected to face at each day's encounters.

A voracious book reader, Madison asked his friend Thomas Jefferson, then in Paris, to send him any new volume that seemed of interest. To Jefferson, this was a delightful command, leading to a deluge of books that shook Madison's modest—in fact, precarious—finances.

A young black man, Paul Jennings, who worked for Madison in the White House before going to work for Daniel Webster as a free man, later had lavish praise for Madison, saying, "Mr. Madison, I think, was one of the best men that ever lived. I never saw him in a passion."

Not in a passion, perhaps, but his quiet toughness could be aston-ishing. Soon after writing to an Italian friend, Philip Mazzei, that "no description can give you an adequate idea of the barbarity with which the British have conducted the war in the southern states," he confronted the way American towns and villages were being set afire and decided it called for a draconian counterattack. Madison's response was to ask the Congress to issue a manifesto directing field commanders to retaliate by executing enemy officers held as prisoners of war. The startled Congress simply tabled the chilling suggestion.

Almost as fearsome was the vengeance that Madison proposed for the British lieutenant governor of the Detroit settlement, Henry Hamilton. On June 16, 1779, he submitted a report to the Congress, citing a study by Thomas Jefferson, showing that "Hamilton had incited the Indians to perpetrate their accustomed cruelties on the citizens of this area without distinction of age, sex, or condition." He noted that the conduct of British officers throughout the war had been savage and unprecedented among civilized nations. He proposed that the said Henry Hamilton and two accomplices be "put in irons, confined to a dungeon of the public jail...and excluded from all converse except with their keeper." In this case, his words were put into action.

Madison served three years in the Continental Congress, often show-ing himself to have, as the French had guessed, one of the finest minds in that disorganized body. But his time there became hopelessly frustrating and financially ruinous, because salaries to delegates were discontinued. When he stepped down, only the small amounts from his father aug-mented the driblets of money that reached him fitfully as a result of his past service in the Congress. The state of Virginia paid him twenty Span-ish dollars (so designated, since the United States had no currency of its own), which came to have only two cents per dollar in buying power. And the state also allowed him £39,000 in paper currency for expenses; this had a cash value of only £547, which was less than half of his skimp-iest living costs. So this man, whom a few knowing persons had begun to look up to as the chief hope for the creation of a solid nation, was virtu-ally a pauper, living on little more than a schoolboy's allowance.

He was frequently resorting, "with great mortification," to the assis-tance of a Jewish banker named Haym Solomon. This rare individual who died almost penniless in 1785 advanced some seven hundred thou-sand dollars to support Washington's army at a time of desperate need. None of this largesse was ever repaid, in spite of pleas that Washington made to Congress in Solomon's behalf. That young Madison made a unique impression on this remarkable lender is clear from Madison's assertion that "Haym Solomon obstinately rejects all recompense."

Jefferson and George Washington, two men who were normally hard to impress, were other important admirers who figured strongly in Madison's career. As a member of the Congress and also of the Virginia Governor's Council, Madison had daily contacts with Governor Thomas Jefferson that quickly flowered into a great and historic friendship. It was partly based, however, on a dark unhappiness in Jefferson's life that Madison insisted on trying to overcome.

Jefferson had left the governorship under a cloud, mainly caused by very unfair charges of cowardice. A sudden attack by British forces had threatened to capture the totally unprotected governor. Rather than allow himself to become a prisoner, Jefferson promptly fled, which was his only other option. If he deserved blame for anything, it was for having made no defensive preparations after Washington warned him that British attacks in his area were expected. Jefferson had many supporters, but the cruel attacks continued and combined with other issues that made his expiring term seem a failure. Madison was more than just one of the supporters. He badgered Jefferson repeatedly to return to politics. Madison's insistence coincided with the period when Jefferson was about to lose his very dear wife, Martha, to a long and debilitating illness. He may have resented Madison's insistence that he take a part in politics again.

Even more powerfully, Madison and other friends contrived to have Jefferson elected as a delegate to the Continental Congress. He refused to serve. The friends made repeated public statements to praise and support Jefferson. They made another attempt to draw him into the Congress and Jefferson refused again. At one point, Madison complained to Edmund Randolph, who had become Virginia's young governor, that he was impatient with his friend's attitude. It was the bleakest time in Jefferson's entire career. But despite what he must have been suffering from Madison's tenacity, a letter complaining about the horrors of public office that Jefferson wrote to the Marquis de Lafayette included the remark that he was consoled by the friendship of James Madison.

But on November 12, 1782, Madison ran excitedly down the street to tell Randolph that he had just received an express message from the Congress telling him that Jefferson had been appointed minister plenipotentiary with the task of taking part in negotiating the treaty of peace with England. It would take him to France, and it would give him an important hand in the peace settlement that would mean so much to America's future. Madison did not even have to wonder whether Jefferson would accept this post. It was clearly a duty.

A unique and historic friendship had been sealed. When a belittling questioner, in 1809, asked President Thomas Jefferson to comment on the qualities of Secretary of State Madison, he responded, "I have known him from 1779, and from three and thirty years' trial (sic), I can say conscientiously that I do not know in the world a man of purer integrity, more dispassionate, disinterested…nor could I in the whole scope of America and Europe point out an abler head."

Madison, as an officer in the Orange County forces that his father commanded, had only brief contacts with George Washington in the course of arranging cooperative moves, but Washington's great talent as a judge of men made him aware of Madison's remarkable ability to find solutions for problems that baffled others. Poor health forced Madison to abandon uniformed duty, but he was never far from military deliberations, the Congress, or work on the Virginia Governor's Council. Later, on at least two occasions, Madison anticipated and put forward ideas that would add luster to Washington's image in history. It is not known that Madison suggested them to Washington, but he certainly used these thoughts long before Washington did—and then, typically, took no credit for them.

One was Madison's statement to the Continental Congress on June 12, 1783, when he said, "The true interest of these states requires that they should be as little as possible entangled in the politics and controversies of European nations." That, of course, is very closely related to a series of statements in Washington's Farewell Address as president several years later. Of the many phrases Madison crafted for Washington on the subject of avoiding foreign entanglements, this was not the most famous, though perhaps the most striking: "Against the insidious wiles of foreign influence, the jealousy of a free people ought to be constantly awake."

And an "address to the states" written by Madison for the Congress in April of 1783 contained a demand "for the gradual extinction of the $42,000,000 public debt," and strictly ruled out any discrimination among the several classes of creditors. In other words, in order to stress the total reliability of America's word, even a speculator who bought an

American bond very cheaply and held it for a very short time would be paid the full amount, exactly like the long-time holders who paid the full price. This courageous statement on a very contentious subject came to be a firm principle of Washington's as well.

The General, who detested the tugging and hauling of politics, marveled at the way Madison could simplify questions so that long-sought solutions often made a prompt appearance. As a result, Washington was almost always inclined to favor any advice or suggestion advanced by Madison. This inclination of Washington's became so well known that a number of insiders made it a rule to consult Madison first when they wanted something from the General, and would continue to do so into the early years of Washington's presidency.

But even stronger was George Washington's close relationship with Alexander Hamilton. Oddly, Hamilton was another person who, like Madison, benefited from Washington's dislike of paperwork and administrative details, although the two young men were not to meet until they both found themselves in the Continental Congress several years later. They would take great pleasure in learning that they shared a passion for wanting to see the separate states joined in a genuinely united nation. Madison arrived in Congress in 1780 and was already disgusted by the impotent government when the twenty-seven-year-old Hamilton appeared there in 1782. The latter's similar sense of mission and more spirited attitude appealed mightily to Madison, who was then thirty.

With hardly any schooling, Hamilton almost supernaturally acquired a command of two languages, a fine writing style, and an instinctive feel for business principles, political strategies, and ways to settle conflicts. These talents made him so nearly indispensable to Washington that the General overlooked instances when Hamilton was nearly insolent in his insistence on being given more opportunities for combat glory.

Only a little taller than Madison, but heavier-set, muscular, and described as having a sensuous mouth and the golden looks of an Adonis,

Hamilton was born on the Leeward Island of Nevis in the British West Indies in such tawdry circumstances that he was never sure of his own age. He was technically illegitimate because his mother had been unable to obtain a divorce from an abusive first husband before she married a man with a great name and no character. Alexander's shiftless father, James Hamilton, a member of a noble British family, was even less caring about family responsibilities than the first husband, leaving mother and child with no visible support when Alexander was only nine. But the slovenly upbringing, his mother's early death, and his father's desertion did not prevent Alexander from becoming well-spoken in English and French, and literate enough to become a clerk in a trading house at the age of about twelve. This was Beekman & Cruger, an export-import company on St. Croix. With branches on neighboring islands and a general store, the firm bought and sold a huge range of products, from livestock to spare parts for ships.

The boy's innate talent and dedication to reading taught him to write well, and his style later flourished to become both elegant and rivetingly precise. His first surviving letter to his young friend Ned Stevens, composed at the age of twelve, revealed seemingly hopeless ambitions. "I'm no philosopher, you see, and may justly be said to Build Castles in the Air," he told Ned, adding that, "I condemn the grovelling condition of a clerk or the like, to which my fortune, etc., condemns me, and would willingly risk my life, though not my character, to exalt my Station." Then he concluded by saying, "I wish there was a war."

That last bellicose remark was due to the fact that Alexander noticed from his constant reading that times of war often allowed adventurous men to quickly improve their circumstances. In his case, the world began to change in a less martial way when his employer, Nicholas Cruger, fell ill and had to depart for New York to seek urgent surgical treatment. Despairingly, he left Alexander in charge, hoping the boy could at least prevent thefts and huge losses. But the apprentice had absorbed so much knowledge of the complex business that he took over with perfect composure, startling tough seamen and even old sea captains who came to do business with Cruger. They could hardly believe that this child was asking them sharp questions, challenging the quality of their wares or the coins they offered, and setting out his terms for trades they had in mind. When Cruger returned, he found that the business had been run as well and as profitably as before.

More evidence of his brilliance caused Cruger and other island people to arrange for Alexander, probably twenty-one at the time, to travel to the mainland early in 1776, aiming toward a full course of study at Princeton University. Within weeks, he was in New York City, enrolled in King's College (later Columbia University) for a brief period of intensive schooling as a preparation for Princeton. But he was dazzled by the new world opening to him, and suddenly felt a great affinity for the Americans who were preparing to fight for their freedom.

Engaging accounts of Hamilton's talents and character were presented by a distinguished scholar of well over a century ago, Harvard professor John Fiske, speaking from a time that was closer to Hamilton's astonishing life, yet sufficiently removed to put his views in perspective. Fiske gave a series of lectures in the 1880s that attributed Hamilton's "shrewdness and persistence, administrative ability, and taste for abstract reasoning to his descent from a noble Scottish clan, joined to a truly French vivacity and grace from his mother's side." Whether this genetic explanation is correct, other points made by Fiske are historically compelling, such as the fact that Hamilton's genius for organization was so great that in many essential respects, the American government in 1880 was moving along the lines that he was the first to mark out nearly a century earlier.

Along with Hamilton's splendid talents, nothing about him was so remarkable as the early age at which these traits developed and the astonishing speed with which he mastered new subjects. With this, he seemed to move instinctively to take advantage of any opportunity that arose. These combined abilities enabled Hamilton to make an almost uninterrupted leap from the island of Nevis to New York City to the pinnacle of American life as a prominent member of George Washington's staff.

The groundwork for this amazing climb was laid when the young man was about seventeen years old. After barely surviving the worst hurricane in the history of the Leeward Islands in August 1772, he quickly collected his thoughts and sent a serious essay vividly describing his emotions to the local English-language newspaper, the *Royal Danish-American Gazette*. The essay captured everyone's memory of the event so perfectly that "The Hurricane Letter," as it was widely known, became a sensation in the islands. It hastened the resolve of Nicholas Cruger, a Presbyterian clergy-man named Dr. Hugh Knox, and other prominent citizens to arrange for Hamilton to travel to the mainland for the proposed university education. About three years were required to raise the needed funds.

Then, in the course of a few months, a great deal of learning and a series of adventures were heaped onto the young islander, beginning with a brilliant pro-revolution speech he gave at an outdoor meeting in New York. Hamilton also wrote numerous anti-British essays that were often wrongly ascribed to some of the most famous older leaders. And he gathered a great deal of military information imparted by a garrulous new Irish friend named Hercules Mulligan, who passed along a variety of artillery skills he learned while fighting British troops in Ireland.

These adventures climaxed in a daring rescue of Myles Cooper, the King's College president who was a leading Tory and targeted for possi-ble assassination by a gang of angry patriots. Despite his dislike of Cooper's position, Hamilton stood and addressed the crowd long enough to give the marked man a chance to flee from the back of the building. Some accounts have insisted that the nearly doomed educator, seeing Hamilton speaking to the mob, thought he was inciting the attackers, and shouted down, "Don't mind what Hamilton says. He's crazy." In any case, Cooper escaped in his nightgown and thus added to the legend of Hamilton's heroism and invincibility.

The short interlude of preparatory study in New York again altered his life. Because the American desire for independence fired Alexander's martial imagination, it led him to give talks and write articles for New York newspapers. Some were composed in the form of debates in print, and Hamilton's words inevitably overcame the opposing views of distin-guished older individuals. In one case, Hamilton wrote an essay on the correct legal position of rebellious Americans who threatened to fight the British. His opponent, who wrote under a pseudonym, was a leading minister who was destined to become the first bishop of the Episcopal Church in America, but the student won handily. The excitement and the endless possibilities to be found in New York City would stay in his memory and pull him back there after the war.

Meanwhile, Hamilton began to fear that the proposed Princeton studies would impede the quick success that he had in mind. He almost convinced university president Witherspoon to break his own rules and allow Hamilton to complete a course of studies there in half the normal time. But while this plan was under consideration, Hamilton saw that the great decision of 1776 was at hand. He quickly thought of himself as an American and gave up the Princeton education to join the Revolution. His boyhood wish for war had come true.

Breaking off his studies, Hamilton was able to volunteer for General Washington's army with no quibbling about citizenship. Moreover, he was given an officer's rank from the start because of the fluency with which he discussed the artillery skills he had learned from Hercules Mulligan. He signed on as Alexander Hamilton, Captain of Artillery.

In short order, Hamilton's tendency to be noticed came to the fore. Looking even younger than his years, and very often giving the impression that he was lost in thought, the new captain somehow made his men look like models of discipline. And even when ill with the gastric problems that plagued him, he rose to fight whenever the opportunity offered.

One of several accounts of how the exceptionally active young man made the personal acquaintance of General Washington reports that another general noticed the intense way Hamilton was ordering a group of soldiers to attack a simple shoveling job. In any event, one of Washington's officers certainly was taken with the young soldier's great looks and active spirit, and brought him in at a moment when the commanding general was grumbling about the mountain of mail on his desk. It looked quite simple to Hamilton, compared to the detail work he had managed in Mr. Cruger's business, and the desperate General Washington asked him to try his hand at sorting some of the letters. Hamilton did more than sort; he wrote answers so crisp that they astonished Washington.

The young captain was invited to join Washington's personal staff early in 1777, and soon was given his first promotion. In time, Hamilton was authorized to write most responses on his own, signing Washington's name to all but the most important letters, and complaining only about how few military actions he was allowed to take part in. He learned a great deal about military strategy by observing Washington, but also dared to think of improvements that the General might have made. When Washington finally gave him a command, Hamilton did brilliantly. He ended the war as a lieutenant colonel, and it was only Washington's concern about arousing jealousy among senior officers that prevented the rank from being higher.

The brilliant immediacy of Hamilton's responses to almost every situation made Washington regard him more as an equal than he did some of his leading generals. A revealing example of this came after Hamilton heard several high-ranking officers seriously discussing with Washington a plan to kidnap British General Sir Henry Clinton, whom Hamilton considered a bumbler. When they left after discussing ways of accessing the place where Clinton took afternoon naps, Hamilton startled the commanding general by asking, "But Sir, if we did succeed in removing Clinton, would it not be our misfortune, since the British could not find another commander so incompetent to take his place?" The plan went no further.

During his three years as one of Washington's principal aides, Hamilton's thoughts frequently went far beyond his military duties—to foreign policy proposals and especially to fiscal decisions that he thought the country's financial officials should make to stabilize the currency's value. This pointed directly toward the aspect of his career for which he is best remembered—his place as America's first and greatest treasury secretary.

Hamilton's almost immediate rise as a junior officer in Washington's "family" of staff members was the General's good fortune as well. Having someone he trusted to write and sign letters in the commanding general's name saved Washington hours almost every day and relieved his mind of many distractions. It will be seen later that as a lieutenant colonel, Hamilton also carried out delicate missions with the authority to act in Washington's name. But he repeated his demands to Washington for a battle command and got into every action that offered an opportunity, once standing on the shoulders of his own men in order to leap a wall and be first in the attack. And he was one of the twenty-four hundred men who crossed the Delaware with Washington for the famous surprise assault that captured nine hundred Hessians at Trenton on December 25, 1776.

Some who knew Hamilton spoke of his effervescence, and of a sentimental attitude that seemed almost feminine. His expressions of sympathy on hearing of a family loss or a child's illness were said to be more like a woman's reaction. This has caused an interest in some of his same-sex friendships that could have contained a romantic element. One of these was with a young officer named John Laurens, who joined Washington's staff and soon became an inseparable friend of Hamilton's. Another was the handsome nineteen-year-old Marquis de Lafayette. In both cases, the word "love" was used freely in notes that were exchanged, but it should be noted that the Marquis also wrote to his wife, "Among the General's aides-de-camp is a young man whom I love very much." Rather than reaching for a conclusion on the basis of an earlier century's use of language, it is more compelling to conclude that he was not homosexual because he was strongly attracted to many women, had a very happy marriage, and fathered numerous children.

In the course of the years, writings about Hamilton have allowed unfortunate parts of his personal life to obscure the fact that his was probably the most brilliant mind among America's early great men. "Surely not more than Jefferson?" some will challenge. But it is at least arguable that while Jefferson was more inquisitive about more subjects, Hamilton probed deeper and proposed more precise solutions.

It happened that an unusually passionate nature interfered in Hamilton's behavior, blurring some of his better judgment. His occasionally emotional responses had passed off harmlessly when, barely into his teen-age years, the precocious boy sent an island newspaper a charming poem that foretold his active libido by describing "a capricious mistress." It must have stunned the adults on Nevis and St. Croix who were anxious to help in this needy child's education, but the easy ways of the Caribbean islands saved him from losing his benefactors. It was more serious when, as a major official of the United States government, he not only had a widely publicized affair with a married woman but then reunited with her after it appeared that she maliciously betrayed him.

Several of his fellow members of George Washington's original cabinet seriously wondered whether his great talents were enough to make them tolerate his flawed judgment. It is not clear whether they realized that his eccentrically forgiving nature extended beyond sexual interests. Acting on behalf of General Washington, Colonel Hamilton was a firsthand observer of the Benedict Arnold affair, and he suffered profoundly from the approaching execution of Major John Andre, the unfortunate go-between. He so regretted the personable Andre's plight as a convicted spy that he argued with Washington about the decision to hang this intermediary. Hamilton wrote a daring anonymous letter to British General Clinton, unsuccessfully suggesting that Andre be traded for Benedict Arnold. To a friend he wrote, "Poor Andre suffers today. Everything that is amiable, in virtue, in fortitude, in delicate sentiment, and accomplished manners pleads for him. But hard-hearted policy calls for a sacrifice. He must die."

Hamilton was even more stricken by sympathy for the turncoat's wife, Peggy Arnold, and her child, writing of her "sweetness of beauty and loveliness of innocence," and wishing that he "were her brother in order to have the right to defend her honor." In truth, she had known about her husband's plan of treason and had approved the idea.

Just below the level of wide public notice, these two rare personalities—Madison and Hamilton—held America's future in their hands. Meeting in popular inns or in informal dinner discussions, they and a few like-minded young Americans took up hard questions, focusing mainly on ways to convince the states that they must contribute tax money if they wished to belong to a nation that could command security and respect. Where Madison relied on his perfect preparations to address these groups, Hamilton was all spontaneity. Even the general agreement that it was unwise to speak out about changing the form of government was a penance to Hamilton. Speaking his mind on any subject came quite naturally to him.

∞

The political half-life they lived was disheartening work for all the men who circled around these two leading figures, mainly because the turnouts at scheduled meetings were usually disappointing. Sometimes half or more of the men who had agreed months prior to attend a gathering would fail to come, pleading financial problems or warnings from superiors in their states that such activities would be dangerous for their careers.

Ideas for a possible union among the colonies surfaced at earlier times, but without gaining much attention. Those, too, came mainly from young people who envisioned greater opportunities in a land with wider horizons than any single colony afforded. And even then, older men with stronger political voices, such as New York's durable George Clinton, Virginia's bombastic Patrick Henry, and Pennsylvania's highly respected doctors Benjamin Rush and William Shippen, suppressed the notion. So the normal, youthful desire for change was a regular feature of the American scene, both before and after the Revolutionary War. But the hesitation or outright opposition by their seniors was not entirely explainable as a typical characteristic of the aging process.

Why leaders who still seemed to be active and vital men were so reluctant to sanction any change in a visibly failing system was, in fact, something of a mystery. Others wondered about it. James Madison was doing more. He sent Thomas Jefferson two anonymous articles, obviously his own, that had appeared on September 17 and October 8, 1783, in the *Pennsylvania Journal*, saying that he was "leaving the author to your conjectures," which was a standard way of avoiding disclosure in case the politically catastrophic words fell into unfriendly hands.

The real Madison, shielded by anonymity, demanded,

Why, at an era so awful and so critical, are the civil institutions of America cursed with the impotence of old age, when they should enjoy the vigor of youth? Why do the horrors of anarchy and domestic confusion threaten to follow the dissolution of the British bond? Ambition, and the desire to exalt communities, is the explanation.

Unhappily then for America, the separate sovereignties of our respective states have left these principles to act with a force but feebly restrained by the weak barrier of a nominal union.

The article, whose shy author had never brought himself to talk this way before an audience, ended with a pledge to "Liberty! The band of patriots who are here thy votaries will instill this holy truth into the infant minds of their children, even as the divine aphorisms of religion, and teach them to hold it sacred…that the SAFETY OF AMERICA will be found in her Union."

Chapter Three

A MATTER OF CLASS

One explanation for America's failure to make itself a cohesive nation as soon as the Revolutionary War ended is that the leaders who might have achieved this goal did not trust their own people enough to put such power into the hands of a single national government. Other reasons played a part, such as the simple wish of some state governments to hold on to power and their fear that larger states might undermine them in matters of trade, water supplies, or boundary claims. There was also the dislike of double taxation that would surely result if strong federal and state governments coexisted. But none of those reasons were as basic and pervasive as the almost unmentionable subject of class.

The country that has always prided itself on being free of social class distinctions was, in fact, composed of a small and elite upper class that was almost as far removed from the large, crude, coarse lower class as it was from the slaves. The founders and nearly all the leaders who were made into instant majors and colonels in order to fight the Revolutionary War were, at heart, English gentlemen who had been schooled by tutors and made to understand the great lessons of ancient history. Regardless of inherited qualities or inborn mental abilities, the performance gap between persons who knew the lessons of the past and those who never even heard of them was bound to be substantial.

Over 90 percent of all workers were simple farmers, hard-working tillers of the soil. And since there was no compulsory education, it was remarkable that so many of those, and so many unschooled factory workers, were at least literate. But among the men, wrestling and fisticuffs, rather than formal duels, were frequent ways to settle neighborly disagreements. The favorite amusements—which they would walk many miles to see on a Sunday afternoon—were bloody cockfights or setting packs of dogs against larger but chained adversaries. There were laws against gamblers and gamesters, but hardly any enforcement.

None of this was specifically related to the lack of a national government, but it was a sign of why the elder statesmen were less interested in making rules for the common people than they were in military or diplomatic affairs. They didn't really expect national laws that might be voted into place democratically by such citizens would be worthy of respect, wise enough to guide the nation, or likely to endure, so they had no incentive to create such a system.

It will become increasingly apparent that Madison did not share this distrust of the people, even though his own background was patrician and, in fact, he was intellectually farther removed from the ordinary American than most of his peers. But although he was well aware of the shortcomings Americans might have as individuals, he was convinced that their collective voice would make choices tending to move a nation in the right direction. This one man's lifelong dedication to a principle that most others only half-believed is astonishing. That Madison turned out to be right certainly is an historic achievement.

In opposition, most upper-class Americans felt it was difficult enough for a state government to maintain a semblance of order and unthinkable that the masses who inhabited the thirteen states should produce anything but chaos. If one big government were workable, they must have thought, the Articles of Confederation would have performed well. If the simple, loose Articles were not working, did it not show that these people lacked the will to govern themselves properly?

Talk about truly uniting the colonies, if anyone dared to try, would not have meant starting from scratch. The idea had been discussed for over twenty years. It predated the Articles of Confederation and the Revolutionary War. The idea of breaking away from England dated back to 1763, when the long war between Great Britain and France ended French power in America. The colonists sensed that they were less dependent on England for protection from the French, but an odd bit of timing had a two-edged effect: the Americans' feeling of "freedom from the French menace" occurred just when the British thought the grateful colonists should be willing to contribute more money to the expensive business of protecting them. The mother country also had the unwelcome idea of asking the colonies to pay for and house a special force of British troops to "protect the colonies against the Indians" (which the Americans thought they could do for themselves). Prime Minister George Grenville had massive problems because of a huge public debt, the result of the war against France. Since he felt that the war was fought partly to protect the colonies, he believed they should have been bearing more of the costs. And even if this was a belated idea, he saw no reason for the Americans to object.

Grenville's ill-fated plan also included, among other annoyances, a new Sugar Act that would have prohibited the profitable smuggling that some of the colonies were conducting with the French and Dutch West Indies. The furious opposition to this new decree came especially from Boston, and it might have stayed with the Massachusetts colony but for a self-defeating decision by the British ministry. On March 22, 1765, Grenville added the Stamp Act, which decreed that official papers— everything from court documents to school diplomas—had to bear British government stamps in order to be legal. By requiring all the colonies to pay this new form of tax, Grenville gave all thirteen colonies a stake in the Massachusetts affair. In this way, a minister in London did more to unite the colonies than anyone ever had done before.

This British mistake brought on the first joint meeting of nine of the thirteen colonies—it was actually given the dignity of being called a "Congress"—and this Stamp Act Congress met in New York on October 7,

1765, at the very time that the young and unknown Patrick Henry was declaring words of warlike defiance in Virginia. The Stamp Act congressmen were more statesmanlike, and their eighteen days of meetings brought a much more moderate declaration to the king that actually led to the repeal of the Stamp Act and a brief period of discretion in both Boston and London.

But a succession of indignities kept frustrating the Americans. Some were trivial but escalated into fighting words. For example, the British general Thomas Gage, commander of all British forces in North America, insisted on housing his officers in New York's most comfortable quarters and pressured the state's governor to make the New York Assembly cooperate or dissolve the body. This led to some of Samuel Adams's most inspired public agitations, as he put together a multi-colony organization to spread anti-British indignation widely. But even more effective in expanding the resistance was the fact that George Mason, a liberal Virginian and a friend of George Washington, persuaded the Virginia House of Burgesses to join the cause by adopting assertive resolutions. The spread of American anger and frustration was leading toward 1776 and rebellion.

An early display of unity came when delegates from twelve colonies (all except Georgia) met in Philadelphia on May 24, 1774, to protest a series of what they deemed "Coercive Acts" that the British had made against Massachusetts. To signify that much of the continent was represented, the delegates collectively called themselves the First Continental Congress. A year later, on May 19, 1775, John Adams took the lead in urging the colonies to stand together, and the remarkable Second Continental Congress met in Philadelphia. This was the supposedly temporary body that would be America's overall government for the next thirteen years. And its early accomplishments were dramatic.

Before even agreeing on its operating rules, this Congress declared the independence of the colonies in 1776, then went on to raise a Continental army, contract an alliance with France, borrow great sums of money by giving lenders the impression of a determination to repay the loans, and build a small navy. Under emergency conditions, the Second Continental Congress asked John Dickinson of Pennsylvania to write suggestions for ways the colonies could operate as a united group of independent states. On November 15, 1777, it adopted a version of his rules, calling them the Articles of Confederation and Perpetual Union. Those Articles were not ratified until March 1, 1781, when the war was near its end, and it was only on this date that the nation could formally be called the United States of America, although the descriptive term "United States" had been used for years and even appeared in the Declaration of Independence. Moreover, apart from terminology or the lack of ratification, the group managed to muddle through the war as if it were a union by pretending that the Articles were effective in the form of "implied war powers."

The reason for delay in ratification was significant: Maryland was the only state that refused to ratify until certain states—especially Virginia, which appeared to have old rights that stretched across the entire continent—surrendered their exaggerated claims to the distant lands. The fact that ratification was impossible until one stubborn state won its point showed an inherent weakness in the Articles of Confederation: many decisions depended on unanimity, and even for the ordinary business of raising money, at least nine of the thirteen states had to agree. Few measures could be carried by a simple majority. This, in the end, would render the Confederation helpless.

The most positive aspect of the Articles, as Harvard professor John Fiske put it a century later, was that "the freemen of each state were entitled to all the privileges and immunities of freemen in all the other states...In all the common business relations of life, the man of New Hampshire could deal with the man of Georgia on an equal footing before the law. But this was almost the only effectively cohesive provision in the whole instrument."

The Articles contained nearly every ingredient for eventual failure. They began by speaking of "perpetual Union between the States," but Article II quickly warned that, "Each State retains its sovereignty, freedom, and independence."

Almost every other stipulation had the same negative aspect—to protect the equal sovereignty of every state, regardless of size. In short, to protect the state against the encroachments of the Confederation itself. No state was to be represented in the Congress by less than two members; no state, whatever its population, could cast more than one vote on any issue. No person could be a delegate for more than three years out of every six. The states, in order to make it clear that they were self-governing, would not allow their own delegates to be paid by the Congress; they would pay their salaries themselves (but seldom did so). The Congress assembled on the first Monday of November each year, and it could adjourn for as long as six months. There was a president of the Congress, but this position proved purely honorific. He had no more power than any other delegate, so there was no executive whatsoever. And there was no fixed meeting place. The Congress often met in Philadelphia, but sometimes in New York, New Jersey, Delaware, or Annapolis.

The treatment of foreign affairs and military matters was somewhat more normal. The states were expressly forbidden to keep any military or naval force, except militia, an exception that was often abused. They could not enter into any treaty or alliance, either with a foreign power or among themselves, without the consent of Congress. And no state could engage in a war, except for the purpose of defense against a sudden Native American attack.

Congress had the sole right of determining questions of peace or war, of sending ambassadors, of making treaties, of managing Indian affairs, and of regulating the value of coins and standards of weights and measures. Congress also was given charge of the post office, but was not allowed to raise any more revenue than the minimum that would cover the cost of the service.

Raising revenue of any kind was, in fact, banned. The fundamental power of taxation belonged to the states alone, and they eagerly grasped this authority—often levying direct taxes on citizens and laying duties on both exports and imports in accordance with their local interests. But the national government could not raise money by direct taxes, excise taxes, or customs duties. Every form of taxation—the fundamental source of funds that nourish governments—was strictly forbidden to Congress. It could make requisitions on the states in proportion to the assessed value of their real estate, but there was no power to make the states obey. They seldom did, so bankruptcy was the clear destination of the national government.

Only the political leaders of the states could have made even a preliminary move toward correcting this unhealthy condition. The citizens who made up most of the populace looked up to their local leaders with a certain amount of awe, and—since street-corner speeches were a principal medium for providing political information—they might have followed their lead if they had heard oratory that called for just a little more orderly cooperation with neighboring states or a little more effort to support the nation's treasury. When, instead, they heard too many of the speakers brashly proclaim why they would not be lectured by the high and mighty officials of New York or Philadelphia and why their state would not hand over the people's hard-earned tax money for the use of the Confederate Treasury, the street corner would inevitably resound to cries of "Hear! Hear!"

Without the right to tax and collect funds for necessary public works there was, in fact, no national government. It was simply a group of neighbors who once found reason to cooperate—acceptably, if haltingly—during the stressful war years, but whose incentive had now vanished. The absence of war was killing the Union.

While the colonies had agreed to unite against a common enemy, they were not ready to merge in other ways. The Articles of Confederation, created under emergency conditions in 1777, showed again how tempted the states were, even in the midst of war, to take only partial and tentative steps toward partnership rather than moving to actual unification. The fact that each state had a single vote offended the great majority of the Union's population, for it angered Virginians or Pennsylvanians to know that their large numbers could sometimes be frustrated by the far fewer residents of Delaware or Rhode Island. And this numerical irresponsibility was raised to near chaos by the fact that states were free to produce wild inflation by creating their own paper money at will. In fairness, nearly all the states were desperately short of hard money, but the resort to paper money made it worse.

Adding to the almost sovereign separateness of these states was the fact that they tried to, and often did, borrow money individually from European sources, that nine of the states had set up their own small navies in defiance of the rules, and that all the states considered their militias to be state armies.

One of the few positive things one could say about the Confederation was that in a handful of superficial ways, the United States did have some of the attributes of nationhood. It had a national citizenship, meaning that anyone living within its boundaries could be called an American, rather than a Virginian or North Carolinian. If an individual traveled from state to state, he would usually be considered a fellow countryman, not a visiting foreigner. And if he went abroad or was sent abroad as a diplomat, he would be received as an American. But while words and names can sometimes be powerful in themselves, they do not compare to economic and political power. And in those areas, the national status had very little significance.

After the fighting ended in 1781, General Washington had held his troops together on the Hudson River until the peace treaty made the victory certain in 1783. But he was as anxious as any other soldier to go home, and as soon as he granted his men furloughs equivalent to a full discharge, he was happily off to Mount Vernon. It was a miracle that the flimsy Articles of Confederation held the Union together that long, for the states had already begun to quarrel more—mainly in their competition with each other for business with the outside world.

No man ever had more right to retire than Washington did. His neatly handwritten memorandum to the comptroller of the Treasury showed that he spent $64,315 of his private funds during the war. He was reimbursed for this outlay, but declined to take any pay for his services. On every side, he was hearing words like those that French ambassador Luzerne wrote to Paris: "It will be useless for him to try to hide himself and live the life of a private man; he will always be the first citizen of the United States."

Yet Washington's wish to be freed from the shackles of power was genuine. He told Martha that he did not mean to leave her for any more public service, and he had business ventures in mind that were his best hope of recouping the heavy wartime losses that had cut the value of his estate in half. To Lafayette, with whom he was always frank, he wrote, "I have not only retired from all public employments, but I am retiring within myself, and shall be able to view the solitary walk and tread the paths of private life with heartfelt satisfaction."

The very thing for which Washington was now most admired—returning home at the height of his glory, like the Roman Cincinnatus—meant the victorious nation would be rudderless. If the commander-in-chief did not feel it right to turn his military power to political power, who else should consider it?

As it was, even the fact that Washington followed the great Roman's example caused him a temporary problem. His closest friend, General Henry Knox, helped to set up a "Society of the Cincinnati" for retired officers of the Continental army, and Washington agreed to become its president general. But it was divided into separate state chapters, and some of these chapters began to make membership hereditary, so that those officers and their descendants were the only persons allowed to join. It became even more aristocratic when only one son in each generation could join, just as a British nobleman could only pass on his title to a first son or an eldest surviving son.

Though uncomfortable with this decision, General Washington overlooked it for a time until there was a storm of criticism from individuals who suspected a plot to turn the country into a monarchy with a hereditary aristocracy. Before long, Washington sent all the chapters a statement explaining his suggestions for the organization's future and virtually demanding that the hereditary feature be eliminated as a condition of his remaining in office. Various chapters reacted in different ways (which has resulted in a variety of garbled accounts), but the hereditary feature was unofficially phased out for the remainder of Washington's life. The public assumed that the hereditary rule had really been eliminated and stopped being concerned about it.

With good humor, Henry Knox, who usually wrote pompously about the organization, once chided General Baron Friedrich Wilhelm von Steuben, who won great affection while instilling new discipline into Washington's tattered army. Von Steuben was an early official of the Cincinnati, and Knox now wrote, pretending to criticize him for inflicting his elegant foreign title on the organization: "Your society, monsieur Baron, has occasioned great jealousies among the good people of New England…who say it was formed by foreign allegiance… You see how much you have to answer for by the introduction of your European distinctions."

The good-natured von Steuben replied with even more garbled witticisms: "A ça, Monsieur le Cincinnatus! Your pernicious designs are then unveiled. You wish to introduce dukes and peers into our republic? No, my lord; no, your Grace; that will not do; there is a Cassius even more far-sighted than this German baron…When I tell him that the young Marquis Henry Knox is already promised in marriage to a Princess Hyder Ali…that the King of Spain wishes to accept the place of Treasurer of the Order, then Blow Ye the Trumpet in Zion!"

The most surprising thing about this banter is that von Steuben could be chided at all, since all his titles had long been exposed as totally false. No one had checked his claims to nobility and to a major general's rank in the Prussian army of Frederick the Great. His willingness to volunteer at no pay and to dispense with any rank in order to avoid creating resentment seemed a godsend because he appeared capable of imparting much-needed discipline and military science to Washington's tattered recruits. He accomplished a real miracle. Despite having no knowledge of English, he worked with his secretary, Pierre Etienne Duponceau, to translate German into French. Then he had an American, Benjamin English, work with Alexander Hamilton to translate the French into English.

Among other surprising points, the manual prescribed behavior by officers that would make them "beloved by their men." The German's good humor enabled him to make the men submit to new ways that seemed far beyond them—cleaning their rusty rifles, standing at reasonably good military posture, even submitting to frequent inspections of their tents and proving that they aired the bedding. Above all, their behavior during battle became almost exemplary.

When a rumor about the falseness of von Steuben's background circulated, he quickly confessed to Washington. He was a poor parson's son, not the least bit noble. He had been in the Prussian army—as a major, not a major general. By this time, however, he was indispensable, and, as the manual prescribed, he had made himself beloved by everybody up to the commanding general. Washington made him an honest man by asking the Continental Congress to name him a major general, and also nominated him to fill the empty post of inspector general of the army. The rare good humor that all Washington's staff managed to maintain under the worst circumstances survived after the war to make the Cincinnati society precious to them.

Von Steuben reminded them of fun times even when they were in tattered clothes and nearly starving at Valley Forge in the vicious winter of 1777. He recalled the merriment of a dinner where "no one wearing a whole pair of breeches" was admitted, and he called those men his "sans-culottes."*

General Washington's wish for a private life could have come true only if someone sufficiently capable carried out four powerful injunctions that Washington himself wrote to the governors of all the states on June 8, 1783, when he was about to disband his army. "First," Washington declared, "there must be an indissoluble union of all the states under a single federal government, which must possess the power of enforcing its decrees, for without such authority it would be a government only in name."

In this letter, which he wished to be regarded as his legacy to the American people, he went on to urge that the war debts incurred by the Congress should be "paid to the uttermost farthing," the militia system must be

---

*George Washington continued to be president general of the group until his death—at which point most state chapters of the Society of the Cincinnati became hereditary again. It lost many members as the original officers died off, but there was a surprising revival when the surge of immigration made many Americans wish to prove their more established ties to the nation. They searched their family trees for evidence of links that went back a few generations, the organization grew more liberal about interpreting heredity, and membership climbed to its current healthy—and prestigious—state. Even the French Cincinnati, a group that had been destroyed by the guillotinings of the Revolution, was reconstituted.

uniformly organized throughout the thirteen states, and the people must be willing to sacrifice local interests to the common good, discarding local prejudices and regarding one another as fellow citizens of a common country, "with interests in the deepest and truest sense identical."

There have been suggestions that this letter, far from being a legacy, was a bid for such broad public acceptance that he would be swept into a new role as a political leader. The falseness of such ideas is shown not only by letters like the one to John Jay, quoted following, but by the many proofs that Washington's exceptional self-knowledge made him aware of his distaste for politics.

As a youth, Washington kept a book of rules for self-improvement. There were one hundred ten entries—all the way from table manners to business discussions with other men—and they show a personality that focused on straightforward ways to use his strengths and avoid weaknesses. Even as an acclaimed national hero, he knew of a weak point in public speaking that had to be compensated for by careful advance preparation. In the same way, he knew and was quick to acknowledge his great reliance on men like Madison and Hamilton for guidance in political matters. The legacy letter was just what he said it was—a wise set of basic rules that he hoped others would carry forward.

And the levelheaded Washington was also aware that bruised feelings had a part in making him even more averse to an active role in public life. He realized that the adulation he received was not accompanied by any sign that this adoring crowd planned to heed the points he made so forcefully. He remembered with embarrassment how a contingent of young girls and women in long white gowns met him near Trenton, New Jersey, and threw flower petals at the foot of his horse while singing a long poem that ended with:

> Virgins fair to matrons grave
> These thy conquering arm did save
> Build for thee triumphal bowers
> Strew ye fair his way with flowers
> Strew your hero's way with flowers.

They spread flowers in his path, but their fathers and husbands clearly scorned his idea that they should "sacrifice local interests and discard local prejudices."

In May of 1786, he bluntly wrote to Henry Knox what he thought of those who did not accept his views: "The discerning part of the community have long since seen the necessity of giving adequate powers to Congress for national purposes, and the ignorant and designing must yield to it ere long."

But his views were being ignored, and on August 1 of the same year, Washington let his resentment show in a letter to John Jay, a leading American diplomat who was to become the first chief justice of the Supreme Court. Disdaining any further role in government, he wrote, "It is not my business to embark again on a sea of troubles; nor do I suppose I would have much influence with my countrymen, who know my sentiments and have neglected them."

Noted observers in America and abroad had even harsher views of the new country's prospects. An Englishman, Josiah Tucker, Dean of Gloucester, who was considered a far-sighted man and who had no ill will toward the young nation, said,

> As to the future grandeur of America, and its being a rising empire under one hand, whether republican or monarchical, it is one of the idlest and most visionary notions that was ever conceived even by writers of romance…They never can be united into one compact empire under any species of government whatever; a disunited people till the end of time, suspicious and distrustful of each other, they will be divided and subdivided into little commonwealths or principalities, according to natural boundaries.

The pessimistic forecasts, often using the terms democracy and republic loosely, did not refer to any precise electoral formula. Any government in which the people hold the ruling power, either directly or through elected representatives, can be called a democracy. A republic is the specific type of democracy in which all the citizens entitled to vote delegate their supreme power to their elected representatives. Those who were pessimistic of America's prospects were not finding fault with the character of Americans, but simply believed they were scattered over too great an area to keep in close enough touch with a capital city for effective democratic government. Nearly all observers pointed out that only tiny states like Venice, Switzerland, or Holland could exist as republics. Some thought an area as large as America might have a hope of surviving by becoming a monarchy, so that decisions made in a capital city would be honored even by distant citizens as a matter of respect.

On the other hand, the usually tough-minded Thomas Paine took an overly optimistic view when he heard that the peace negotiations had been concluded and the army disbanded. He rejoiced with the words, "The times that tried men's souls are over." Allowing for the celebratory spirit of the moment, this claim seems to fall far short of Paine's earlier acute judgment. An end to trials was never in sight, but he might have said that a time worth waiting for was coming into view.

Chapter Four

A REBELLION
PAYS OFF

A postwar business slump that came after the peace treaty of 1783 proved to be an alarm bell that signaled the need for a new government. But the political response to an economic turn is often slow. In this case, it took three years for the right people to sense the danger that lack of a real government was causing.

The slump's first effect was to sour the country's mood, and to make the states further reduce their payments into the federal treasury. Only Pennsylvania was paying a substantial part of its assessment now. The Confederation was nearly bankrupt. Madison was surprised at the apparent disinterest of the people. In good times or bad, it appeared, the great majority of Americans esteemed their state far above their country. Compared to one's home state, the unknown quantity called "national government" had almost no magnetic attraction for most Americans. Their leaders did not want to lift their states onto a broader national stage, and the people apparently had no wish to see any such elevation.

This attitude was promoted not only by governors, but also by state legislators who, as political speakers, were as closely followed as theatrical personalities later came to be. Many had the great personal influence that long familiarity brings, and they used this aggressively to defend their own status quo. They valued their prominence as local leaders too much to risk gambling on some new political scheme that might make them expendable.

Individuals with great ambition might have thought differently, reasoning that their own opportunities could be greatly enhanced by having a thirteen-state area in which to develop careers. But there were probably few who thought this out for themselves. Only after expansion actually occurred would many of those "self-made men" that America was said to be producing learn to think in this larger way.

Madison, having left the Continental Congress in 1783, was an example of how even the brightest might find himself at loose ends. Highly qualified as he was, highly skilled in the more elevated forms of law, he made a good enough impression on some of his elders to be offered several high positions in the Congress. In each case, he declined the offer, saying that he felt himself unqualified for the honor, although his real reason was a distaste for the hopelessness of the work. So with limited funds but ample time, he read and wrote prodigiously, always arrived a day or two early for meetings, and then waited and studied while wondering how many others would show up.

Most of the other young men who came were all finely educated and a few even had Madison's own Princeton background and bent for studying the philosophies of Greece and Rome and the famed legal foundations of the British system. Yet, as they saw a decided tilt toward lawlessness, an altered and tougher attitude began to be noticeable among them. The virtual revolution they talked of that would overturn the Confederacy could not put so much emphasis on "the consent of the governed" that it overlooked the need to restrain the governed.

Talk of social compacts in the early days of the Revolution—when several state constitutions were written—was remarkably optimistic about the character that was expected of both citizens and officials. The rules were based on the assumption of a well-behaved citizenry, governable by benevolent and understanding authorities, along lines envisioned in Jean-Jacques Rousseau's 1762 doctrine of the social contract. The experience of just a single decade told perceptive Americans that more restraining forces would be needed to ensure a government that would neither invite corrupt behavior nor become corrupt itself.

Early in 1786, something more exciting than a business slump was afoot—a growing popular fury over a foreign outrage. The terrible acts of the Barbary Pirates, based on the southern shore of the Mediterranean, in capturing American ships, holding the sailors for ransom in filthy pens, and sometimes torturing them caused angry outcries from enough Americans to convey a clear sense of national unity—with no distinction between states. A livelier attitude could be sensed in the news and the talk among delegates to the Congress. Here was an ill wind that created the same irate sensation in every state and made them all feel as one. The dormant feeling of being American showed signs of renewed life.

The pirate states were taking large sums in tribute money from the trading countries and often failing to honor their promises to release ships and crews. The British or the French could have destroyed this menace, but they virtually admitted that the great maritime powers found it useful, for it kept weaker nations from competing for a share of the lucrative shipping trade. Benjamin Franklin described how London merchants were heard to say, "If there were no Algiers, it would be worth England's while to build one." And England's protectionist Lord Sheffield had shamelessly published a pamphlet to that effect. In America, even Congress members began to say that a government that failed to protect the lives and property of its citizens no longer served them and should be discarded.

In March, a Continental congressman from Virginia, William Grayson, said he was speaking for several other Congress members when he told Madison, "I am in no doubt about the weakness of the federal government. If it remains much longer in its present state of imbecility, we shall be one of the most contemptible nations on the face of the Earth."

It would be years before the pirate threat would be put down, beginning with Stephen Decatur's daring move to set a stolen American ship on fire and then blockade Tripoli harbor. The belated creation of a strong American navy was to follow. But long before this, the sense of American unity against all enemies was a force in itself.

Madison already sensed that the winds might be shifting, and he talked repeatedly to George Washington about what might be done to strengthen the Articles of Confederation. Washington said he agreed, as he usually did with Madison's views, but he showed no desire to become personally involved. So Madison employed one of his usual techniques—a slight divergence in a direction that he knew to be a special interest of the other person.

He knew Washington was a keen businessman. The subject of trade as a way to help develop the country was dear to his heart—and especially when the Virginia–Maryland area was involved.

Madison remembered the time when Washington invited a small group composed mainly of Virginia legislators to Mount Vernon to discuss the development of the Potomac River area. On that occasion, he voiced agreement with Samuel Chase, a leading Annapolis businessman who became almost boisterous in demanding that there should be no tolls or other restrictions on trade along the river.

"The truth is that making everything open and free is the way to build this nation," the heavy-set Chase cried, slapping the General's table in a way that guests seldom did. "I'm a merchant, and I can tell you that we only tie our hands when we try to charge fees and duties every time some goods go from here to there. The more we share and trade, the more good fortune we promote for ourselves."

Washington joined in agreement, in effect confirming a new economic theory promulgated in Adam Smith's *The Wealth of Nations*. That groundbreaking work had been published in 1776, the same year the United States Declaration of Independence declared the freedom of a people to choose its own political direction. Smith declared that two trading parties must both be gainers, or otherwise one would have to stop trading. (Smith's work was particularly relevant because he pointed out that the rule could be evaded when dealing with colonies, but only at the cost of great harm to both parties.) General Washington and Samuel Chase had probably not read Smith's work, but their business sense agreed with Adam Smith's destruction of the old notion that achieving a monopoly was the acme of success.

Understanding this view of Washington's, and knowing his great wish to develop the Potomac area, gave Madison an opening. When Madison proposed another meeting of limited scope involving men from Maryland and Virginia, the General reacted positively. Seeing that his interest was aroused, Madison suggested that they might expand the meeting to include Delaware and New Jersey, or perhaps even invite all the colonies, though still limiting the subject to trade alone. Washington was in favor, the meeting was set for Annapolis, and the state legislatures were asked to appoint commissioners who would represent them. The date set was September 11, 1786.

Madison typically arrived three days early at Mann's Tavern, one of the nicest hostelries in Annapolis, to begin gathering his thoughts and papers. But when the meeting date passed and succeeding days came, it was clear that not even Washington's name had spurred interest on the part of the states. Madison and eleven other representatives from only five states (Delaware, New Jersey, New York, Pennsylvania, and Virginia) were on hand. John Dickinson, who authored the Articles of Confederation, was chairman. Also included were Alexander Hamilton; Edmund Randolph, governor of Virginia; and two men from Delaware who would be heard from in the months ahead, George Read and Richard Bassett. But their number seemed far too few in the spacious first-floor room that the tavern provided. Maryland itself, the site of the meeting, had not even bothered to appoint a delegation. No one found it necessary to debate whether a quorum was present, nor whether the event would be called a failure.

Now, however, both Hamilton and Madison rose to the occasion. Hamilton refused to talk of success or failure, but instead proposed that they plan a larger and more comprehensive meeting. They should invite all the states to send substantial delegations to a gathering that would discuss not only trade, but all the aspects of making the Confederate government work more successfully.

There was a stunned silence. Hamilton appeared not to realize the folly of calling for a larger event when this modest meeting had failed, nor did he see that such rashness might end a political career. The lack of interest in substantial change should now be clear. But Hamilton continued confidently, as if the silence of the others signified approval.

Instead of bristling about the younger man's leap forward or slyly reminding him of the risks they would be taking, Madison saw at once that this initiative might be well-timed to concur with the new and more aggressive mood he had been sensing.

He also seemed to believe that this very different mindset of Hamilton's could be an asset to his own plans. "Agree and then diverge" was one of his regular principles for dealing with dissenters. First agree with them, then watch for opportunities to gradually diverge toward a compromise. So now, instead of the expected disagreement, Madison reviewed the details of Hamilton's plan approvingly. But, he pointed out, it was not yet time to propose this meeting to the Continental Congress. That do-nothing Congress was jealous of its prerogatives and might sense danger in the proposal.

But why not prepare a report from the few commissioners who were present at this meeting addressed to the states they represented? Doing so would allay fears by showing that the states were in full control and the delegates were very properly keeping them informed. Then suggest that these five states invite all the other states to join them in sending delegates to a larger meeting in Philadelphia. The country's largest city was an impressive site that usually drew great attendance, for it was a place to see and be seen, with modern attractions—theaters, balls, wax works, elegant shops that featured European finery—and the assurance that many important people would be there. If the states responded well, it would be time to write to the Congress for its approval.

Hamilton saw the merit of these thoughts and willingly drafted the suggested report, presuming to speak for the whole group with some telling words that would eventually lead to the overthrow of an already outworn government. "Your Commissioners," he told the states, "cannot forbear to indulge an expression of their earnest and unanimous wish that speedy measures may be taken to effect a general meeting of the States, in a future Convention, for the same, and such other purposes, as the situation of public affairs may be found to require." Even a suggested date, "the second Monday in May next," was included, and the little group that could not achieve a quorum was on its way to an honored place in history.

What a fine team Hamilton and Madison seemed to make. Together, they turned a failed meeting into an exciting initiative. Fateful September 11 first achieved prominence as the date of what historians know as "The Annapolis Meeting," and the "other purposes" that Hamilton proposed in his report became major steps toward creating a nation.

While the revolutionary report from Annapolis wended its way to the appropriate state officials, other rebellious groups were contributing far more dramatically to the same cause. They were reacting with violence to the wave of hardships caused by the postwar business slump. However trivial or ominous the threat may have been, it roused George Washington to use passionate language that he rarely resorted to, and it undoubtedly helped assure that a great political convention would be held.

A former officer of the Revolutionary War, Daniel Shays, had organized a group of neighboring Massachusetts farmers who, like him, were in danger of losing their farms and even going to prison because the slump combined with bad harvests and heavy state taxes to make it impossible for them to pay their bank debts. Massachusetts was slow to respond to their demand for debt relief, as some of the other states had, and its delay invited dangerous passions. When a previous insurgent leader named Job Shattuck was captured by the state and treated as a criminal, it only inflamed the rebellious farmers. Shays's followers grew to some twelve hundred, and he decided to dramatize the farmers' plight by arming his comrades—with pitchforks for those who had no shotguns. For two months he gave them military drills while threatening to attack the courthouses that conducted bankruptcy actions.

The justices dodged trouble by keeping the courts closed, but the state's Governor Bowdoin wanted action. He raised an army of forty-four hundred men, paid for mainly by wealthy Bostonians because the Massachusetts treasury was without funds. This larger force stamped out the insurgent movement in two pitched battles. There were a few fatalities and the rebels were jailed. Some were given the death penalty, but all were pardoned after a dramatic delay.

Shays's Rebellion was magnified by the fact that similar disturbances had recently occurred in New Hampshire and Vermont, so the likelihood of spreading disorder could not be ignored. In newspapers and on street corners, it was as hotly discussed throughout the states as a major war, which was justified by the pivotal role it played in American history. The rebellious farmers had many sympathizers and the rightness of their cause came to be confirmed by changes in the treatment of debtors, even if the threat of violence was condemned. Shays died in poverty some years later, but he had unwittingly made an important contribution to the future of the United States. The hapless little band reinforced James Madison's program to interest major political personalities in the changes he had been preaching to less influential men.

The admiration of two of the country's most prestigious individuals could now help Madison's cause, but each one had to be managed with special care. His old friend Thomas Jefferson, who once referred to him as "the greatest man in the world," was such a charismatic figure to Americans at all levels that his support, even from a distance, proved powerful and influential. Jefferson, who had long valued every word that Madison spoke, was in Paris as the American envoy, so he could only encourage his younger friend by mail. His extensive correspondence with many of the other men who were destined to be at the Philadelphia convention might well become a positive influence if he chose to send other delegates ideas in support of Madison's positions. Such specifics would be slow to develop. And Madison had to factor in the two months it would take for any letter he might ask Jefferson to contribute to reach some other key delegate in Philadelphia.

A letter Jefferson wrote to Madison on January 30, 1787, typified the wide-ranging nature of their exchange of confidences. While it was not tough enough on Shays to be useful in Madison's endeavor of the moment, its tone gives evidence of how these two closest of friends seldom exchanged letters that failed to be historically significant.

The dozen subjects that this letter took up, ranging from serious to playful, included a report on his own dislocated wrist, a theory on the job status of France's envoy to America, great praise of the Marquis de

Lafayette, his description of a new pocket telescope and walking stick, and the expensive news that he was sending Madison a portable copying machine that he found to be indispensable—and which cost 132 livres, including all its appendages (roughly equal to twenty-two to twenty-six dollars—a considerable amount in that day).

But Jefferson started with:

> I am impatient to learn your sentiments on the late troubles in the Eastern states...This has produced acts absolutely unjustifiable; but I hope they will provoke no severities from their governments...Societies exist under three forms: Without government, as among our Indians. Under governments wherein the will of everyone has a just influence, as is the case in England in a slight degree, and in our states, in a great one. And under governments of force, as is the case in all other monarchies and in most of the republics. To have an idea of the curse of existence under these last, they must be seen.

This subject closed with Jefferson's much-quoted remark, "I hold it that a little rebellion now and then is a good thing and as necessary in the political world as storms in the physical."

Jefferson went on to the first intimations of a subject that he and Madison would jointly make into one of America's most astonishing events sixteen years later—the Louisiana Purchase:

> I feel very differently about another piece of intelligence, to wit, the possibility that the navigation of the Mississippi may be abandoned to Spain...I have had great opportunities of knowing the character of the people who inhabit [the west]. And I will venture to say that it would be an act of separation between the Eastern and Western country...I have the utmost confidence in the honest intentions of those who concur in the measure; but I lament their want of acquaintance with the character of the people who, rightly or wrongly, will suppose their interests sacrificed on this occasion to the contrary interests of that part of the confederacy. If they declare

themselves a separate people, we are incapable of a single effort to retain them.

Madison's other great admirer was General Washington, near at hand and accessible, but hitherto unwilling to become personally involved in public life. Happily retired as the master of an estate in Virginia, Washington enjoyed the obvious admiration of many but he did not in the least miss the pomp of power. He took a great interest in the Potomac River area and talked with other local individuals about wise and broad-minded policies that would encourage growth near his Mount Vernon estate, but his only national interest seemed to be concerned with the eventual selection of a site for the nation's capital city.

Shays's Rebellion, however, brought an instant change of attitude. Washington received direct word about it from General Henry Knox, the Confederation's secretary of war, who had just returned from Massachusetts. The cheerful, three-hundred-pound Knox was one of the few confidants who Washington completely trusted, partly because of Knox's superhuman wartime feat of having once brought forty-two cannon, some weighing over a ton, from Fort Ticonderoga to Dorchester Heights. Few Revolutionary War memories could compare to Knox's ingenuity in assembling a team of carpenters to build forty-two huge wooden sleds to hold the cannon, then finding eighty-four yokes of oxen to drag them over three hundred miles of winter snow. When the British saw all this artillery lined up on the heights that faced them, they promptly quit Boston.

What made Knox's feat more unusual was that it was based on mere book-learning plus exceptional inventiveness. He was a book-seller by profession, and became a self-taught artilleryman by reading some of his own books. Anyone who showed long and steady courage in disheartening times won an unusual level of regard from Washington. If that person struggled to learn a difficult subject on his own, the admiration doubled. This trusted friend now explained how ominous the Shays affair might become if it gave rise to similar behavior in other areas.

"This dreadful situation has alarmed every man of principle and property in New England," Knox wrote to Washington. "They start as from a dream and ask, what has been the cause of our delusion? What is to afford us security against the violence of lawless men? Our government must be braced, changed, or altered to secure our lives and property."

Washington was reminded of all the ideas for action that Madison had given him. Suddenly, he saw how right Madison was. Not even in the dark days when he was commanding half-starved and frozen troops at Valley Forge had the usually taciturn General erupted with so much emotion. Suddenly, he was the one exhorting Madison.

The letter Washington wrote to Madison on November 5, 1786, included these ardent words:

> Let us look to our national character and to things beyond the present period. No morn ever dawned more favorably than ours did; and no day was ever more clouded than the present! Wisdom and good examples are necessary at this time to rescue the political machine from the impending storm. Virginia now has an opportunity, I hope, to take the lead in promoting this great and arduous work. Without some alteration in our political creed, the superstructure we have been seven years raising at the expense of so much blood and treasure must fall. We are fast verging to anarchy and confusion!

It was everything Madison could have wished for. The outline of how a still-unauthorized convention in Philadelphia should be run must have begun to form in his mind as he read Washington's letter, and he surely would have thought that the General could not protest too strongly if his name were inscribed on the list of Virginia delegates who would attend. Before even consulting Washington, Madison already planned the role the General would play there.

The dawn of a new attitude toward union could be sensed, but it was not yet ready for the full light of day. Too many eminent persons had to back down carefully. Men in leadership roles had previously pronounced themselves basically satisfied with the Articles of Confederation when they should have known that a government without a chief executive would be too weak to succeed. Why would anyone have expected, as many Americans pretended to do, that a large congress with no leader would know when important actions should be taken? And the idea that unanimity was required in order to make a decision, so that a single small state could and often did frustrate the will of a dozen other states: how had anyone ever favored such a rule? Some very delicate shifting of positions was in order. Individuals with political instincts were, as always, the kind who began to point these things out as if they had been trying to say them all along.

But the younger men who had, indeed, been trying to say such things were coming to the fore. The quiet, patient Madison was the unquestionable leader, but the rather turbulent and decidedly impatient Alexander Hamilton was well able to make a place for himself in the group, even though George Clinton, the governor of his own state, considered Hamilton a rival to be held at bay.

Madison and Hamilton successfully joined together on several occasions, even when they appeared to possess divergent ideas. Now there was a special need for a concerted effort. The excited group of young political thinkers who were longing for change wanted to push ahead at once with the idea of a great convention in Philadelphia, which would, as the Annapolis meeting had urged, "Bring together enough persons from all the states to make a more substantial review possible." But that would have been highly improper without the consent of the Continental Congress. One could not simply form a new government without asking the old one to agree, for that would mean two governments opposing each other, essentially creating a civil conflict. So the term "review" was carefully stressed to show that this meeting only proposed to consider the need for improvements, not to do away with the old.

This was easy enough to say in a group of twelve or fourteen like-minded young men whose average age was little more than thirty years. But was the Congress not likely to react like a roused old porcupine, turning its usually torpid self into a determined enemy?

The plotters were conscious of their insecure status. They could tell that Madison was doing an expert job of managing the strategy to get them national attention. But Madison was not yet a nationally known figure, and they had no great names such as Adams, Henry, Mason, or Jefferson at the forefront of their movement. Madison promised that Washington would be there, but the General usually remained subdued in political meetings; George Mason, a brilliant Virginian who could have been a great national leader, was always more interested in his family and estates. He had lost his wife and had nine children to raise alone; he might come to Philadelphia but not stay the course. And Franklin, at eighty-one and ailing severely, would be fortunate if he made it at all, even though the convention would take place only a few blocks from his home.

But these insiders may have underestimated their own strength. There were other politically perceptive citizens who told each other what the men who attended the recent small meetings already knew as a fact: an aggressive young leadership was coalescing around the two men. Madison, now thirty-five, already a veteran planner and debater, despite his youth; and Hamilton, some three years Madison's junior, was a man whose years had all been spent at double-time. It was reassuring to see that the pair were on friendly terms at this point and spoke favorably of each other, but those who worked with them were made apprehensive when they noticed that the two so often seemed about to go in diametrically opposite directions on important issues.

A sharp division threatened time and again, but Hamilton somehow seemed a different man when Madison was in the room—quieter, but not entirely content. Madison's placid manner somehow caused Hamilton to look pensive, to seem on the point of speaking, but then to let an objection fade wordlessly. For the moment, at least, they may have been drawn together by the fact that both had serious political problems within their own states, Virginia and New York. These would play a great part in every phase of the Constitution's creation, even extending to the heart-stopping ratification.

Chapter Five

STATES IN DISARRAY

For both Madison and Hamilton, achieving national goals was made doubly difficult by standing on shaky ground in their home states. In 1784, Madison's career became curiously entangled with that of the far more famous Patrick Henry who, after first disdaining this younger Virginian, had grown to detest him as a challenging upstart. Henry was the first American to raise his brilliant oratory against the British ten years before anyone else mentioned the possibility of independence. But as he aged, he developed into a religious zealot.

While serving several brief terms as governor of Virginia, separated by periods of highly successful private law practice, Henry used his political prestige to promote a scheme that Madison considered a move toward the "established" church that existed in New England. Declaring that only Christianity could save the nation from the moral depravity that engulfed it, Henry offered a loosely worded resolution "for the people to pay a moderate tax or contribution annually for the support of the Christian religion or of some Christian church, denomination, or communion of Christians or of some form of Christian worship." Henry insisted that he saw no bigotry in this position, for he was not promoting any single denomination—as though no one could object to the insistence that it must be Christian.

Madison and Jefferson deemed it an embarrassment for Virginia, which was used to being looked up to as the home of great minds, to be planning something they considered a deplorable attempt at "thought control." It was unbearable, they thought, for the great state of Virginia to have such backward legislation when a lesser entity like North Carolina had ruled explicitly that "in the relationship between church and state, there is to be a disestablishment of the Anglican church. No person should be compelled to pay a tax in support of the clergy of any denomination to which he did not belong."

Madison, Jefferson, and the Virginians who looked to them for leadership considered the idea of compelling everyone to support Christianity as an attack on freedom of thought. But there was no Constitution to bar this mingling of church and state at that time, and the Anglican and Presbyterian clergy declared themselves in favor of Henry's proposal, having been seduced by the promise of new and easy money. The House of Delegates put this resolution off until the following year, but by then Henry's eloquence in a series of outdoor speeches appeared likely to carry the day.

Henry had the advantage over any other politician of being able to reach a substantial audience at will. All he had to do was stand on a street corner in Richmond, start a conversation with a few citizens, then gradually raise his clarion voice to enlarge the audience. His ideas were cleverly structured, his pace and meter were captivating, and soon heads would be nodding in excited agreement. If the weather was fair and remained so, Patrick Henry could speak for hours. On this subject, he pointed out—to the satisfaction of the mesmerized crowds—how every dead city named in ancient history could have been saved by Christianity. His powerful oratory seemed so persuasive that Jefferson suggested there was just one pious way to defeat him—"devotedly to pray for his death."

In fact, the soft-spoken Madison found another way. Madison, who was to play so great a part in the architecture of the United States government and then in the doubling of the nation's size with the Louisiana Purchase early in the next century, had been thirty-four years old at the time the verbal duel with Patrick Henry began. While Henry had been a national figure for two decades—since the time that he risked being condemned as a traitor for attacking the Stamp Act and calling for war—Madison's reputation remained within his own state. Even in Virginia he was most often thought of as "Jemmy," the son of a father who had long been respected for splendid management of his estate and firm leadership in Virginia's Orange County. It was known that the senior James Madison had the highest regard for his eldest son, having made him a colonel and second in command of the Orange County militia during the Revolutionary War. Still, this son was hardly a celebrity or even a known quantity who could have been expected to cross swords with Patrick Henry on the latter's favorite subject.

Madison, who normally slept no more than three or four hours each night, was even more profitably wakeful as April 1785 approached. He normally kept a candle lit to allow him to jot down thoughts that might occur at a moment of wakefulness; in this case, a few words he scrawled held the kernel of a perfect idea. His note suggested that if petitions against Henry's bill were suddenly submitted from all parts of the state, the effect might be devastating to the ominous legislation—whereupon he wrote a compelling paper called "Memorial and Remonstrance Against Religious Assessments," gave it to a supporter, exacting a promise that the man would distribute it without changing a word, and had one hundred fifty signatures in the first day.

The statement gave fifteen clear reasons for opposing Henry, written in what Madison called, "the language of the people." It made clear the obvious: that Virginia's state constitution guaranteed every man the right to exercise religion according to his own conscience, and it included a declaration that "rulers who overleap the great barrier which defends the right of the people are tyrants, and those who submit to it are slaves."

These thoughts, with no competition from Henry's seductive voice, allowed Virginians, by simply signing, to send a message they really meant (which may have been just "no new taxes"). An avalanche of these petitions soon cascaded back to Richmond, some bearing a hundred signatures. Henry's proposed measure was dead. The usually undemonstrative

Madison was so delighted that he allowed himself the only boast ever ascribed to him: "I flatter myself," he wrote to Jefferson, "that this has extinguished forever in this country the ambitious hope of making laws for the human mind."

But although his religious initiative was dead, Patrick Henry was far from finished. In 1787, he appeared on every available street corner, talking about the ills of tampering with the Articles of Confederation. In turn, many of his listeners shouted their agreement. It was more than just a grudge against Madison. The great firebrand who was willing to defy a monarchy twenty years earlier had turned ultraconservative in his determination to resist change of any kind. Mercifully, Henry would refuse to join the group going to the convention in Philadelphia, so he would not have an effect on the negotiations until the time came to seek approval of what the coming convention might propose.

Without Henry, the Virginia delegation would consist of seven men who were more or less like-minded; Madison's managerial skill made it relatively easy for him to prevail on contested issues even in spite of the cautious Governor Randolph. He knew, however, that anything he might achieve in Philadelphia would encounter Henry's eloquent opposition when it needed to be ratified by the state of Virginia.

Alexander Hamilton's problem in his home state proved more crippling. The great power of New York state was divided because its longtime governor, George Clinton, was determined to hold fast to the Articles of Confederation, with no revision at all. The reason was a selfish personal one, but politically formidable. Clinton simply feared that any change might dislodge him from his secure position as head of the state, which he had already held for more than ten years. Nonetheless, Hamilton, although even younger than Madison, was forceful enough to have made himself a rising power in New York. His surge from indigent young man to leading New York barrister and socialite (owing to a very advantageous marriage) was so miraculous that it was no wonder he thought he could accomplish anything.

When he returned from the war to civilian life, Hamilton studied law books for three months, passed the New York bar examination, and began to practice, quickly gaining a reputation as a leading lawyer.

Loving challenges as he did, it is not surprising that some of Hamilton's most spectacular cases were either for or against Tories who were involved with lucrative property settlements while being regarded as unsavory persons. As long ago as 1777, as a soldier in Washington's army, Hamilton wrote a letter to the committee of the New York Convention, urging that no halfway course be taken toward individuals who chose to remain loyal to the king. His letter of April 20 read, in part, "I believe it would be in general a good rule either to pardon offenders entirely or to inflict capital and severe punishments. The advice given by a Roman general to his son, when the latter had the Roman army in his power, was very politic: Either destroy enemies entirely or dismiss them with every mark of honor and respect. By the first method, you disable them from being your enemies; by the last, you make them your friends."

In one unusual case, he agreed to take on the markedly unpopular cause of a rich Tory who had strongly opposed the Revolution and who was personally detested by the entire community. This defendant held an estate that had belonged to a very popular widow who fled from it when New York was captured by British General Howe. She was suing for its return, citing the Trespass Act that favored all persons who quit their homes because of enemy action, and it was assumed that no one could possibly find any winning argument to make in the Tory's favor.

Hamilton, however, delightedly agreed to handle the case because he had discovered a much older law that favored the odious defendant, and he would maintain that his client should not be penalized on the basis of public opinion. Hamilton argued brilliantly that both the common law and the law of nations had a firm principle that "immovable properties belong to the captor as long as he remains in actual possession of them." He sympathized with the widow for having "suffered one of the gross instances of wickedness wrought by the war," but he proved that the Trespass Act contravened all established law and must be set aside. Even officials who were infuriated by the Tory's victory and personally angry at Hamilton for having brought it about had to admit the brilliance of his argument.

Within months of becoming a lawyer, he also became an important but virtually impotent political figure, for New York's perennial Governor Clinton found ways to stifle Hamilton's activism. In the course of a few months, the enmity between Hamilton and Clinton became vicious, the attacks going beyond all bounds. Hamilton denounced Clinton as "a man high in office preserving power and emolument to himself at the expense of the Union." Clinton responded with anonymous letters in which he gave Hamilton a foul name and surmised that he was "not only a foreigner, but a quadroon, that is partly black," and ready to do anything for the treacherous people he served.

But Hamilton was not deterred from pressing on with his thriving legal career. He was also thinking of a project that had been in his mind since his military days. He was reading heavily in the field of finance, formulating plans for the new nation's monetary stability, and hoping that his New York political career would at least help to propel him toward a leading government position in the financial field. Hamilton had long felt that financial strength could be one of the principal pillars of American power and influence in the world, and he thought himself the man who could make this happen.

Governor Clinton's influence, he knew, would serve as a roadblock. The governor's sole interest was the preservation of his own position, and he preferred to see the least possible change in New York. Even if Clinton thought at all about the well-being of New York and its people, he would have seen no need for change because he believed that his state, more than any other, could continue and prosper on its own. A number of states had visions of becoming independent nations, but New York alone considered this seriously and thought it could succeed as a totally separate country if need be. Clinton, therefore, felt no pressure to accept the notion that major changes in the shape of the Confederacy were needed. He wanted no changes at all.

To Clinton's distress, one of Hamilton's opposing moves in the New York legislature was to keep calling for a convention to rewrite the state constitution. No one knew what he would put into it because even the outspoken Hamilton had to hide his most far-reaching ideas in deference to the prevailing fear of change among the people. But Clinton's control of a three-man New York delegation that was sent to most meetings gave the governor an automatic way of handcuffing Hamilton. This was demonstrated at one of the preliminary meetings, when the other two men representing New York were Clinton's choices, and their two votes—firmly against any attempt to alter the status quo—effectively cancelled Hamilton's vote.

On February 15, 1787, a final attempt to raise revenue for the Confederation failed, owing to Governor Clinton's opposition. It became clearer than ever that some new approach to rescuing the Union was needed. Five months after the failed Annapolis meeting that stirred so much unexpected activity, its reverberations grew louder with each passing day.

Since the time when the scarcity of support for change seemed to sound the death knell of the United States, an electrifying new attitude had begun to be felt, making it seem that nothing would prove impossible. The proposal of Madison and Hamilton to examine the existing system of government and formulate "a plan for supplying such defects as may be discovered" was being taken seriously. To those who prayed for change, the speed of this seemed too good to be true. And if some were superstitious individuals who expected that such favorable winds or such daredevil navigation foretold rough sailing ahead, they had a point.

In the spirit of the moment, Madison sped to Richmond and persuaded the Virginia legislature to act at once on the Annapolis recommendation. Showing more assertiveness than usual, he helped his entreaties prevail. The Virginia body promptly declared that a delegation would go to Philadelphia and set about selecting the group's makeup. The unaccustomed pressure that Madison applied—sensing a moment when minds might be changing and carefully quoting Washington on the need for action—made his initiative seem prescient.

There was a moment when Washington slowed the pace, for he was reluctant to attend what might be considered an "irregular convention" before the Congress approved of the plan. But judicious reminders about Shays's adventure and the danger of more such uprisings made things move with unaccustomed ease. By late March, New Jersey, Pennsylvania, North Carolina, Delaware, and Georgia had also named delegates. New York led a few other states to hesitate on the ground that such a convention would be working illegally unless the Continental Congress consented. But the answer to that objection was clear.

It was obviously time for the planners to seek the approval of the Continental Congress so that the event in Philadelphia would go forward with as much legitimacy as possible. Strangely, they were heartened by the fact that the Congress had recently taken two rare initiatives—including a rather aggressive one. These signs of life made the usually torpid group seem more approachable because there was more normalcy about it.

First, the Congress heeded Henry Knox's warnings about the dangers threatened by the Shays affair. Knox benefited from his reputation for coolness. If even he saw the country in peril, something clearly must be done. Typically, the Congress did half of something. It called on the states to form a continental military force, without saying what it was to be used for. There were hints that it had something to do with protection against Native Americans, but no one took that seriously. The true enemies— rebellious American farmers—must not be mentioned aloud.

The second action was truly the grand accomplishment of this much-maligned Congress. Like the bad king of whom it was said, "Nothing in this life became him like the leaving of it," the Continental Congress approached its end with rare bravado. This Congress was in control of long-disputed western territories that seemed a problem too deep for resolution for many years. Control of lands to the north and west of the principal area occupied by the thirteen states had been disputed from very early colonial times because old royal charters loosely gave Massachusetts and Connecticut lands "from sea to sea" at a time when the Pacific Ocean was thought to be only half as distant as it really was. This, and similar excessive rights owned by Virginia, created strips of territory right across parts of Pennsylvania, and four states had claim to territory north of the Ohio River.

In 1784, Thomas Jefferson was the guiding spirit who promoted an ordinance that made these disputed western lands national property that could eventually be formed into states when a sufficient population had grown. Immigration was now building in those areas, and in 1787, Congress found a way to turn a problem into an opportunity and also to get real money from this territory. In July, at a committee session where less than usual opposition was present, an ambitious young congressman named Rufus King took control and convinced enough delegates to recommend the Northwest Ordinance. With no precedent to go on and no referendum, it set up rules for the operation of a speculative venture called the Ohio Company and the interim government of the territory. The one-house Congress passed the bill and grandly ordained that this interim government would have a two-house legislature. It specified that there should be division into states when population warranted. Ohio, Indiana, Illinois, Michigan, and Wisconsin would be born as a result.

Madison thought this more spirited old Congress might be more receptive to an announcement that its condition was about to be examined—with its permission, of course. To the astonishment of the young Virginians around him, Madison, who was expected to write the fateful letter himself, asked Hamilton to prepare a draft. It was now evident that Hamilton was becoming a bigger factor in Madison's planning. The latter did not, as most men would have, show irritation at the entry of such an opposite personality into his carefully arranged world. A new facet of Madison's leadership was to take the Hamiltonian manner and abilities into account, then test them as a possible way to energize his own plans.

However, Madison appeared to have miscalculated this time. He must have been thinking that Hamilton's ability to seize the moment might produce an overwhelmingly persuasive argument. Instead, the pugnacious Hamilton wrote a paper that declared "the imperative necessity for a powerful government" that would "cement the union." Such a statement, virtually saying that the Articles of Confederation must be dissolved, hardly seemed like a route to winning approval of the doomed chamber. Madison looked pensive, as if casting about for a comment. Hamilton looked truculent. He was not accustomed to having his brilliant letters greeted with disdain.

Before either of them spoke, Virginia's governor Randolph bristled about the impropriety of such an affront to the Congress. He threatened to quit the delegation.

Madison quickly stepped into the dispute and told Hamilton quietly, "You had better yield to this man. For otherwise, all Virginia will be against you." To everyone's amazement, Madison's steady voice had just the right effect. Hamilton took the letter wordlessly, then rewrote it with such a mild tone—changing "cement" to merely "adjustment of the Federal system"—that all the others said it sounded exactly as if Madison had written it. The effect that Madison and Hamilton had on each other seemed, at that moment, to be positive and supportive to each man's views, adding new thrust to Madison's quiet ways and smoothing Hamilton's excessive combativeness.

The Congress gave its astonishingly prompt approval to the proposed meeting. Some leaders of this old Congress may well have seen the chance that the convention would provide answers that finally gave them real power, or a few may even have expected that a new body would be created—with a place for them.

And so it was decided: on February 21, 1787, the Congress agreed that on the second Monday in May next, less than three months away, a convention would be held in Philadelphia. The approval, however, was "for the sole and express purpose of revising the Articles of Confederation and reporting to Congress and the several legislatures such alterations and provisions therein as shall when agreed to in Congress and confirmed by the States render the Federal Constitution adequate to the exigencies of Government and the preservation of the Union."

Many of the delegates who would be going to Philadelphia did suppose that a revision of the articles was their purpose. Several hoped the changes would go beyond mere revision. One mind was clear on what it wanted. James Madison was training all his mental power on moves to blow away the old Confederation and install a new republican government.

This was also one of the high points in Madison's close relationship with George Washington. The General seemed to be excited about the great political move ahead, and he realized how authoritatively Madison could assess, manage, and even dominate a great enterprise. A letter he wrote to Madison on March 31, 1787, as the planning of the convention intensified, was noteworthy for the humorous strain that Washington rarely adopted, treating Madison as an equal by pretending to apologize for his own failure to write, but begging Madison to write to him even more—and comparing the exchange of letters to the swapping of paper money that was so current a topic.

My Dear Sir,

At the same time that I acknowledge the receipt of your obliging favor of the 21st Ult. from New York, I promise to avail myself of your indulgence of writing only when it is convenient to me. If this should not occasion a relaxation on your part, I shall become very much your debtor—and possibly like others in similar circumstances (when the debt is burdensome) may feel a disposition to…pay you off in depreciated paper, which, being that or nothing, you cannot refuse. You will receive the nominal value, and that you know quiets the conscience and makes all things easy—for the debtors.

Washington then went on to say he was pleased that Congress recommended that the states join in a convention to be held in Philadelphia. Continuing, he said that those who lean to a monarchical government have not consulted the public mind or are living in a region where they find it too easy to forget their level upbringing. He called for a reform of the present system.

Washington also hoped the convention would avoid evasive expedients and probe the defects of the constitution to the bottom, providing radical cures, whether they are agreed to or not. Washington explained this startling statement by saying that many of those who fail to agree will come around to agreeing in due course.

The two vastly different personalities of Washington and Madison are vividly shown when this letter of the General's is compared with a study by Madison, "Vices of the Political System of the United States." Washington had great respect for the man who wrote such a study. He would wisely conclude that such flights of theory were not for him, but were a good reason to have Madison nearby, turning the ideas into practice.

Madison's study opened with the startling thought that he considered one aspect of the Constitution to be even more important than direct election by the people. That is the power of the federal government to negative state laws in all cases whatsoever. (In modern usage, where "negative" is an adjective and not a verb, the word would be "negate.") This, he explains, means giving the federal government the power that was once held by the British king. The United States could not consider itself to be in control of its own territory and inhabitants until that royal power had been replaced. This federal veto, he said, would be the foundation of the new system, making the thirteen states into one indivisible sovereignty. The reason for this conviction on his part, he said, was that the absence of this provision seemed to have been fatal to the ancient confederacies.

Madison's historical studies convinced him that the tendency of federal systems was rather to create anarchy among the members than to produce tyranny in the head. Also, he added, the federal negative would have the happy effect of providing greater security for private and minority rights.

Madison was never satisfied with simple statements that most others might make without supporting them. He pointed out several examples of encroachments on the federal authority that had been going on in America all along: the wars and treaties of Georgia with the Indians, the unlicensed compacts between Virginia and Maryland and between Pennsylvania and New Jersey, and the troops raised and to be supported by Massachusetts. He showed how one state after another had already violated the American treaty with France and the treaty with Holland, which also caused complaints to be made to the Congress. And he listed twelve separate types of "aggressions" by American states against each other, such as a Virginia law restricting foreign vessels in certain ports, New York and Maryland's favoring of vessels belonging to her own citizens, the misuse of paper money, and a new practice of making property into a form of legal tender. Madison said he had proof of all these self-serving acts in his pocket. Presto, what seemed such an exaggerated remark about the federal government's life-and-death need for a certain absolute power became a reasonable statement because it was so thoroughly supported by existing proofs.

But the man with this powerful mind was far from being a cold-blooded conspirator. His mental state was best revealed by a friendly letter dated April 22, 1787, that he sent from New York to Edmund Pendleton, an older man who was president of the Virginia Convention of 1776 and who therefore could commiserate about the tension of such critical events. Madison wrote:

> We are flattered with the prospect of a pretty full and very respectable meeting next month. All the states have made appointments except Conn., Md., and Rd. Island. The last has refused. The absences of one or two states will not materially affect the deliberations. Disagreement among those present is much more likely to embarrass us. The nearer the crisis approaches, the more I tremble for the issue. The necessity of gaining the concurrence of the Convention in some system that will answer the purpose, the subsequent approbation of Congress, and the final sanction of the States, presents a series of chances which would inspire despair in any case where the alternative was less formidable.

All the states except Rhode Island, whose highly negative administration refused to risk any change of government, soon appointed delegations. And George Washington confirmed that he could now officially be considered part of the Virginia delegation. Although reluctant to risk being drawn back into national affairs himself, he was strongly moved to do this by the fear that if he failed to attend the Convention, his countrymen would suspect that he had lost faith in the republican form of government. In any case, it was a hard decision for a happily married man, for Martha reminded him that all her plans for the future were based on his promise that he was leaving public life for good.

Chapter Six

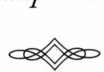

SPRINGTIME IN PHILADELPHIA

Philadelphia was not like any other city in the New World. The thought was exciting to visitors, making them conscious not only of being in the largest American city, with its population of more than forty thousand, but of its varied attractions and its sense of superiority. Some resented its display of community pride, but few denied that it was based on real accomplishment.

Regrettably, James Madison, who had been here many times as a delegate to the Continental Congress, felt no such happy anticipation on this visit. In fact, the memory of a broken romance more than three years earlier made Madison hesitate before writing to tell Mrs. Mary House, who had been his landlady in Philadelphia, that he would be coming to her place again early in May and that he planned a stay of several months. Her comfortable rooms, at 5th and Market Streets, a block from the Convention's meeting place, and her reliable table were costlier than Madison usually allowed himself in other cities, but very definitely worth the price.

It was at Mrs. House's that the thirty-one-year-old Madison met and fallen in love with Catherine Floyd, the exceptionally pretty daughter of

William Floyd, a signer of the Declaration of Independence and a New York delegate to the Congress who was also one of Mrs. House's boarders. Young Kitty was then five months short of her sixteenth birthday, but her parents seemed delighted with the match. Her father, at fifty-three, only two years younger than George Washington, must have viewed Madison, who was some twenty years younger, as an appropriate son-in-law. Madison rode with the Floyds partway when they left for home on April 29, 1783. It was agreed that he would go to their Long Island home for the wedding within a few months.

Jefferson, who had become an important part of Madison's life, had met Kitty and heartily approved of his friend's choice. With typical Jeffersonian brio, he wrote encouraging letters to Madison on this subject (one of them in cipher!). It is also known that Madison and Kitty exchanged one or more letters, with Jefferson's eleven-year-old daughter Martha acting as go-between, and one of these enclosed a copy of a song.

But all this romantic promise vanished in August, when the disappointed suitor sent Jefferson a letter that later became partly illegible. Its one telling sentence is: "The necessity of my visiting the state of New York no longer exists." And it also contains the phrase, "a profession of indifference at what has happened." Madison later recovered this letter (presumably from Jefferson's personal effects), and its impact on him can be judged from the fact that even as an elderly man, he seemed to attach an odd importance to it. Madison inked over parts of the old letter, but did not destroy it. Sources of unproven reliability have said that a separate message from Madison told Jefferson that "it would be improper by this communication to send particular explanations, and perhaps needless to trouble you with them at any time."

Not unnaturally, young Kitty Floyd had decided she preferred a nineteen-year-old medical student to a man twice her age. But it was years before Madison could develop the "state of indifference" that made this change so easy for Kitty. In 1787, not even the drama of traveling to magnificent Philadelphia with a plan to overturn a government could keep him from being distracted by the memory of that rejection.

Friends and colleagues were tempted to ponder why this man who sometimes struck observers as someone entirely involved in matters of the intellect was still, after almost four years, struggling to forget a wisp of a girl who had thought nothing of dropping him. Some have thought his long distress over this setback is evidence of an unusually sensitive nature. Detractors have imagined that Madison was so absorbed by his ability to win whatever he set his mind to that any defeat was abnormally traumatic. Despite the fact that his rising fame made an increasing number of unmarried women look at him with interest, Madison let seven more years slip by without risking any further romance until he met and determinedly wooed the charming twenty-five-year-old Dolley Todd.

In any case, the daunting prospect of coming back to Mrs. House's did not prevent Madison from arriving, as usual, well ahead of everyone else except the local Pennsylvania delegates. He arrived in the first week of May, more than a week before the set date and almost three weeks before a sufficient number of delegates were on hand to start the formal meetings. And whatever his sentimental feelings were, he counted on this city's great attractions to enhance the chances of a successful convention. He suggested Philadelphia as the site because it improved the likelihood of good attendance and of delegates staying the course, in case the meeting dragged on and tempted some to leave for home. It was unusual, of course, to think a nation's fate could hinge on the choice of a popular location, but Madison never overlooked anything that improved the odds.

Remembering his own first visit to Philadelphia, made while he was a student in Princeton, he wrote about it as "the cultural and intellectual capital of the new nation. The Quaker imprint was everywhere, and it remains strong." The editors of that Madison memoir wrote, "Philadelphia was enlightened, wealthy, moral, and staid. The neatly patterned and trellised streets with their rows of sedate, red brick and white-trimmed houses expressed a sober charm."

By now, 1787, most of the arriving delegates had been in Philadelphia before, a few for meetings that preceded the Revolutionary War and many more for meetings of the Continental Congress. But, like European visitors who marveled at the elegance of Philadelphia, those who did not know the nation's largest city well were captivated by its splendid appearance and the array of innovations that it offered. Here, one was always conscious of being in a place unmatched by any other. New York and Boston were its only rivals, but they could not compare in size or in quality of attractions.

Americans and foreigners were still like explorers, regarding every part of the new country as something that invited discovery. They often talked about a city's place in the still-obscure geography of the continent, so when they came to Philadelphia they examined the scenery around the Schuylkill River and several streams that flowed into it. One unusually observant visitor said, "On the banks of the Schuylkill, about two miles from Philadelphia, there is a wild scene of rocks, breaking the river into several rushes and falls. The metallic brilliancy of these rocks, whenever their strata is (sic) broken up, indicates the ridge of granite…from Long Island to Roanoke, and which probably extends on as far as Savannah."

But it did not take such a probing eye to understand how William Penn's plan for a "greene countrie towne," symmetrical, rectangular, and spacious, had given way to a city that spread far along the Delaware waterfront. Penn wanted it to fill an eight-block-wide band between two rivers, but it achieved a size and shape he never imagined. Philadelphia made room for cluttered center city streets, where narrow houses were squashed together, contrasting with the elegance of the four great public squares and the refinement of fine homes on residential avenues. All this was presented with a distinctively gracious style.

The completely urban impression and feeling of security were increased by the paved streets. These were twenty-four-hour streets, well-lit all night with the use of whale oil, and a watch could be seen patrolling the neighborhoods. When most other American cities were still only tentatively urban, clearly awaiting further refinements, Philadelphia gave the impression of completeness, rewarding each newcomer with the feeling of cosmopolitan urbanity.

It was typical of Benjamin Franklin to have opted for a home in the cluttered area. It was just off busy Market Street, and even in his eighty-first year, and ill, he had it enlarged so he could have more room for entertaining. Everyone knew where Mr. Franklin lived, for the busy foot traffic passed by a large arch that opened to reveal his welcoming front door. His love for the city and its people was summarized when he said, "If there exists an atheist in the universe, he would be converted on seeing Philadelphia. Everything so well arranged proves that there must be an arranger."

The shops were apt to attract the most attention—large bookstores; Whiteside's fancy drygoods shop, with its display of mulls, muslins, and chintzes; other ladies finery that appeared to rival Parisian elegance (and prices!). Nor were gentlemen overlooked. There were bespoke tailor shops, as the English called tailors who made suits to order; superb hatmakers; and custom shoemakers, some claiming London connections. A lady who once accompanied the compulsive shopper Thomas Jefferson on a morning walk along some of these attractive streets was stunned at seeing him buy the finest gloves in three neighboring shops, all enormously costly.

The city had its full share of hurly-burly streets, too, with pedestrians pushing each other and street vendors creating a din. Only a short walk away were squares that were triumphs of design in themselves, partly populated by learned societies. Franklin started the American Philosophical Association in 1743, and it was still there on South 5th Street, between elegant Walnut and Chestnut Streets, an unmatched center for study and research.

Although he was once a slave owner, Franklin showed his amazing ability to keep growing throughout his life by becoming Pennsylvania's leading abolitionist. He was elected president of the Pennsylvania Society for Promoting the Abolition of Slavery and the Relief of Free Negroes. The second half of that title meant that Franklin's group was the only place in the nation that would make efforts to locate unfortunate free blacks who were kidnapped by thugs and sold into slavery.

Franklin's grandson, Benjamin Franklin Bache, was a smart young man who would have been happy to know that he was *dans le vent,* as the French indicate a person whose name is being heard everywhere. Born in 1769, he was not yet twenty at this time; he accompanied Franklin to

Paris and received part of his education in France. But while there, he also showed an interest in the family business by taking up printing.

Young Bache mastered French, while his grandfather only pretended to, and this had a funny result when they both attended a cultural event in France. Franklin, not understanding the oratory, watched his lady friend, Madame Helvetius, and applauded whenever she did. His grandson later told him, "But, Grandpapa, you were applauding when they praised you—and louder than anyone else." If he was embarrassed, Franklin never showed it. The incident delighted him.

On his return to America, Bache studied at the College of Philadelphia, then started the *Aurora* and *General Advertiser* in 1790. But his strong support for the French Revolution greatly displeased George Washington, who opposed the violence that accompanied it.

The Society of Friends—the Quakers—were not quite as untroubled as Madison's youthful memoir indicated, but they were still prominent in Philadelphia, despite several blows to their standing. Some Philadelphians still recalled that many years earlier, William Penn Jr., son of the founder, was arrested by Philadelphia police for "riotous conduct" that was never publicly explained. It was only reported that he had been brought before Quaker magistrates, but the disposition of his case was not revealed. The only known detail was that he was "treated without regard for his dignity," presumably meaning that there had been no favoritism. This incident did not seriously damage the great influence Quakers had in Pennsylvania, since the first William Penn, the original "Proprietor" of Pennsylvania and Delaware, had three other sons who were his legal heirs.

A much more disruptive force was the Revolutionary War, which had quickly made Quakers unpopular with many Americans. Their refusal to bear arms, which previously won respect, now caused them to be jeered by Americans who had become militaristic. They had been exempted from serving in the military, but required to pay taxes for the support of soldiers. Now, six years after the fighting ended, there was still a cleavage between Quakers who had clung to their old principles, and groups of "Free Quakers" who had served in the army or otherwise aided the revolutionary cause. Many called the latter the "Fighting Quakers."

This group petitioned for a plot of land and built their own separate two-story church on the west side of 5th Street, having been given a prime spot to repay them for their patriotism.

But discord among the Quakers was noticeable mainly because this was so different from their normal behavior. The truth is that aggravated feelings "between the loyal and the disloyal" continued to exist in almost every religious group and in most American cities for years after the war's end. It tended to be less aggravated in Philadelphia than almost anywhere else.

The city's press was flourishing, always claiming "fearless devotion to duty," with duty being interpreted in a variety of ways. Among the respected papers were the *Independent Gazeteer*, a weekly that was considered moderate because it was friendly to the popular revolutionary cause, Francis Bailey's the *Freeman's Journal* and the *North American Intelligencer*, both of which claimed to report on all sides of an issue. The latter had a motto: "Open to all parties, but influenced by none."

Apart from the usual claims for medicines that described wondrous properties in the Philadelphia newspapers of the time, there were also commercial articles that told of artists and sculptors who clearly expected a more discerning clientele. A number of portrait artists claimed to be having very full schedules around Convention time, and some had specialties that they touted as extraordinary, judging from their exaggerated terminology. Austin Florimont, for example, described himself as a limner (a pretentious word for one who sketches, draws, or illuminates manuscripts). Florimont claimed to produce "peculiarly happy likenesses—miniatures and crayon pictures of all sorts."

Another unusual artist was Joseph Wright, whose mother Patience Wright, of Bordentown, New Jersey, had been famous for modeling portraits in wax before the Revolution. She went to England and succeeded in establishing a patronage there, meanwhile giving her son Joseph a fine English education. She also arranged for him to study painting with the esteemed Benjamin West. Joseph returned to America in 1783 and painted portraits professionally, some being of the unusual wax variety that was practiced by his mother. General Washington and Mrs. Washington were among his early patrons. But he suffered a disaster when the Continental

Congress asked him to take a cast of Washington's features to be sent to Europe for use by sculptors. The General submitted to this troublesome process, but Wright broke the mold by accident. Washington would never allow it to be done again. Wright surfaced once more at Convention time, however, and painted a portrait of Madison. He was stricken by a fatal case of yellow fever soon after. This dread disease, which was particularly pernicious in Philadelphia, caused a great many residents to quit the city in summertime.

Another artistic specialist of a totally different sort was William Rush, who learned to carve wood as an apprentice to a ship carver. He went to many foreign ports and attracted a great deal of admiration for the beauty he could add to the prow and decks of a ship from simple blocks of wood. Returning to Philadelphia, he found that he was obtaining orders from places abroad where he had no previous contacts. Because a ship goes from place to place, the figures that are seen on it may become known much more widely than most artistic works. His fame spread even more when he received a commission to do a full-length wood figure of George Washington for a ship that would be named *The Washington*, which was later sold to the city of Philadelphia.

Some publications published articles that were uncanny precursors of the slightly daring looks at fashion and style that would become regular features of later leading newspapers and magazines. For instance, wigs and extreme styles of hairdressing for men were featured in innovative stories of an nature not yet known in other American cities. This began with a markedly simple style for men's hair, called the Brutus Crop, when the French Revolution made its influence felt. Would-be innovators soon produced weird variations, and these gave rise to pretended feuds among the newspaper writers. Contributors from the reading public were invited to take part. Of course each fracas ended inconclusively, but with a boost for newspaper circulation.

Some of these sallies rose to the level of appearing in the respected *American Historical Record*. Their sorry quality would make them unworthy of notice, but for the fact that when the Convention delegates, including General Washington, were dinner guests in the homes of leading Philadelphians, subjects like these were discussed and pro-voked rippling laughter. Well-bred Philadelphians had the British atti-tude that business or serious affairs should never be talked about on social occasions when ladies were present. Men who mentioned subjects drawn from their normal occupations were considered boors. The great Duke of Wellington, for example, was rated a delightful dinner guest for engaging in banter with the ladies that sounded almost stupid, but momentarily diverted the mind from serious cares. This was true even at the Duchess of Richmond's famous ball in Brussels, when he knew the Battle of Waterloo was hours away.

One such article of this kind featured a brigadier general named Lord Stirling who was said to consider himself the pinnacle of male sar-torial excellence. He was thought to be a fictitious character or a buffoon when he was shown to have 31 coats, 58 vests, 43 pairs of breeches, 30 shirts, 119 pairs of hose, 14 pairs of shoes, and 4 pairs of boots. When the last line revealed that he had 54 cravats and only 2 pairs of gloves, the disdain and the diverging opinions about his judgment had leading Philadelphians laughing for days. The unexpected end to this story was that the real Lord William Alexander Stirling, although he spent most of his hours in an alcoholic haze, proved to be a ferocious fighter whenever the cry of battle was heard. He especially distinguished himself in the Battle of Brooklyn, and the jests about him dwindled after that.

∞

In an era when most homes were made of wood and protection from fire was woefully inadequate, firefighting became a major preoccupation almost everywhere. But hardly any place attacked the danger as firmly as Philadelphia did. With little concern for cost, the city proudly supported a unique assemblage of equipment and personnel. The number of fire companies doubled in the last quarter of the eighteenth century, with the establishment of twenty-six new ones. As costly as equipment purchases were, most of the profits stayed close to home, for there were four fire-engine-building companies in the city. And Philadelphians' pride in their well-trained and well-equipped men was often on display, as they were honored with special parades each year.

The city's pride was matched with interest in the military forces that stood ready to protect Philadelphia. In August 1787, the city's entire force was turned out to be sure its wartime skills had not declined. Five light infantry companies, two companies of artillery, and the entire city troop of horses exercised on the commons, with firings and "other incidents of battle." All this was reviewed by Baron von Steuben and French general Duplessis. The baron, a great favorite, complimented the entire force on its efficiency.

Convention delegates who had a mind for business would have noticed something even more significant for Philadelphia's future—the pace of industrialization. It traced back to 1722 when early businessmen convinced the assembly to establish a bank to help provide ready money for the foreign trade deals they were already doing. Fifteen thousand pounds of legal tender were issued, and the results were so good that another thirty thousand pounds followed. These issues kept succeeding for another half century, but when the Revolutionary War intervened, a flood of paper money proved so destructive that by May 1781 the approaching victory at Yorktown was accompanied by Philadelphia newspaper headlines saying, "The Congress is now bankrupt."

Tories were noteworthy conservatives and opponents of paper money who had usually laid low during the war. Now they could not resist coming out gleefully. They festooned their hats with scores of paper dollars to show their worthlessness. As another sign of disdain, they had a dog tarred, with masses of the paper dollars in place of feathers. But while the gold and silver they had hoarded were indeed superior to paper money, these conservatives were wrong to think hard metals alone would ensure permanent prosperity. Philadelphia businessmen kept concentrating on invention and innovation as the keys to future success.

They correctly judged that iron would replace wood in a great many modern products, and they began to excel in this form of production. When the superiority of steel became apparent, Pennsylvania plants were found at the forefront in this transition as well. By the time of the

Constitutional Convention, Philadelphia had the largest and finest steel furnace in the nation. And the state of Pennsylvania became the unchallenged leader in the production of iron and steel.

Even when their investments were not successful, they were forward-looking. In March 1788, the *Freeman's Journal* published a paper showing a plan for moving a wagon by steam power. Philadelphia had lured an inventor named Oliver Evans to come and work on his ideas. Two machines for carding wool and cotton resulted, followed by a flour mill in 1783. Then came his principle of using steam to move heavy objects, resulting in an elevator and an endless chain of buckets to raise flour or grain to any desired height. His more dramatic plan for a steam-powered wagon was sent to England, but largely ignored there. Which, thought Philadelphians, was England's loss.

⚘

While science is often advanced by a single researcher in a small shop, there was also a special place for people like the earnest Philadelphians who added their own time and money to boosting their city's place in the advancing world of invention. Here again, the protean mind of Franklin played a major part. In 1787 he encouraged and then became president of another forward-looking organization, with the seemingly endless title Society for Political Inquiries, for Mutual Improvement in Knowledge of Government, and for the Advancement of Political Science. This was composed of fifty resident members meeting each fortnight. They were expected to come to every meeting and to follow up and report on every project that was assigned to them.

This organization was so thoughtful that it took note of how other aspects of life in the city might affect the business future. It led them to ask, "Might the subject of penal law interact with the city's industrial policies in any way?" Signs of a more enlightened and merciful attitude appeared when an attempt was made to reform the old practices by using criminals condemned to hard labor to take part in work on the city streets. They were to be paid one shilling sixpence (about thirty-five cents) per day, and the plan was hailed for its wisdom.

But the prisoners did not take well to it. "Some scoundrels tried to drop their confining iron balls in a way that would hit passers-by," said an observer. Also, "they had too easy access to friends, many of whom gave liquor to prisoners, making them intoxicated and very unruly." One prisoner grandly pulled out a gold watch he had stolen and "obligingly informed his keeper the hour of the day." When convicts were moved out to work on rural roads, they groaned and objected furiously, putting the whole project in jeopardy.

A prisoner named Jacob Dwyer, though convicted only of burglary, said he preferred death rather than this form of kindness. He was sentenced to be hanged, but then judges ruled that his desire for death was, in itself, a sign that he was mentally unfit to be executed. He was pardoned by the Supreme Executive Council, headed by Benjamin Franklin, and discharged, though with certain conditions. These were soon broken, and Dwyer came before the Supreme Court of Pennsylvania. He was again ordered to hang, but a legal standstill occurred between the Court and the Council, since both were "supreme." The Council again pardoned Dwyer, after which history lost track of him.

But one of the Pennsylvania delegates who was waiting for the Convention to begin, Gouverneur Morris, had the last word on this affair, as he often would have in the weeks ahead: "I cannot conceive a government in which there can exist two supremes."

No single ethnic group can take credit for setting the high standards of Philadelphia, for the city had one of the most diverse populations in the country—Scots, Irish, Poles, Danes, Italians, French, Greeks, Swiss, Czechs, Christians of several denominations, and Jews from many nations. All took part in the remarkable defenses that Philadelphians erected on both banks of the Delaware River under Polish-born engineer Tadeusz Kosciuszko to prevent the British from supplying their army. And all took part in the city's speedy revival after Britain's withdrawal.

It was, in short, a community that served as a sterling example of what most of the delegates wanted the whole of America to be—perfectly adapted to the historic role it was about to play.

CరఏO

Only in the third week of May did a substantial number of delegates begin arriving. The leisure time before that gave an early bird like James Madison an opportunity to study all the state constitutions that had been drawn up in recent decades and to take special note of features that all of them appeared to have, such as bills of rights.

One thing Madison studied with special interest was the site of the coming meeting, so he could picture some of the movements and juxta-positions of people who might have a bearing on his plans. Soon after arrival, he walked to nearby Chestnut Street and to the empty State House (later called Independence Hall) between 5th and 6th Streets, where the meetings would be held. The graceful Georgian building was the most ambitious public building in all the colonies when it was started in 1732, the year of George Washington's birth.

Now Madison found it locked, but having attended so many meet-ings there when he was in the Congress, he was well-known to the chief of guards who controlled all security in the area. With his instinctive flair for talking to an average person as an equal, he explained very frankly that he had arrived early in order to plan ways to make the coming meet-ing go smoothly. The guard, concluding that he personally bore a heavy responsibility for the meeting's success, instructed his underlings that Mr. Madison should be admitted to the empty building at any time, and that they should stand guard to see that he was not disturbed.

In this way, Madison spent hours in the large main assembly room on the ground floor. Not all the chairs and tables were in place yet, but he learned that the room would be rather crowded with about thirty tables and two chairs for each table if all the expected delegates arrived. Madison paced the length and breadth of the room, trying to picture where he would prefer to be seated for the purpose of judging each speaker's manner and signs of confidence or uncertainty. This meant first pinpointing where the presiding officer would be, which called for several assumptions.

Madison guessed that if health permitted, Benjamin Franklin, as the leading Pennsylvania official, would preside over the opening session, say a few welcoming words, then make a motion proposing that George Washington be named president of the Convention. He knew this proposal would pass, probably by acclamation. Washington would promptly take the chair, after which each delegate who rose to speak would stand quite close to the president's chair. Madison pictured the approximate spot where he would like to be seated in order to see each speaker at close range. This would be helpful if, as he expected, he was going to take the fullest possible notes of the proceedings; and it would be even more important in trying to judge when the debate called for him to make an objection or addition to what was said.

The early time was also precious because Madison was able to conduct personal talks with Pennsylvania delegates who were already on hand. And it developed that some of those discussions were as much a part of the event as were the regular sessions to come.

He was welcomed by financier Robert Morris, who had done the most during the war to supply George Washington with enough money to keep his army intact. Because of draconian measures that Morris sometimes took to control the money supply, many people called him a "dictator" and "profiteer." But Madison, as a delegate to the Congress, had supported him at every turn, so now he was received warmly in Morris's magnificent home. And it was clear that Morris would be as determined as any man in the State House to make sure no weakness in the nation's finances would lead to disunion.

One of Madison's most significant acts consisted of a series of talks with James Wilson, a Pennsylvania delegate whom he knew to be a close friend of Franklin's. Madison knew him only slightly up to this time, but he now grew hopeful that he had found a new ally. In fact, Wilson would prove to be one of his major supporters throughout the Convention. They were a strange pair, both inscrutable, yet somehow having the kind of instant interplay between them that would lead to dazzling teamwork in controlling the course of crucial arguments.

Wilson, born near St. Andrews, Scotland, came to America after a fine education at Glasgow and Edinburgh. He was first employed as a Latin tutor, but soon left teaching to study law under John Dickinson, a universally admired lawyer. While still young, he set up a successful practice in land law, and also began to speculate successfully in land. In addition, Wilson defended Tories in their struggle to regain part of their expropriated properties, and the rewards for this onerous job that most others avoided were great. At one point, these specialties had combined to make him a very rich man, but as in many other cases, his dangerously speculative investments in turbulent times led to painful losses. Even though he signed the Declaration of Independence, and President Washington later named him a Supreme Court justice, his life would end in turmoil as his investments collapsed and left him bankrupt.

The treatment of Tories, and those who were suspected because they stayed behind and dealt with the British occupiers when other citizens fled, was more lenient here than in most other states. Returning Philadelphians could have been infuriated when they found a dirty city, damaged buildings, and plundered personal property. Some Tories (or Loyalists) had seized important property, even as large as a steel furnace, so the initial bitterness was great. But the officials and the people were reluctant to take extreme measures.

In order to forestall tension, Chief Justice McKean and two other judges sat in City Hall day after day to invite the surrender of 345 persons who had been accused of aiding the British or stealing property. Forty of these appeared voluntarily, but no accusers came to present evidence against them. McKean commented, "The inhabitants appear to be rather afraid of one another, or the Whigs cannot yet believe that their friends have the government of the city." Other officials recommended "lenience and forgiveness in order to limit passions and prejudice of the population." Such high-minded behavior was hardly found anywhere else.

Nevertheless, James Wilson knew there was enough anti-Tory feeling to make his legal activities in their behalf very unpopular. And his own personality did not make for popularity. So it seemed strange that Wilson shared Madison's interest in empowering the same public that looked askance at him. It is apparent, therefore, that Wilson had an elevated mind, given to putting the rational above the emotional. At this time, he was in low spirits because he had recently lost his wife and faced years of struggle to raise a large family alone. Yet Wilson was able to focus on the coming Convention, and he quickly took to the ideas that Madison shared with him. Their long sessions paid off remarkably well when the telling moments came.

Madison also was able to hold advance talks with some southern delegates, especially two from South Carolina, the most determinedly slave state in the Union. These delegates proved to be essential to compromises that would have to be made in the meeting. One was John Rutledge, whom Madison encountered earlier in interstate negotiations, and another was Charles Pinckney, from a leading family that also included Charles Cotesworth Pinckney, his cousin. All these South Carolinians were staying at the Indian Queen, which many considered the finest tavern in America, though there were six taverns in the country with that name, honoring Pocahontas. Thomas Jefferson stayed there in 1776, but he moved to a quieter place to draft the Declaration of Independence. It was described dolefully as "a large pile of buildings with very spacious halls."

But its greatest attraction was the multiple convenience of being between Market and Chestnut Streets and so full of delegates that a stroll through its public rooms would, after all the expected guests arrived, often result in fascinating encounters with such brilliant Massachusetts delegates as Caleb Strong, who had graduated from Harvard with the highest honors, or Nathaniel Gorham, who was born to poverty and had little education, yet gradually made himself a prosperous businessman, lawyer, judge, and uniquely trusted politician. Or one might meet the delightful though unknown William Pierce of Georgia, or Virginia's famed George Mason, who had framed his state's Declaration of Rights, a model for the first part of Jefferson's Declaration of Independence.

Everyone was of potential interest to Madison, but especially the southerners he knew well enough to sound out how they might plan to deal with any attack on the slave trade that might come up. If any one subject had the potential to put an end to the Convention, Madison felt slavery was it. Three-quarters of a century before the issue led to war, he already feared a secession by southern states and a terrible test of wills.

Both Pinckneys were well-educated individuals, more respected than some other major slave importers and owners who often seemed unsavory to the non-slave states or to Virginians, even though the latter were major slave owners themselves. The Pinckneys managed to give a superior impression despite the great number of slaves they owned. Charles, the younger of the two Pinckneys at the Convention, was a particularly attractive and even elegant young man of nearly thirty years (who would later be sent abroad on major diplomatic missions). He and Madison came to a virtual gentleman's agreement in advance of the sessions, based on Pinckney's warning to Madison that he and John Rutledge would be forced to leave and take their entire delegation with them—"for the state would feel that we were not wanted in the Union"—if any concerted attempt were made to impinge on the South's right not only to retain their slaves but to import more of them as well.

In arranging to speak with other delegates, Madison might not have been known to them as a person of great means or position, but nearly all the others knew that he had a hand in bringing this meeting about. And he was further recommended by the very positive fact that he was a Virginian. At least three other states—Massachusetts, New York, and Pennsylvania—carried themselves with a certain swagger of superiority. But the one that was more often considered the most important state was Virginia, based on population, pivotal position, and the number of great men that it had produced. The fact that one of these luminaries, Washington, had saved the Union added luster to this image of importance. Also, since Virginia's insistence on states' rights was beyond question, the other states were confident that Virginians would guard against granting excessive power to a federal government.

In the late eighteenth century, it was seen as a most impressive fact that Virginia insisted on separately ratifying the peace treaty with Britain in 1783, as if an act by the Union's Congress had to be blessed in this additional way. Virginia then refused to carry out points in the treaty about treatment of Tories and debts owed by Virginians to British creditors. The fact that Madison came from this premier state was capped by the known fact that he was close to General Washington. So when he wanted to hold pre-Convention talks with any other delegate in Philadelphia, there was no question of a ready response.

Chapter Seven

WASHINGTON'S WAY

George Washington's trip to Philadelphia began in a seriously troubling time. Early in the year 1787, his beloved brother, John Augustine, died after a long illness. Then George's mother, a chronic complainer living in Fredericksburg who invariably contrived to make her son feel guilty, found herself in seriously declining health. She also wrote more insistently about her lack of funds and hinted that she might come to spend the rest of her life at Mount Vernon. Washington was firmly against this, and he exhausted himself in writing and rewriting a careful letter to her that said she was always welcome of course, but warned her at great length of how much she would dislike all the company and bustle "of a place that may be compared to a well-resorted tavern, as scarcely any strangers who are going from north to south or from south to north do not spend a day in it."

It was not at all like Washington to use such exaggerated figures of speech, and the fact that he did added to his distress. It was one of nature's oddities that the General, who could bear up under the greatest physical hardships and not even appear to notice deadly danger, had a sensitive nervous system that buckled under psychosomatic stress.

Martha knew how guilty his mother made him feel and how her troubling behavior affected his health. Just as she feared, ten days before he was scheduled to leave for Philadelphia he contracted a cold accompanied by rheumatism so severe that one arm had to be put in a sling for several days. He warned Governor Randolph, who would head the Virginia group in Philadelphia, that he might have to delay or even cancel his planned departure. As days passed, however, Washington improved and his spirits began to brighten.

But on Thursday, April 26, as he began to look forward to the journey, express mail (mail that was delivered very quickly at a higher cost) from Fredericksburg told him that his mother and his sister Betty were both extremely ill, suggesting they might not recover. They begged him to come at once, which meant traveling in the opposite direction of his trip to the north. He had no choice but to leave the next morning, hastening southward and wondering what he was going to find. Fortunately, when he arrived at 2 p.m., he found his sister out of danger and his mother "debilitated by age and her disorder," but not in immediate danger.

His feelings were alternating in a way that was unusual for him, but he somehow felt relieved and relaxed enough to stay an extra day, lodging at his sister's home. He left on Monday, April 30, near sunrise, had a slow trip, and reached Mount Vernon in a mild rain shower at six o'clock.

Overcoming the Fredericksburg problem so promptly seemed to improve his spirits and his health. But there was another factor that tells a great deal about George Washington. It has been shown that he was a devoted man of business, enjoying the art of developing properties and building wealth. But he was also a dedicated farmer who found real joy in the details of farm work. His diary written when he was at Mount Vernon supervising his people makes it clear that nothing else mattered to him in those single-minded hours. There are long weeks at a time when the record of his daytime hours contains nothing but farming information.

The reason for his better spirits after the Fredericksburg visit may, in fact, be best attributed to a fortunate encounter he had with Charles Yates while he was there. Yates was a specialist in farming techniques whom

Washington admiringly described as "a gentleman on whose veracity entire confidence may be placed," an encomium almost never accorded to any of his military or political associates.

This exceptional man told Washington of "raising Irish potatoes by placing them on unbroken hard or grassy ground and covering them with straw. He found them to succeed admirably." The General then filled an entire diary page, which usually served for six or seven days, with careful measurements of how large an area Yates used, showing that one acre would produce seven hundred bushels of fine, well-tasted potatoes. This was followed by the exciting revelation that some potatoes were accidentally discovered in a cornfield where they had grown through the old corn stalks and yielded a fine harvest. He ended with "Query: Must find out whether this covering, laid on thicker, will not do as well as straw." Like any person engrossed in a hobby that also shows signs of profitability, these very thoughts clearly acted as pacifiers on the General's troubled mind.

Washington finally left for Philadelphia very early on the morning of Wednesday, May 9—a day later than he had planned—because he wanted an extra day or two to cushion the possibility of delay en route and still arrive in Philadelphia on May 13, so that he could appear at State House early on the appointed date of May 14. Even though he knew from dreary experience how few others would take the starting date seriously, arriving in Philadelphia a day or two late himself was anathema to the exceptionally punctual General. It was not only habit, but military experience that told him how often an early arrival meant victory and a late arrival spelled defeat. But he put aside his doubts and was optimistic about making the desired arrival date, so he climbed jauntily into his new light traveling coach, with his man Jackson riding beside it, exactly at sunrise. He gave Martha a last assurance that he wanted nothing more than freedom from public duties, and that he looked forward to their own quiet life together. She reminded him again that all her plans had been made on the basis of his earlier promise to that effect.

He was in excellent spirits by then, clearly looking forward to the trip. The first stop was a few hours away, in Bladensburg, Maryland, some twenty miles from Mount Vernon. He dined and then lodged at a

Major Snowden's. But he retired early, for he was "struck by a violent headache and sick stomach."

He felt better the next morning, but an early rain was falling, so he delayed setting off until about eight o'clock. Many men would have traveled in the rain, but Washington was very thoughtful of his employees, and he disliked forcing his men to ride in a steady rain unless time was really of the essence. He also customarily made a mental note of where he might stop if a slight rain worsened.

By one o'clock he had traveled over thirty miles and reached Baltimore, where he enjoyed dining at the Fountain restaurant. Later, still in Baltimore, he supped with Dr. James McHenry, who was an aide to Washington during the war, remained a close friend, and would later serve as his secretary of war.

On Friday, May 11, Washington set off before breakfast, rode twelve miles to Skerretts Tavern, but did not pause for food because the weather was threatening. He continued to the ferry at the small port town of Havre de Grace, and dined there, but could not make the crossing because of a squall. He decided to lodge in the town.

On the next morning, Saturday, the Susquehanna River was crossed, despite a difficult wind. Time was made for breakfast at the Ferry House on the east side of the river. He continued as far as Hollingsworth's Tavern, where Washington stopped to dine and met up with Francis Corbin, an acquaintance and a member of the Virginia Assembly. Washington was feeling more convivial than usual, so they talked at length, and it was decided that "Corbin would take a seat in my carriage to Wilmington." Along the way, both men lodged at another favorite tavern of Washington's, Flinn's Sign of the Ship.

The General and Corbin set out early on Sunday morning, May 13, covered nearly forty more miles at a fast pace, and reached Chester in time to dine at Mrs. Whitbey's, the widow of a British military officer, whose Columbia Hotel was considered one of America's best. But at Chester everything changed, for a scouting party was on the lookout for General Washington, and he found himself surrounded by General Mifflin, who had become Speaker of the Pennsylvania Assembly, Generals

Knox, and Varnum, Colonels Humphreys and Minges, and Majors Jackson and Nicholas, all of whom were members of the Cincinnati, and all determined to escort him to Philadelphia.

It was one of the few times when General Washington is known to have suffered the uneasiness of a social misstep that most others have experienced; he had been caught declining an invitation on a false excuse. Months before, when the public outcry over the hereditary practices of the Cincinnati made him wish to reduce his own participation for a time, he told these devoted officers that he could not attend their forthcoming general meeting because of ailments that he greatly exaggerated as agonizingly painful and life threatening. As it happened, this meeting was to be in Philadelphia and the Constitutional Convention turned out to be starting in the very same month. Washington's deep sense of courtesy made him determined not to offend his officers by showing up for another meeting after refusing their invitation. "But you must certainly be in Philadelphia for the Convention, Sir," came the pleas from Madison, from Virginia governor Randolph, and even from Thomas Jefferson, writing from Paris. After all, this gathering concerned the future of the nation, not just a social misstep.

Washington had pretty much made up his mind that he would simply attend both meetings and hope the Cincinnati would accept his explanation about a remarkable improvement in his condition. But now in Chester, the officers showed their old dash, overrode all humbug, and made sure of the outcome. By meeting on the road, in a flurry of warlike whoops, the whole thing passed wonderfully.

George Washington's arrival in Philadelphia on May 14 was one of the many great moments that would brighten the Convention days. In the few years since his retirement, this man, who was generally acknowledged as the father of the new country, had become almost as controversial a figure as he was a revered icon. The workings of the great American political machine, which somehow seemed to have sprung into life fully grown, had already created a ready list of enemies for Washington. The number of western-minded Americans who suspected Washington of being in the pocket of the northeastern shipping interests was great enough to constitute a major faction. Others in many of the states were rabid enemies for more ideological reasons, thinking that Washington belonged to a monarchist clique. There were some so bitter that they made up odious nicknames and jested about his alleged pomposity, kingly pretensions, and long list of misdeeds. But let it be known that he was in the neighborhood, and all this ugliness disappeared. Observers had the impression that young girls in garden-party dress magically encircled him bearing spring flowers, or so the newspaper accounts reported, whatever the season.

This time, of course, it *was* spring. While still miles out of Philadelphia, but rolling along the expected path, Washington was suddenly confronted not only with a number of flower-bearing girls, but also by a prolonged ringing of the city bells. Washington never ceased to be embarrassed at being showered with flowers, but he learned to take some of these welcoming festivities in stride. For instance, his diary for that day carried the rather routine note: "When I came into town, they rang the city bells."

Washington's entry into the city itself had still other high points. As his carriage rolled up to Mrs. House's establishment, a messenger came running up and handed the General a note. It was from Robert Morris, a man who was more than merely a friend of Washington's. After sailing to America from Liverpool as a boy of fourteen, Morris prospered to become the nation's richest man for a time, although too many of his holdings proved to be shaky. The major role he played in the Revolutionary War in repeatedly supplying important sums of money at moments when Washington's troops were in dire straits led Hamilton to write to Washington in 1783, hoping a way might be found to have the Congress repay Morris. "Mr. Morris," he said, "certainly deserves a great deal from his country. I believe no man in this country other than himself could have kept the money machine a-going."

Now Morris, living in Philadelphia's finest private mansion, was repeating his invitation that General Washington should "come and spend any amount of time" with him and Mrs. Morris. Washington had turned down the invitation earlier, feeling that a long stay might make him a burdensome houseguest. But this repetition of the offer made

Washington feel that he must accept, even though it disrupted Madison's wish to house the entire Virginia delegation in one place to facilitate after-hours talks about the events that would soon be under way. So two declined invitations were reversed and accepted before Washington even emerged from his carriage.

∞

The next morning, Washington went first to visit Benjamin Franklin. In his diary, Washington very primly noted that he "waited on the President, Dr. Franklin," because the latter was president of Pennsylvania's Supreme Executive Council, a grandiloquent title that amused Franklin. He would have preferred to receive a nice piece of land as a grant for his services—something he felt the Congress should have given him for all the favors he wrested from France.

The visitor could not fail to approve of the delightful approach that the Franklins had prepared, making it seem that passage through the large arch on Market Street opened onto a rural scene. The yard was of modest size, but its gravel paths were flanked by grass plots and flowering walks, with much of the area shaded by a mulberry tree.

These two great Americans were totally unalike, and yet they cherished every opportunity to meet. The remarkable amount of credit that Franklin and Washington were given would be fiercely summarized by the angry John Adams just after he became vice president in 1790, writing privately to Dr. Benjamin Rush, another skeptic: "The history of our Revolution will be one continuous Lye from one end to the other. The essence of the whole will be that Dr. Franklin's Rod smote the Earth, and out sprang General Washington. That Franklin electrified him with his Rod—and thenceforth these two conducted all the Policies, Negotiations, Legislatures, and War."

Feeling underappreciated, as he often was, Adams was responding by underappreciating others. It was true that Franklin's achievements were partly based on showmanship, but they were of a high order. And if Washington thought back to his childhood book of good and bad behavior, Item # 38, which read, "In visiting the Sick, do not presently play the Physician if you be not Knowing therein," would have told him that Dr. Franklin never had any need of such strictures. He saved at least two lives—an English lord's, by simply advising him to quit a deadly treatment, and his brother's, by inventing an instrument that medical science came to call the multipurpose "flexible catheter."

It was well known that Franklin was slow to cast his lot with the revolutionaries at the time of the hated Stamp Act, and Franklin had once been inclined to stay in England as a Tory, loyal to the king. But after he made his choice and supposedly created that memorable sentence—"We must all hang together, or most assuredly we shall all hang separately"—no other man was more important or produced such diplomatic successes for the new nation.

George Washington had a long memory for a stupid act or a splendid one, and he knew that Franklin was a towering figure. When Franklin returned from Europe in September 1785, Washington wrote to him, "As no one entertains more respect for your character, so none can salute you with more sincerity, or with greater pleasure, than I do." It is not clear whether he realized that Franklin's genius as a practical scientist may have surpassed his political dexterity, but he would have considered this morning's meeting itself well worth the arduous ride from Mount Vernon to Philadelphia.

Now, sipping tea with Franklin in his huge, newly remodeled house near the Convention site, Washington became aware that the older man again was not fully committed to the political business at hand. He was not at all sure that the Articles of Confederation needed to be discarded. The reason was Franklin's chronic optimism. He had written to a French friend that Americans were happy in their independence and that British newspaper accounts of distress, confusion, and disorder in the United States were either ignorantly or deliberately misleading. He understood the problems of a weak government, but he was not yet sure they were severe enough to risk a major change. Strangely, considering the power of Franklin's mind, he was seldom quick to announce a decision on any subject. It may have been due to a principle he had of "never forcing a subject...I let events show me how I can make the best use of them."

Washington was not misled by Franklin's support of the status quo. He remembered several times, starting with the decision to join the Revolution, when Franklin was slow to adopt a common position that others were rushing into. He had been slow to endorse the Articles of Confederation, but then proposed his own version to the Congress of that day—an astonishingly strong central government that would have been much like the plan Madison was now about to put forward. (There have been suggestions that Franklin's plan had borrowed liberally from an ancient Iroquois "constitution" and that these ideas were then reflected in the document produced in Philadelphia. It is true that Franklin took an exceptional interest in the Native American heritage, but it is drawing a long bow to find any effect of this on the new American Constitution.) Franklin had called for a congressional government with an executive committee to manage "general continental business and interests, conduct diplomacy, and administer finances." His plan covered everything from the conduct of foreign affairs to the settling of disputes within the colonies, with costs to be paid from a common treasury supplied by each colony in proportion to its male inhabitants.

The plan was too radical for 1775, but brilliantly farsighted. Franklin also pretended, untruthfully, to be reluctant about going to Paris for the assignment that turned him from a celebrity into a legend. And even when he proved that lightning and electricity were the same, he spent so much time rechecking the facts and waited so long before announcing his discovery that a Frenchman was the first person to tell the world about it—though fortunately, he gave full credit to Franklin.

Now Washington surely pretended that his own interest in changing the form of government was still open to question. He listened to Franklin's doubting remarks, but—based on Washington's low-key approach in his correspondence with other respected persons at that time—it is very unlikely that he labored to sell any new plan to the other man.

They talked about the Cincinnati because of the coincidence that this contentious organization was now the subject of a current meeting in Philadelphia. But Franklin was undoubtedly too courteous to let Washington know of his disdain for the martial group. The idea of giving the next generation a way to share in the glory of their fathers' wartime accomplishments seemed wrong-headed to him. He praised the Oriental attitude that prestige should flow backward, rather than forward. In the Orient, it is parents who are singled out for honor if they have an illustrious son, because they were the ones who created and raised him. This is wise, Franklin thought, because it engenders a society in which people are given an incentive—and even a selfish motivation—to raise their children well. In Franklin's view, to glorify a son for what his father did served no good purpose.

Chapter Eight

WELCOME ARRIVALS

On Monday, May 14, the day the Convention was to open, George Washington duly entered the State House at 10 a.m., even though it was known that no quorum existed. His diary entry said that "such members as were in town assembled at the State House," and he could have added "because I set them an example." He also wrote that the only two states represented, Virginia and Pennsylvania, agreed to attend at the same place on the morrow. Again, it would be a mere show of propriety. Only the same two states had enough individuals to be officially "on the floor of the Convention," which failed to constitute a quorum.

Madison felt a sense of relief as more individual delegates arrived, even though their states' rosters were not complete. It soon became clear that this would not be a repeat of the Annapolis fiasco, but Madison's anxious state of mind is still detectable in a brief letter he wrote to Jefferson the next day, May 15.

Monday last was the day for the meeting of the Convention. The number yet assembled is but small. Among the few is General Washington who arrived on Sunday evening, amidst the acclamation of the people…There is a prospect of a pretty full meeting on the whole, though there is less punctuality at the outset than was to be wished. Of this, the late bad weather has been the principal cause.

Madison was eagerly waiting for more people of the Virginia contingent, and happily, the Virginians were the only group, other than the Pennsylvania locals, who were settled in only three days after the official opening day. Edmund Randolph, for whom Madison had big plans, was the fifth Virginia delegate to arrive, at a late hour on May 15. He was followed by Dr. McClurg on the next day. And the seventh and last Virginia man, George Mason, came on May 17. In his independent way, he brought his eldest son, and the two of them stayed at the popular Indian Queen tavern rather than at Mrs. House's. (Mason, tight with his money, even though he was wealthy, noted that the Indian Queen charged him only twenty-five shillings of Pennsylvania currency per day for "self and son, including servants and horses.") But Mason's crusty attitude was apparent when, even before settling in, he began to complain of "the etiquette and nonsense of dining in this place."

Now, with only Washington and Mason staying elsewhere, Madison, even though he was outranked by others in age and position, could arrange to have most of the Virginia team on hand at Mrs. House's to hear his private thoughts on how the Convention's deliberations should proceed; and these sessions went on until quite late at night. The hour made little difference to Madison, as he was quite content with three to four hours of sleep each night.

As the delay went on, waiting for enough arrivals to make up a quorum, the delegates on hand decided to meet in the State House each day for brief informal talks, usually lasting only one to two hours. These leisurely times covered some of the subjects that later—when the formal meetings began—made it possible to move quickly on rules of order, courtesy, and comity that enabled the Convention to run smoothly. During this time, somewhere between May 20 and 25, George Washington spoke informally, but in a way that left a lasting impression.

Although Washington would speak only a few times during the formal Convention, he stood now and made a brief statement that is often overlooked, but deserves attention because the General's solemnity and the expression of suppressed emotion that he conveyed set a special serious tone. Even if Madison planted this approach in Washington's mind in preceding days, simply by stressing the new mentality that had to be created in this diverse gathering, the solemn cast was the General's own. No one else could have matched it.

As best we can tell, based on personal comments made by other delegates, Washington's words contained these sentences: "It is too probable that no plan we propose will be adopted. Perhaps another dreadful conflict is to be sustained. If, to please the people, we offer what we ourselves disapprove, how can we afterward defend our work? Let us raise a standard to which the wise and the honest can repair; the event is in the hand of God." He was challenging them all to face the fact that the right solution could not be a politically pleasing one, for the people back in their home states were not yet conditioned to accept great change. Even if their deliberations led to conflict, he reminded them, nothing could be as bad as stifling their own best judgment for the sake of an easy way out.

Also during these pre-Convention days there were many times when men gathered to form into interesting discussion groups in taverns or in their lodgings. Much of the early talk was simply get-acquainted chatter, rather than exchange of opinions, for a great many of these men knew little or nothing about each other. Some of them later admitted that they had come with foreboding about the delegates they would meet and the nature of the states they came from. Some northerners expected the men from major slave states to be crude boors with whom they would hardly be able to hold a civil talk, while William Pierce of Georgia, who proved to have a rare sensitivity, said he expected to be treated like a pariah. Some of the men who misunderstood each other most ended by appreciating each other best.

A few had been born abroad—Wilson in Scotland, Thomas Fitzsimons, also of Pennsylvania, in Ireland. George Wythe and John Blair had studied law in London's Middle Temple, while Dr. James McClurg—a last-minute

Virginia delegate who was appointed to membership after Patrick Henry refused to attend—had the equal cachet of holding a medical degree from the University of Edinburgh. He had virtually no experience in the political world, but was highly respected for his service as a surgeon in the Revolutionary War.

More than half of the delegates had legal training, and twenty-nine also had university degrees, which was not yet common. Madison was a Princeton graduate, while Gouverneur Morris, a year younger than Madison, had a degree from King's College, in New York City, which later became Columbia.

As they looked back on these early talks, several of them spoke of how surprised they had been—pleasantly, for the most part—at the things they learned about their new colleagues. Pierce Butler of South Carolina said, "The manner and modes of thinking of several states differed nearly as much as in different nations of Europe." Rufus King, the brilliant member of Congress from Massachusetts who engineered the Northwest Ordinance and would later run for the United States presidency, said he distrusted the meetings at first, but made the startling confession that he had been overwhelmed when listening to Hamilton, of New York, "who revolutionized my mind." On the other hand, Delaware's George Read began to suspect that the delegates from small states must keep a close watch on propositions offered by the larger states "who will probably combine to swallow up the smaller ones by addition, division, or impoverishment." This fear would have a major effect in the next few weeks.

In the last week of May, most of the remaining delegates arrived, almost filling the boarding houses and taverns where they would lodge for the next four months. A majority arrived too late to get into the Indian Queen and, as a result, made the large City Tavern their next choice. Their late arrivals reflect the nature of time and punctuality in that era. It did not entirely indicate a lack of respect for the others who were waiting for them, as Washington felt, but simply the impossibility of foretelling how long each person's trip would take. Even a simple steady rain that might seem no impediment at all to travelers of a later century could cause days to be lost if a thoughtful man wanted to spare his drivers a daylong drenching. Or an accident on the precarious roads, even if it were not serious, might damage an axle or a wheel, resulting in a delay and requiring a search for new parts. Regrettably, most travelers set out full of optimism rather than allowing extra time for such mishaps. It was the accepted custom to set a fixed date for the start of any meeting or event, but it would be regarded as astonishing if everyone arrived on that very day.

General Washington nevertheless longed to have promptness all around him. And Madison condemned himself to the same frustration, for after so many experiences with waiting he still called the non-arrivals "a daily disappointment." After the first week of waiting in Philadelphia, Washington wrote to Arthur Lee, a Virginian and member of the old Congress who was serving abroad as one of America's trade representatives, "The delays sour the tempers of punctual members who do not like to idle away their time." He thought of being on time not only as a military trait, but also as simple courtesy and thoughtfulness. But to most of the others, any time within a week of the set date was considered approximately on time. As a result, they gave substance to the belief that "the only thing wrong about punctuality is that there's nobody on hand to see it."

When more than half a hundred persons were expected, as in this case, and some coming from five times the distance as the near neighbors, a two-week span in the actual arrival dates was not at all dismaying. Consequently, the pace of the event itself was then expected to be leisurely. It would have been unseemly for the delegates to wrap up their deliberations in a month—a sign of disinterest. There was never any danger of this. But some delegates actually thought in terms of two months, and they would become edgy as the proceedings clearly headed for a much longer time. Richard Spaight, age twenty-nine and impatient, wrote to his North Carolina governor, "The length of the Convention is entirely uncertain and a great concern. This seems to promise a Summer's Campaign." In mid June, the astute Pierce wrote that "the Convention will not rise before the middle of October." He was the only one who overshot the mark.

It was the absent Thomas Jefferson, serving as America's envoy in Paris, who had a sparkling phrase to describe the negotiators—"An assembly of demigods," he wrote to Madison when he saw the list. Jefferson's assessment has been deemed an exaggeration, because most of the men who came, while successful, did nothing spectacular with their lives before or after this convention. One could easily argue in favor of that objection. Or one could find at least three separate reasons to agree with Jefferson's label. First, that it was even more exciting to see these rather "normal men" rise to the heights that enabled them to take such a tangle of conflicting ideas and make them into a positive jewel of law and communication. Second, that they were in any case far above the average level of education for their day, as more than half were lawyers and many had been near the top of their college class. Third, that since the older founding fathers are thought of as America's "divinities," these second-generation men can quite naturally be called "demi" or lesser gods. But it is very likely that none of these explanations is what Jefferson had in mind. Almost certainly that supreme egotist was jealously wishing himself there, certain that he could have written a document superior to what they were going to produce, and therefore giving them a title that he expected them to recognize as a piece of elegant sarcasm.

Their fellow Americans seemed to think there were indeed demigods among them. The entire country's air of expectation was astonishing. After so calmly enduring the "incompetent" government of the Confederation, having given the impression that no other government was wanted, the American people were excited to learn that carriages from most of the colonies had rolled into Philadelphia. This was conveyed in letters that delegates received from their friends at home. Few people of that day knew the names of Madison and Hamilton, much less those of Morris, Wilson, Pinckney, or King. But just knowing that George Washington was on the scene seemed to tell these same Americans that something truly momentous was about to happen.

General Washington, meanwhile, sought after by everyone, tried to accommodate as many invitations as possible. Some of the other delegates brought their wives to Philadelphia, and most evenings included a supper or entertainment that local matrons and visiting ladies all hoped Washington would attend. He struggled to avoid offending anyone, so there were nights like Friday, May 18, when "after dining at a club at Grey's Ferry [over the Schuylkill] I later accompanied Mrs. Morris and other ladies to hear a Mrs. O'Connell read (a charity affair) to obtain a little money in her reduced circumstances. Her performance at the College Hall, on 4th street below Arch, was tolerable."

Even though Washington was used to a fine table at Mount Vernon, he specially noted that he dined "in great splendor" one night at the home of William Bingham, a Philadelphia banker who was considered a leader of the "aristocratic set." Mrs. Bingham lived through a succession of reputations—first as a young beauty who was considered "loose" in her ways. Otto, the major domo of the French Legation, then in Philadelphia, said he had seen her ride off from home in a single-seated sulky, sitting in the lap of Gouverneur Morris, and spread the story all over Versailles.

Following her marriage to Bingham, a banker who became rich while working with Robert Morris, she assumed a new identity as a leading hostess. But this elevated position was further exalted by a reputation as a leading woman thinker who felt that women should play a political role, like Madame de Stael in Europe. It was in this incarnation that Thomas Jefferson wrote her a cutting letter, seeming to depress her pretensions (see chapter 19). The thoughtful Washington was always careful about his diary entries, and would not have wanted to disparage his hostess if his words were seen during or after his life. But the term "great splendor" in this case may have meant "excessive" and was slightly derogatory. In contrast to many European aristocrats, America's leaders believed that an upper class existed, but it was based on real accomplishment or learning, not on money and lavish display.

Washington had a less splendid, but probably livelier, dinner with his beloved Cincinnati members who had already started their meetings at spacious Carpenters' Hall just off Chestnut Street. When he attended the Cincinnati's business meeting later in the week, Washington laid down a set of strictures about altering the society's hereditary rules. The officers appeared to accept all his words as they had always obeyed his commands, and then, as noted earlier, the various chapters went off to make their own confusing decisions that the public, and even Washington—still president general of the group—were blissfully unclear about.

There was hardly ever a quiet moment when the Cincinnati came together. They never tired of reminding each other of deadly perils and humorous endings. Magnanimously, their memories included a long roster of foreigners who had come to share their fate: not only Lafayette, who was beloved by all, but also General Deborre, a French general who commanded a brigade; Brigadier General Conway, a gallicized Hibernian who fought in Stirling's division; and Louis Fleury, a French engineer who had offered his services from the beginning and won a captain's commission from Washington. One of the most admired was Count Casimir Pulaski, a Polish officer who had already been famous throughout Europe for defending his country against Russia, Austria, and Prussia. He volunteered to fight in the Light Horse, and Washington soon suggested to Congress that he should be given the command of it.

They talked a lot, too, about Harry Lee, of Virginia, who was only twenty-one when he became renowned as Light-Horse Harry for harassing the enemy's pickets with special brilliance and stealing wagonloads of food. The commanding general always noticed him, they said in whispers, maybe because he was the son of Lucy Grimes Lee, a celebrated beauty who first touched Washington's heart as a schoolboy, leading him to write rhymes about her at Mount Vernon. But they also knew that admiration for Harry's unequalled daring and skill was long-standing. As Colonel Washington, he received the fourteen-year-old Harry and his father at Mount Vernon, and declared then that he had never seen the boy's equal on a horse.

Seven years later, General Washington had just abandoned New York to the British and had General Howe nipping at the heels of his starving troops when his aides wakened him to report a miracle: Harry's troop had just brought in twenty British wagons loaded with food. After waiting all afternoon for just the right moment, it had taken Harry just five minutes to accomplish this feat without a shot or a scratch.

Although these men were always deferential to their commander-in-chief, making sure that the humorous barbs they traded were never aimed in his direction, they had a special way of letting him know that he was a part of their lighthearted banter. For example, they were amused to recall Washington's typically calm reaction to a very severe loss to Britain's General Howe in Pennsylvania. Some of them could recite lines from his letter to Connecticut's Governor Trumbull with the understated words: "We have reason to wish it had not happened, but I hope a little time and perseverance will give us some favorable opportunity of recovering our loss and putting our affairs in a more flourishing condition." Sounds of "oh, yes," and "exactly so," would follow.

Or they might pretend to make sport of Henry Knox's almost unbelievable three-hundred-mile movement of cannon to Boston, but then laughingly do an impersonation of the blasé commanding general calmly acting as if he had expected nothing less. Washington, far more sensitive than anyone suspected, loved the self-image they gave him and gloried in it.

Some of the interchanges among various delegations before the formal opening of the Convention were highly significant. Apart from Madison and the Pinckneys of South Carolina, Roger Sherman of Connecticut, was one of the most active. Sherman was like no one else there—sixty-six, older than all except Franklin, with a brief, blunt way of talking that always made a telling point. Although the precise thoughts exchanged in those preliminary talks were never recorded, it is clear that important compromises in the Constitution would have their origin in these informal sessions.

Also special, but in a different way, was John Dickinson of Pennsylvania, who probably received more respect than any other delegate save Washington himself. Fighting against serious illness most of his life, Dickinson had been a loyalist who understood the wrath of the colonies, but stood firmly against separating from Britain. He made it plain, however, that he would never fail to support his friends and neighbors if they insisted on independence. And when the die was cast, he immediately enlisted in the American forces and served throughout the war to the best of his ability. Now, in this turbulent time, he saw the need for stronger government, wanted to make sure the change was made in a legitimate fashion, and showed his impeccable judgment in every question that arose. Even though he could not become an all-out supporter of Madison's ideas, the two men had an affinity based on their style and their almost identical devotion to rational approaches.

There were many who thought—and a considerable number who said aloud—"Where is Hamilton? Has he been seen?" In all these encounters, the young leader who was thought to be Madison's equal in the enterprise was looked for but had not yet appeared. He had his own agenda, which called for undertaking many pursuits at the same time. Although he married into a very wealthy family, it was a point of pride with him to make his own way. So until there was something close to a quorum in Philadelphia, he preferred to be in his New York office, taking care of the law practice that meant so much to his family's future.

Hamilton's absence, however, made some wonder whether he was in accord with whatever plans Madison was clearly concocting, or whether he had a low regard for the value of these informal discussions. They realized that, hampered as he was by having two New York delegates who would nullify any vote he might cast, he might find it hard to see what part he could take to help carry out the plan that Madison was working at so industriously.

The private talks could not have flatly decided in advance what subjects might be considered out of order and left unmentioned during the formal sessions, for no one could foresee what others might say, but they arranged understandings between key individuals who then realized the need to avoid or downplay certain dead-end issues. As an example, the nature of the action when the formal meetings were under way made it clear that the two interlocked issues of slavery and secrecy had been considered in advance. Secrecy would never have been agreed on so swiftly if preliminary talks had not paved the way. And the slavery issue would have threatened an end to the Convention if Madison had not made his closest supporters aware of the shattering fact he learned from Pinckney: significant political forces in South Carolina had already considered seceding from the Union, and they would certainly insist on abandoning the plan for a Constitution if the Convention made any move that was unfavorable to slavery. This meant that Pinckney and his delegation would have no choice but to leave Philadelphia if attempts were made to tamper with his state's right to keep importing slaves without limitation.

It might be asked how Madison could be sure this warning was not a trick of Pinckney's—a formula for crying "Caution! Do not touch," at any mention of slavery. The question surely occurred to Madison, even though he and other Virginians admired and trusted Pinckney as an honest man. But apart from trust, Madison concluded that the latter would have known any dissembling might be exposed in the course of events, weakening his position in future dealings with other states. And during the coming year, events did reveal the truth—which was that Pinckney had been entirely reliable. When the delegates went back to South Carolina to prepare to ratify the Constitution—confident that they had won unexpected benefits for their slave-based economy—they encountered a storm of public complaints from pro-slavery factions who still thought the delegation had been too compliant in the few concessions it had made.

Some critics of the Convention's work have gone so far as to charge that slavery was totally ignored in Philadelphia, simply because the subject made so slight an appearance and the word was never used in the written Constitution. But in fact, although slavery as an institution was only sporadically attacked in the formal meetings, certain differences in slave and non-slave states played a big part in other major subjects, such as voting rights, taxes, and customs duties. Everyone present knew, when those issues were discussed, that slavery was being talked about even if it was not named aloud. Voting rights in the Lower House of Congress automatically led to the question of how many votes a slave owner might command as a result of owning these other persons. And any delegate who questioned the standing rule to avoid publicizing the Convention's deliberations would have threatened to create publicity that might destroy the Convention.

Most delegates knew or suspected that slavery had been taken up in private talks, especially between Madison and Pinckney—discussed and then ruled out as a separate subject for the Convention. Firm written proof of this was avoided as carefully as a strategic plan would be protected in time of war. But letters on other subjects occasionally indicated how unspecified arrangements were under way. For example, William Grayson, a congressman from Virginia, exchanged letters with Madison that hinted at plans that could not be put into writing. On May 24, 1787, when the first session of the Convention was at hand, Grayson wrote to Madison:

> A little flurry has been kicked up about Philadelphia. Carrington, I assume, has given you full information [Edward Carrington was also a Virginia legislator]. The enemy wanted to raise a mutiny in our camp by proposing to go to Georgetown at a certain time…Since the matter has blown over, some particular gentlemen have offered to join us in getting Georgetown fixed as the capital of the Federal Empire. They say they will vote money for the buildings…I am not certain when all the Eastern States come forward, but some good may come of this, provided we act with delicacy and caution…Entre nouz [sic] I believe the Eastern people have taken ground they will not depart from respecting the Convention. One legislature composed of a lower house, biennially elected, and an Executive and Senate for a good number of years. I shall see Gerry and Johnson as they pass, and perhaps give you a hint.

Apart from the fact that Grayson's letter, before any formal meeting had been held in Philadelphia, spells out almost exactly what would be arranged during the next four months, it is quite likely that the "particular gentlemen" were southerners who were also accurate in pinpointing the distant decision for a capital site just where they preferred to see it. And, in that case, their promise to produce "money for the buildings" would probably indicate their great prosperity, based on the promise of uninterrupted slave trade.

Even if there were a gentleman's agreement, which Madison and Pinckney might have made known to their own and allied delegations, it would not have been enforceable as a rule for other delegates to follow. Consequently, several delegates who may have hoped to see a dramatic fight on the issue attempted to raise the slavery question, but were usually deterred by the rules of order and civility they had agreed on. Such indicants cannot provide specifics, but they are proof that secretive arrangements were discussed.

In opposition to this view, George Mason of Virginia has been highly praised for his principled stand that the Constitution must not be created without a clear attack on the institution of slavery. He rose repeatedly to brand slavery with titles such as "this vilest of all evils," hoping he might rouse talk of its abolition or at least some resolution about its eventual end. He ultimately broke away and went home, partly because the Convention's leaders refused to attack the southern states on this issue. But no possibility existed that any action at this Convention might have moved the whole terrible custom toward an end nearly a century before a Civil War had to be fought. Mason's hope for this casts doubt on the long-standing notion that he had the mind and the potential to have been a great statesman. His attitude was honorable, but impractical in contrast to Madison's.

Mason had the mind of a philosopher instead, and the courage of his firm convictions. It may be a pity that the duties of managing a large family and important estate did not leave him time to write extensively about his decidedly original thoughts. One of his unusual ideas that should have been made known to the world (and especially to people of wealth, who had time for philosophy) was this: he wondered "how the superior classes of society could be indifferent to the well-being of all others," for no matter how affluent they themselves might be, he pointed out, it was a certainty that some of their own posterity would be distributed through the lower class of society. "So every selfish motive, every family attachment, should recommend a system of policy that would provide for the happiness of all orders of citizens."

It is a fact that most wealthy or important families over the course of a few generations produce impoverished members. Alexander Hamilton's father was descended from a noble and wealthy family. Yet, in a single generation, this errant family member became penniless and behaved in a totally irresponsible fashion toward his sons. Madison's own widow, Dolley, was driven almost to poverty after his death because a ne'er-do-well son by an earlier marriage lost most of her money. A considerable number of America's presidents have had very troubled descendants, and the same is true of most citizens of distinction. Mason was, in effect, reminding all these families of their own blood ties to "the poor." He was rousing them to his own strict sense of familial responsibility, saying, "It is a matter of simple self-interest to encourage policies for educating or otherwise aiding disadvantaged persons, for some of your blood relations are likely to be included among them."

But even if Mason had a supply of interesting thoughts, Madison was the more practical achiever. His adroit lobbying efforts that lined up the two South Carolinians, Pinckney and Rutledge, for the times when he would need their acquiescence on a key issue were masterful. It was a matter of knowing which of his acquaintances from his days in the Congress had the power and the willingness to meet his minimum negotiating needs.

Although Virginia had the most slaves, South Carolina was the state that relied most on the institution of slavery. There were more slaves than white people in South Carolina, and the whites always lived in fear of a slave uprising but gloried in the state's soaring profits from exports. Pinckney made it clear to Madison that if there were any thought of challenging this slave operation, at least three delegations—his own, North Carolina's, and Georgia's—were determined to go home at once. There was not the slightest chance that South Carolina would make any concession on this subject, he said, and he could not prevent his state from using its great leverage over North Carolina and Georgia to quit the Convention as well.

Though a strong antislavery advocate, Madison knew these men and their home situations well enough to be sure this was the truth. He knew they could not go back and report that they agreed to any limitation of their slave-based system. Georgia, although it had a very small white population and fewer slaves, was basing its hopes of growth on building up the number of slaves by importing black persons from South Carolina. Madison realized that Georgia's threat was a little less firm than South Carolina's, for that state's delegation was anxious to see a strong central government that might protect it from both Spanish and Native American forces that threatened its southern border. But its threat to secede rather than make any antislavery concession was nonetheless quite credible because Georgia had no alternate program for economic development.

Madison saw that any attack on slavery would simply break up the Convention and do great damage to the strong abolitionist trend that was under way in the northern states. Later in the Convention came compromises that were called "scandalous," but among all the compromises the one regarding slavery was the most despised, partly because it seemed to fit hand-in-glove with the decision to have absolute secrecy about deliberations, votes, and record-keeping.

The deliberations under way were so thoroughly and successfully conducted in secret that some popular records of events taking place in Philadelphia in 1787 do not even mention the Constitutional Convention. One such collection did say that "in August, while George Washington was in the city, he lent his presence and reputation to the attempts to interest the public in favor of manufactures by visiting the steel furnace of Nancarrow & Matlock," which was said to be "the largest and best constructed steel furnace in America." But it gave no reason for his being in the city. Ever the business enthusiast, Washington employed a free day for the purpose of publicizing the new plant. But even though the nation knew of the General's presence at a great political event, he clearly gave the impression that newspaper chatter on that subject was to be avoided.

Although the need to compromise has to be regretted, nothing proves the absolute determination to save the Union as these two decisions do—the rule of secrecy and the avoidance of a fight over slavery. Despite the fact that his great friend Jefferson, when he heard about the decision to conduct the convention in secret, said that it was abominable "to have tied up the tongues of their members," Madison said later that a Constitution could never have been written if the deliberations had been publicly known. He even imposed a fifty-year embargo on the notes he made of Convention proceedings, and they were not seen until years after his death.

If Jefferson had been present in person to hear Madison's calm explanation, he surely would have been forced to agree, as he almost always found himself swayed by his friend's logic. An especially delicate example of how this came about in practice occurred early in Jefferson's presidency, when he developed a close relationship with the young and very forthcoming Emperor Alexander of Russia. On learning that Alexander had interceded on the United States' behalf in a dispute with the Turkish government, Madison commented pleasantly on the event, but immediately added, "I wish, however, that with this obliging temper, there may not be included some little view of drawing the United States into the politics of Russia." Although Jefferson could not have been pleased to have his brilliant new friendship examined in such a different light, he quickly saw that Madison had put his finger on a point that he had overlooked. And he did proceed to observe this caution in later contacts with the emperor.

Any violation of the secrecy rule leading to public discussion of what was afoot in Philadelphia would have caused opposition forces to form in various communities throughout the country. Since word-of-mouth reports inevitably exaggerate and distort the facts, the public outcries would have increased and the Convention delegates would have heard even more frightening versions of how their home front was reacting. Some of these delegates would surely have tended to pull back from any commitments they were preparing to make so that the room for compromise would have shrunk to an unworkable level.

Madison's decision on the subject of slavery was hardly a compromise; it was virtually a surrender to the slave forces. But the alternative was to abandon the idea of a new Constitution altogether, leaving a huge slave population intact in both the Carolinas and Georgia, with not even the hope of eventual liberation. Instead, Madison and his intimates assessed the fact that slavery was already declining sharply in most of the

Union. Massachusetts had already banned slavery in its own territory and New Hampshire was on the point of doing so. All of New England was abandoning the practice. Most other states introduced laws that ruled out any new enslavement and that tended to promote liberation of the children born to slaves. Virginia and even North Carolina took steps in that direction. It made sense, even though it proved to be wrong, to think that a wave of antislavery action was under way. So keeping the entire Union intact and hoping that all the states could be weaned away from slavery over time seemed far preferable to an all-or-nothing solution that would have removed any hope for eventual emancipation. This reasoning, reached after long, late-night talks that must have been extremely distressing, left the discussions on the Convention floor mainly free of unwinnable debates on the issue of slavery.

Chapter Nine

A STRIKING START

On Friday, May 25, with a light rain falling, the delegates entered the State House and went to the same large first-floor room that Madison had studied so carefully. This time they arrived for the first formal session of the Convention. With the New Jersey delegation complete, seven states were now represented. The twenty-nine delegates in the room included sufficient numbers from Delaware, New Jersey, New York, North Carolina, Pennsylvania, South Carolina, and Virginia to make those delegations official. A quorum had been reached. The fifteen tables, each with two chairs, were neatly arrayed and covered in green baize, leaving room for more tables as new delegates arrived.

Pennsylvania delegate Robert Morris, temporarily presiding in place of Benjamin Franklin, who was ill, welcomed the delegates and made a motion to declare George Washington president of the Convention. It was seconded by John Rutledge of South Carolina. These steps normally would have led to a discussion of the nominee's personal qualities and fitness for the office, but it was deemed improper to have any such talk about General Washington while he was present. The usual procedure was to ask the nominee to leave, but after a few moments of hesitation, the thought of doing so brought on a little muffled laughter that under-scored the silliness of supposing that anything negative was going to be said about this nominee.

Morris hesitated only a moment before simply declaring, "Let us pro-ceed to take the ballots." When the votes were counted, on the agreed basis of one vote per state, George Washington was unanimously accepted as president. In his diary, he said only, "By a unanimous vote, I was called up to the Chair as President of the body. Hamilton and Charles Pinckney were chosen as part of a committee to prepare regula-tions and rules for conducting business. Then adjourned till Monday 10 o'clock. Dined with a club at City Tavern."

There was actually a little more pomp than Washington described. He had been seated near the middle of the room, intentionally avoiding a front chair that might have indicated an expectation of this honor. After the unanimous ballot, there was a round of enthusiastic applause. Morris and Rutledge walked to where the General was sitting, positioned them-selves on either side of Washington's seat, and then escorted him to the president's chair.

This brief ceremony occurred exactly as foreseen by James Madison, who had selected a chair near the front of the assembled delegates and begun at once to take the copious notes that were destined to remain unseen for a half-century. But apparently Madison allowed Thomas Jefferson to read these notes, for in 1815 Jefferson wrote to John Adams, saying, "Do you know that there exists in manuscript the ablest work of this kind ever yet executed of the debates of the constitutional convention of Philadel-phia? The whole of everything said and done there was taken down by Mr. Madison, with a labor and exactness beyond comprehension."

The meeting turned next to the choice of a secretary, whose record of the proceedings would be largely mechanical—not an account of what was said, like Madison's, but a listing of persons present, who spoke, who intro-duced motions, and other factual accounts. There were two candidates: One was Major William Jackson, whose military career had consisted largely of helping higher officers in their work on diplomatic issues. After retirement, he tried aggressively to become a fixture at as many political meetings as possible. The other candidate was Temple Franklin, another of Benjamin Franklin's grandsons, who offered little in his favor except his grandfather's recommendation. He had been a poor student in Paris. He was suspected of disloyalty because his father, William Franklin, had been the royal governor of New Jersey and remained a devoted loyalist. And Temple lived miles from the Convention on a New Jersey farm, while Jackson lived in Philadelphia, which seemed to promise prompt arrivals.

Major Jackson was nominated by Alexander Hamilton, speaking for the New York delegation, and he was waiting outside the hall with what some considered his usual poor sense of propriety. He was elected by a comfortable margin, and some believed that Benjamin Franklin was absent from the first day of real debate that followed to protest this disregard for his personal choice. Gouverneur Morris told a friend, "Old Dr. F. was much mortified that he had not enough influence to procure the place for his grandson."

In any case, Jackson later came to be generally considered a poor selection, for many called him lazy and inefficient, saying that his account of the points he was supposed to cover was dry and incomplete. It seems likely that this poor performance was due to Jackson's disappointment at finding that the secrecy rule made him nothing more than a record-keeper. Earlier, Jackson was heard saying that his future would be assured if he could be named secretary, for he estimated that he could realize thousands of dollars from the sale of his report. As it was, the Jackson account had little commercial appeal.

Credentials were then read and accepted. As in the Continental Congress, it was declared that voting would be recorded in geographical order, north to south from New Hampshire to Georgia, and would be cast by state rather than by individual delegate. A very important point was decided—that decisions made by a majority on any question would not necessarily be final, but could be reconsidered and revoked during the life of the Convention.

Nine states were represented in the room at that time, but two had incomplete delegations, and men from three other states were thought to be on the way to Philadelphia. So the quorum was far short of the full number of delegates expected, and there were complaints about the combined effect of the rules on quorum and voting. Since a majority of the states represented on any day could decide any question, and since a quorum of seven states meant that four could be the majority, the net effect was that just four states could potentially decree drastic changes in the Articles of Confederation or create major rules for a new Constitution that thirteen states would be pressed to accept. The impropriety of this rule was discussed but never acted on, probably because the rule providing for reconsideration made any such distortion almost unimaginable.

After completing the normal housekeeping events that precede a large meeting, the plan of work was set up and rules for presenting and discussing ideas were established, with a notable emphasis on civility. There were stipulations for not interrupting or crossing in front of a speaker. Even reading printed materials while another member was speaking was an unallowable discourtesy. This emphasis on civility was in keeping with the much-remarked fact that Samuel Adams was not included in the Massachusetts delegation. Not long ago, Adams was one of the country's leading personalities, and his masterful stage-managing of protests was widely credited with many of the nation's early successes. But now it was not a talent for disruption that was needed. This Convention aimed for orderliness and assured secrecy.

To have secured a majority's approval of the rule "that nothing spoken in the house be printed or otherwise published or communicated without leave" was an astonishing accomplishment. (Washington's diary abbreviated this as "no com'ns without doors," meaning no communications to be given to the outside world.) A few months earlier, it would have been considered in poor form and decidedly against American principles to discuss the future of the nation in secret. To have brought this about was a first real victory for Madison. They now formally agreed on his prior decision—there would be no public disclosure of their deliberations as the meetings went on, nor any record kept for disclosure when the meetings ended.

Madison made it known that he alone would attempt to keep an accurate written journal of the proceedings, but that this record would not be made public until fifty years had passed. Only then did the nation learn the nature of discussions in the Convention that had previously been known by their final results. Madison's notes proved to be remarkably accurate, and they also contain speeches given by many other delegates in very exact form because some speakers gave Madison copies of their own speeches and asked that he incorporate them in his notes.

It is worth noting that during the proceedings, several delegates said they would be satisfied if the Constitution were to survive and serve a good purpose for as much as ten years. Madison, in setting the fifty-year rule of secrecy, clearly had far higher hopes. And it was a canny move. If anyone were to contest the legality of the Constitution on the basis of some allegedly improper argument found in the original notes, this opponent would have been attacking a document that was already hallowed by a half-century of existence.

After these matters of detail were settled, the weekend recess ran through Monday despite the apparently erroneous statement in Washington's diary that they had adjourned until Monday. This diary became a simple two or three line entry each day, as Washington scrupulously observed the rule that not a word was to be written about events at State House.

It was Tuesday, May 29, when the meeting resumed, and Madison struck early by having Governor Edmund Randolph take the floor to speak for Virginia. By writing to the governor more often than usual for the past several months and making repeated subtle references to the great need for a stronger government, Madison had been preparing Randolph for this role since February, when the likelihood of a great convention appeared.

Since the plan to be presented was Madison's, why should he not have made the proposal himself? It must be borne in mind that Madison was not a person who carried great weight at this point. His work in the Congress had been noticed several times for its hard-hitting precision. More than once, he was proposed for promotion to head some new department of the existing flimsy government. On each occasion, he declined the opportunity, saying that he did not feel qualified (although the real reason was a poor opinion of the office). Now he had no state or national office at all and no record of official accomplishment. As noted earlier, he was not even a property owner yet—a major gauge of maturity at that time—but a young man financially dependent on his father. A relatively small circle of leading individuals valued every word he said, but most of the delegates would have wondered, "Why is this young man presenting Virginia's plan? What has he done to deserve our attention? Why has this, our greatest state, put so much power into his hands?" Recognizing this view existed and having no wish to put himself forward, Madison decided three months earlier that he wanted the state's governor to make the formal proposal.

There was one problem. The very correct Governor Randolph— three years younger than Madison, but decades older in his rather stolid approach—did not want to suggest a new form of government. The old Congress granted permission only to review the Articles of Confederation and possibly recommend certain modifications, so Randolph had to be promised that he would be doing nothing more than was proper. The Virginia Plan that he was to propose, Madison told him, would simply help the Convention organize its "review."

No public speaker has ever been so thoroughly tricked as Randolph was on that occasion, and it is remarkable that a man of considerable intelligence should have walked innocently into the trap, seen it close on him, and yet not stomp furiously from the meeting. Somehow, he let it happen without any sign of rancor. The plan that Randolph first laid out on May 29 contained fifteen "resolves" (as the resolutions were called because each began, "Resolved that…"), and it so clearly called for a new form of government that someone was virtually certain to ask, "Why are we talking of this as merely an adjustment of the old Articles? It is obviously a new plan. Why not give it that title?" It seems quite possible that Madison, with his meticulous way of leaving nothing to chance, prepared at least one of the delegates to raise this very question. It turned out to be Gouverneur Morris who, with his flair for light banter, opened the next morning's session (May 30) by cheerfully asking Randolph exactly that question.

Apparently Morris's lighthearted way of raising this point made it seem less weighty to Randolph; and perhaps he felt satisfied that he had done enough to obey the Congress's instructions for nothing more than a review. In any case, Randolph changed his whole approach and switched to a flat statement that he was acting "at the action of Gouverneur Morris" in asking for a postponement of debate on his resolution of the day before. Instead, he offered a new proposal for a national government. He plunged ahead to describe in greater detail what would now be called the Virginia Plan. It was Madison's plan, pure and simple.

After such a bizarre beginning, the handsome Randolph seemed perfectly composed and introduced the new plan by saying,

> The Confederation was made in the infancy of the science of constitutions...when no commercial discord had arisen among states, when no rebellion like that in Massachusetts had broken out, when foreign debts were not urgent, when the havoc of paper money had not been foreseen, when treaties had not been violated, and when nothing better could have been conceded by states jealous of their sovereignty. But it offered no security against foreign invasion, for Congress could neither prevent nor conduct a war, nor punish infractions of treaties or of the law of nations so that there is a prospect of anarchy from the inherent laxity of the government. As the remedy, the government to be established must have for its basis the republican principle.

The Virginia Plan that he went on to present would make the federal government directly reflect the individual's wishes by establishing a national legislature in which the combined wishes of the American people instead of the American states would be represented. If the heart of the Constitution had to be described in a single sentence, that would be it.

Randolph then described a Congress with two houses—the lower house elected by popular vote with the number of delegates proportioned to the population of each state. This provision, of course, survived all the buffeting of the Convention and is triumphantly alive today. The other part of Congress did not last in its original form. The upper house was to be selected by the lower house from candidates proposed by each state's legislature, and these upper members would have longer terms. The two houses would join in selecting an executive whose term would be short and not renewable. The key point, which was pure Madisonism, was that the common people would be dominant because both houses of Congress and the executive branch would derive from the people's original election of lower-house members and of their own state legislatures. And because that lower house was proportioned to population, the larger states, with their greater number of persons, would have the most influence.

The day was also brightened by the arrival of Benjamin Franklin in a great carrying chair that was handled by four brawny prisoners from the Philadelphia jail. They deposited it gently in the room, allowing Franklin to move to a comfortable chair as the delegates applauded wholeheartedly. After all this, George Washington allowed his diary to allude to "a superb entertainment given on the evening of June 1st at Bush-hill by Mr. William Hamilton." And on Monday, June 4, he told of "having reviewed the Light Infantry, Cavalry, and part of the artillery of the City, at the importunity of General Mifflin." But he was punctiliously adhering to his promise that "nothing will be suffered to transpire. No minutes of the proceedings have been or will be inserted in this diary." Only a line each day told of attendance at the session.

The number of clashes that the Virginia Plan set up was indeed daunting. To say that the large states appeared to have an advantage is one thing. But to picture the enormity of that advantage was another. Virginia would have sixteen representatives compared to only one for Georgia. Then there was the additional shocker that the national legislature would not only have great power to propose new laws, but also power to set aside state laws that it deemed unconstitutional. Madison himself spoke in defense of this power for dealing with states that passed unacceptable laws. "A negative on state laws," he said, "is the mildest expedient that can be devised for enforcing a national decree. The negative would render the use of force unnecessary." In other words, only by having the power to overrule a recalcitrant state could the federal government avoid the necessity of brutalizing that state into submission. It seemed obvious to Madison, dreadful to others.

This point would prove to be Madison's greatest disappointment, for it apparently never had any chance of passing. Yet, to the very end, he felt that there was danger of uncontrollable state actions, saying that either this provision or actual armed coercion were the only two alternatives if one were to have a true central government. His feeling of failure in connection with his view on this issue was considered strange, as most delegates saw no need for such a provision. Clause 2 of Article 6 was thought to accomplish the same objective without dealing the states another insulting slap. This clause says that the Constitution and the laws of the United States made under its authority "shall be the supreme Law of the Land," regardless of anything that might be found in the laws or constitution of any state. Obviously, then, if the Supreme Court finds any law, federal or state, to conflict with the Constitution, it is invalid.

It must be conceded, however, that Madison's point seemed well taken at least once, when, during the presidency of Andrew Jackson, South Carolina, after months of warning that it would not stand for the imposition of high tariffs on imported goods, proclaimed on November 24, 1832, that the federal government's tariff charges were void "and not binding upon this state or its citizens." It further declared that the use of force to collect duties would cause South Carolina to secede from the Union. In the stormy national debate that ensued, President Jackson sent seven cutters and a ship of war to Charleston, saying, "Nullification [meaning the state's attempt to nullify a federal law] means insurrection and war. Other states have a right to put it down. No state has a right to secede." Congress made things worse by being conciliatory, saying nothing about the use of force. Former president John Quincy Adams said, "The message goes to dissolve the Union and is a complete surrender to the nullifiers." Some others were urging Jackson to "recede with dignity."

On the day the president's message was to be read to Congress, Jackson was peering over the shoulder of his brilliant secretary of state, Edward Livingston, who was writing hastily. Livingston had already given Jackson a long lecture on the catastrophic damage to federal power if nullification were allowed. Now, as Livingston wrote, the combative president kept saying, "Good. Give it your best flight of eloquence."

The Proclamation on Nullification was proclaimed on December 10, 1832. The words were Livingston's, the spirit was Jackson's, and it was acclaimed as the greatest state paper of the Jackson era. Jackson presented the thoughts with his unique forcefulness. He called nullification an "impractical absurdity." He showed why "if this had been established at an earlier day, the Union would have been dissolved in its infancy...I consider the power to annul a law of the United States incompatible with the existence of the Union. It is contradicted expressly by the letter of the Constitution."

The reception by the Congress made it clear that South Carolina must give way, for everyone was on the side of the president and the Constitution. Bells rang across the nation. Men paraded. Volunteers offered to help if the military called, but they were not needed. Yet, this obvious foreshadowing of what was to come three decades later showed that Madison had been right. An explicit statement in the Constitution about nullification and secession would have strengthened a president's hand in such a crisis.

There were other moments in Philadelphia when Madison's need to "win" may have been due to extreme fatigue, as some historians suggest. But most agree that he was wrong to insist later that he "had no claim" to be called the "father" of the Constitution. Even though other stars emerged, Madison's extensive preplanning already laid out many basics and gave a sense of direction to the men who would play major roles.

This early point in the proceedings brought the first comment by Roger Sherman of Connecticut, and the more experienced men in the room knew this was probably a precursor of something serious to come. Sherman reminded the meeting that they were operating under the Congress's permission to conduct nothing more than a review, and he asked Randolph, on behalf of the Virginia delegation, to please explain how far they were willing to go in making changes. Randolph seemed to have the bit in his teeth by that time, and his reply was, "We have no intention of making changes, but only studying and proposing possible changes that the people could then consider."

Wilson spoke incisively, perfectly summarizing the question of how far the Convention could go. "As I see it," he said, "we are authorized to conclude nothing, but to propose anything."

Nonetheless, many delegates began to call the Virginia Plan an audacious scheme, enough to take the breath away. "Under the original Virginia Plan, the smaller states would have been virtually swamped," as one early historian puts it. So when the first vote was taken, the four most populous states—Virginia, Massachusetts, Pennsylvania, and North Carolina—voted in favor and carried South Carolina with them. The smaller states of Connecticut, New Jersey, Delaware, and Maryland voted against. The vote was considered inconclusive because the New Hampshire delegation had not yet arrived.

If they were to begin this way, they might as well go home, some were saying. They were not sent there to abolish the Confederation and set a revolution afoot. But Madison was not discouraged, for he noticed that most such comments went on to resolve themselves into specific details. Known enemies of change, like Hamilton's bitter New York colleagues Robert Yates and John Lansing, were against the whole Virginia Plan, as expected. But George Read, of Delaware, while saying that his delegation might feel obliged to withdraw from the Convention, added the words, "if the election of representatives according to population should be adopted." This comment with a specific objection made it into a point one could haggle over and work toward compromise. The sarcastic remark of South Carolina's Charles Cotesworth Pinckney would prove to be more to the point than it first appeared: "For all the talk against a national government, just give New Jersey an equal vote, and she would have no objection to a national government."

But even before that, an unlikely ally who did not really agree with him, as Madison knew, would prove indispensable. Gouverneur Morris, known to be very conservative in his basic views and independent-minded enough to show it, was nonetheless anxious to see a strong government emerge, even if it were based on Madison's policy of popular representation. He and Madison had talked enough to understand and respect each other. Now Morris used his quick mind to assist Madison by promptly proposing that such a basic principle as Read questioned was too important for a hasty answer. It would require time for deliberation, and he tactfully suggested that it be postponed for a small committee discussion a few days later.

Everything about Morris's remarks, even the warm tone of his voice, somehow carried a promise of accommodation and good things to come; so Read nodded his acceptance and the incident passed. Equally important, the technique of referring thorny questions to small committees set a precedent that would prove to be invaluable on many occasions.

The basic idea of a national legislature with two houses had not been vigorously opposed, so Madison pressed hard to decide at least that much. And surprisingly, this basic matter drew no opposition at all, nor even any substantial comment. Without argument, it was approved at once, which led Madison to test his luck further. He asked if members of the legislature should be selected by the people, and in a rather offhand manner, he answered his own question. "It would surely be the way to put this government on firmer ground." The opposition to this new thought built up slowly. Because several of the states chose their assemblies this way from the beginning, the idea felt comfortable at the start. Even so, it gradually became clear that many delegates had real doubts about the safety of this supremely important principle.

Several of the older men insisted that the people were wayward and unreliable. A favorite son of Massachusetts, Elbridge Gerry, who was trusted implicitly by his followers, showed that he did not return the compliment. He said outright that the people could not be trusted. "The people do not want virtue," he proclaimed. "But they are the dupes of pretended patriots." Many heads nodded in agreement, for—as Gerry reminded them—they all remembered so often seeing crowds swayed by hearing the words of a facile speaker.

Sherman, Rutledge, and both the Pinckneys took the same negative view, dealing Madison a hard blow on the most important point of all. He knew it was true that many people could be swayed, but he felt that a large enough body of people would find their way to the right decisions more often than a few elite leaders would. Shaken as he was, Madison would not be silenced on this issue. He would normally have let it slide and waited for another occasion; now he took a great risk and pushed grimly ahead. But a heated argument was not the kind for which all his careful preparation had readied him.

The roomful of delegates saw with surprise that Madison was not himself. They were accustomed to his ready answers whenever opposition loomed. They expected perfectly chosen historical quotations or clever reminders of remarks his opponents made a year or two ago. His hesitation was unsettling. The moment might have proved very destructive if Madison had been humiliated by a wave of opposition, but the disappointing Hamilton, whose silence was a great question mark in many minds, came smartly to life.

Amazingly, in view of what was to come later, Hamilton came to Madison's aid with a firm and perfectly timed declaration: "It is essential to the democratic rights of the community that the first branch, at least, must be directly elected by the people." George Mason rose immediately with a powerful follow-up: "The proposed assembly," he said, "is to be, so to speak, our House of Commons, and ought to know and sympathize with every part of the community. It ought to have at heart the rights and interests of every class of the people, and in no other way could this end be so completely attained as by popular election."

It was like a well-rehearsed performance. As soon as Mason sat down, Madison's pre-Convention chats paid off handsomely when his new friend, Wilson of Pennsylvania, made another of his moves to increase support for Madison by saying, "Without the confidence of the people, no government, least of all a republican government, can long subsist...The election of the first branch by the people is not only the cornerstone, but the foundation of the fabric." After that torrent of support, Madison's friends allowed him to speak, and a few softened words from him carried the day.

Because this power of the people to select their representatives was Madison's greatest desire, the day could have been seen as a triumph. But he was not fooled. There were going to be severe challenges at some point. The small states, which enjoyed the incredible luxury of equal representation in the old Congress, must certainly be preparing to object—or even walk out—if they saw their protests as hopeless. Most of the delegates, young as they were, were sophisticates—and they wondered when and how the opposing forces would decide to strike. Madison's initial victory put people on record in his favor, but he knew the rules of the Convention allowed the question to be reopened.

Already, that warning shot from Roger Sherman, the elderly Connecticut man who was never known to waste a word, seemed to spell trouble. But it was manageable trouble, for he knew that Sherman wanted union. So any problem he presented would be subject to compromise. A highly intelligent person who had been a key player in every event since the Declaration of Independence, Sherman now pointed out that the destruction of the existing system hardly seemed like a way to create respect for the work of this Convention. In other words, he was objecting to the style of the Virginia Plan rather than its content.

Madison was heartened by noting that most of the men who spoke seemed ready for changes in the form of government. It would take different approaches to deal with such persons, but they were not major threats. Madison felt that individuals to be feared were those delegates who said little or nothing. He knew some of them were men who objected to far more than style, and he could only hope that in the end they would be outvoted.

Chapter Ten

SMALL STATES
STRIKE BACK

The Convention was nearly demolished by a great issue that came up on June 4, interrupting a routine discussion of the Virginia Plan. The subject was no surprise, but the force of the attack was startling.

The smaller states revealed their absolute determination to reject the Virginia Plan, for they felt the larger states would have so many more votes—based on population—that small states would count for nothing. Beyond the practical aspect of this disparity, they seemed to feel disrespected and insulted by the nature of the proposal. The small states had full voting equality under the Articles of Confederation. Why would anyone think they should readily accept a demotion to lower status? The answer might have been: "To keep the Union together." But they were now giving a credible display of little regard for a union that held them in such low esteem.

The leading example of why the smaller states felt trampled was New Jersey. The state delegates insisted they knew what it was like to be tyrannized by powerful neighbors. New York and Pennsylvania were the behemoths that carried out their own ways of trading, exporting, and rearranging fees or discounts with an eye to maximizing profits for their businessmen and gains for the state treasuries, regardless of the effect on small states. Connecticut and Delaware felt some of the same pressures; and to some extent Maryland expressed similar views. But it was New Jersey that spoke out angrily and threateningly as the champion of the whole group in early June.

William Paterson, leader of the New Jersey delegation, compared the relations between large and small states with the status of rich and indigent individuals. "We do not say that the rich man should have fifty times as many votes as the poor man. Why then give the large state three times the votes of the small one?"

Paterson was only five feet, two inches tall, but he suddenly rose to dominate the room. He now proposed to amend the Articles of Confederation, but to amend them with a plan of his own, which came to be called the New Jersey Plan. It was made to appear structured enough to be called a "plan," but it was not really an innovation. It called for an executive, but in the form of a council chosen by the Congress rather than an individual. It also provided for a federal judiciary, and for a revenue plan based on a Stamp Act.

But much like the Articles of Confederation, it proposed a single house. This seemed hopelessly outdated in view of the fact that the tired old Continental Congress had already decreed a bicameral system for the Northwest Ordinance. Weakest of all was the fact that New Jersey copied the dying system by failing to give its proposed congress the power to enforce its rulings. Also, much like the old Articles, it proposed a federal legislature that would represent states, rather than individuals. And the states were to vote equally, regardless of population. In short, it did not even address the main weaknesses of the Confederation, so it was strongly opposed by Madison, Hamilton, Wilson, and Rufus King.

The New Jersey Plan's chief appeal was its claim to be legitimate because it did not exceed the powers granted by the old Congress, as the Virginia Plan clearly did. But Governor Randolph, gathering fire with the passing days, shot back, "When the salvation of the republic is at stake, it would be treason to our trust not to propose what we find necessary."

And Hamilton came forth with the propitious reminder that the newness of any plan they might adopt would not be a violation of the stricture from Congress, for they would not be bringing a new government to life, but only recommending a scheme that would have to be submitted to the states for acceptance by the people. If ratification succeeded, it would mean that the people had chosen this new document, making it their own creation.

David Brearly, of New Jersey, stood up stoutly for his colleague Paterson, charging that Virginia, Massachusetts, and Pennsylvania were about to carry everything before them, proving New Jersey's point about the dominance of the large states. A dozen years earlier, Brearly had been such an outspoken revolutionary that the British had arrested him and charged him with high treason, putting him in danger of hanging, until he was rescued by friends. Now he cited his own less daunting experience that even in state affairs, the large counties always carried their point. So what future, he asked, could the small states look forward to unless they at least had voting equality with other Americans who pretended to be equals.

Paterson then sarcastically added that if one really wanted a nation ruled by individuals, all state distinctions must be abolished. "Throw everything into a hotchpot and have just one huge nation peopled with equal citizens," he advised, "taking care that a rich citizen should not have more votes than an indigent one." But the truth is, he said seriously, that if the great states wish to unite on a plan, "let them unite if they please, but let them remember that they have no authority to compel the others to unite…Shall I submit the welfare of New Jersey with five votes in a council where Virginia has sixteen? I will never consent to the proposed plan."

But James Wilson pointed out the absurdity of giving one hundred eighty thousand men in one part of the country as much weight in the national legislature as seven hundred fifty thousand in another part. "The gentleman from New Jersey is candid," Wilson said. "I commend him for it. I will be equally candid…I never will confederate on his principles."

It seemed that a real brick wall was being raised between the opposing parties, and the debate grew more intense, more visibly nervous. No one wanted to see the meeting collapse, yet they could not find a way to end the heated dispute.

John Dickinson, with customary wisdom and courtesy, pointed out that the nation had greater security for the future because of the "accidental lucky division of this country into distinct states," and he hoped this would be preserved by giving states equal votes in at least one branch of the national legislature. The phrase "at least one" was clearly the way to a solution, but no one appeared to notice it at that moment.

Madison tried his hand at pacification, saying quietly that if a union should finally be formed, they would find that this rivalry between large and small states was hardly an issue at all, especially as compared with the real clash between northern and southern states. It was the first time anything this ominous had ever been said in an official setting—a forecast of the Civil War, which was over seventy years away. He did not use the word "slavery," but put it this way: "The great danger to our general government," he said prophetically, "is the great southern and northern interests of the continent being opposed to each other." In saying this, he showed how desperately anxious he was to win a compromise on the present issue, for he risked offending the South Carolinians. But prophetic as his words were, simply bringing up a greater problem failed to impress the delegates as a cure for the one that lay before them. No one seemed to take great notice of what he had said. The impasse went on.

Rufus King, who was destined to be America's diplomatic representative in London, called on an overseas example to placate the small states. "Take Scotland's rights, for instance," he reminded them. "These are surely safe from violation, even though its representation in Parliament is so much smaller than that of England. Why on Earth does anyone assume that the number of seats held is such a threat?"

But that view only roused Delaware's Gunning Bedford to greater fury. A large and forceful man who was a classmate of Madison's at Princeton, he barked:

Pretences to support ambition are never wanting. You insist that if the general government's powers are increased, it will be for the good of the whole. And although the three great states form nearly a majority of the people of America, you say they never will injure the lesser states. Gentlemen, I do not trust you. If you possess the power, the abuse of it will not be checked.

And here Bedford shocked even his own closest colleagues, adding, "Sooner than be ruined, there are foreign powers who will take us by the hand."

There was a moment of complete silence. Everyone knew that European powers had made lavish proposals to some of the small American states, hoping to win a profitable outpost in the New World. But no state had ever spoken of this before—and certainly none sounded so seriously enticed by the offers. In a roomful of men arguing over high principles, Bedford's remark sounded like a refined lady's sudden suggestion that prostitution was one possible career she had in mind.

The silence was finally broken by Rufus King, saying somberly, "I am concerned for what fell from the gentleman from Delaware. Take a foreign power by the hand? Indeed. I am sorry he mentioned it, and I hope he is able to excuse it to himself on the score of passion." Although King was young, his comment carried just the right tone of quasi-parental disapproval. It reminded everyone present that they were all Americans—impervious to the blandishments of foreign seducers.

At that dramatic point on June 27, a forty-eight-hour loss of time occurred. Maryland's puffy, tired-looking Luther Martin, whose heavy drinking sometimes blurred his superior legal mind, did himself and all the others a real disservice when he took the floor and began a most unwelcome departure from the strict subject of discussion. It turned into an angry speech that rambled on for nearly two full days. Somehow, Washington, as presiding officer, could think of no way to end it, for it was not entirely unrelated to the subject that was under discussion. The people who were trying to take notes could not even follow Martin's reasoning enough to put anything down. But they understood his basic point that the general government was meant merely to preserve the state governments, not to govern individuals. And he made clear his repeated threat that he would rather see the Union break up into partial confederacies than unite on a plan like Virginia's. To underscore how dangerous the situation had become, he insisted that "the convention is on the verge of dissolution. You must give each state an equal suffrage, or our business is at an end."

When Martin finally sat down, the weary delegates heard Franklin ask for the floor. He began in a low, soft voice, speaking directly to George Washington, as if it were a personal conversation, saying,

> The small progress we have made after four or five weeks and continual reasonings with each other is methinks a melancholy proof of the imperfection of the human understanding. We have been running about in search of wisdom, have gone back to ancient history for models of government, and we have viewed modern states all round Europe, but find none of their constitutions suitable to our circumstances.
>
> In this situation, Sir, how is it that we have not once thought of humbly applying to the Father of Lights to illuminate our understanding?

He went on at some length, recalling previous times when prayer had been part of their approach to problems. "Therefore," he said, "I beg leave to move that henceforth prayers imploring the assistance of Heaven be held in the Assembly every morning before we proceed to business." It is likely that Roger Sherman seconded the motion.

More than one twentieth-century history of the Convention reported that Hamilton rudely said, "I see no need to call for foreign aid in solving our problems." While clever, this remark neither sounds like Hamilton, nor conveys the respect he had for Franklin. It gained currency because Hamilton did speak against Franklin's idea. But rather than a cutting remark, he said and later personally confirmed that he would have favored prayers if they had been the rule all along. But he feared that if word got out about prayers just starting, the public might believe a serious deadlock had occurred. Several other delegates agreed with this reasoning and regretfully decided to forego the use of Franklin's idea.

Roger Sherman then thought of just the right thing to say. He looked at Franklin, as if thanking him for having tried. He looked then at King, as if thanking him for his dramatic rebuke to Bedford. He even glanced at the tiresome Martin, and he seemed to be rephrasing that man's last words by saying, "Then we are come to a full stop." It could have been taken to be a tough declaration that the Convention could not go on. But this was not so, for there was a double meaning. It was interpreted as a way to say that the weekend recess was about to begin, while implying that "we've done all we can do for now."

It was Sherman who, together with his Connecticut colleague, Oliver Ellsworth, talked with numerous other delegates during that weekend, mainly in the drinking rooms of the Indian Queen tavern. They proposed the celebrated arrangement that is often and quite logically called the "Connecticut Compromise." (The names linked to the various compromises vary greatly. This one and another that some call the "Great Compromise" are the only ones that will be used in this book, because the others cause more confusion than clarification.) Sherman suggested that the lower house be elected as the big states wanted, on the basis of proportional representation; the makeup of the upper house would placate the small states, for here they would have exactly as much representation as the large states—two seats per state. He also proposed different methods for electing representatives: the lower house directly chosen by the people, and the upper house appointed by the state legislatures.

The widespread assumption that this Connecticut Compromise was a great stroke of fresh thought that fell from the minds of two New Englanders is difficult to accept. Recall that only a few days earlier, John Dickinson had voiced the hope that equal representation would be preserved "in at least one house," which clearly foresaw two houses with different rules of membership. It was heard and apparently disregarded. It is hard to think that a chamber full of men with such agile minds, having fixed on a bicameral plan almost from the start, could have gone on for long in a quandary over how to resolve the clash of large and small states—never seeing the obvious way to put this two-house system to flexible use. Why two houses then? Was it only to imitate Britain? Or to make a place for persons of different caliber? Each of these reasons could play a part, but many delegates would certainly have thought, "Why not use this bicameral arrangement to solve one more problem—make the states all equal in one house and have proportional representation in the other." The compromise was too obvious to be a surprise.

But in that case, if many men present were thinking of such an arrangement all along, why did no one mention it much sooner? Almost surely for the reason that so many bargaining sessions—in politics, in salary disputes, in industrial strikes—go on at tiresome length even when the midway point of eventual agreement is predictable. It is because the first participant who suggests an accommodative arrangement puts himself or herself at a disadvantage. The opposing side thinks, "Ah, they are ready to talk of a compromise. Let's see how much more we can get from them." The playing field is already tilted against the player who shows a willingness to make a concession. In Philadelphia, it seems likely that the delegates all kept waiting for a moment so full of tension that one brave soul would dare to show his hand and to imagine that the momentum of the instant would make his opponents realize the virtue of his suggested solution.

When the canny and courageous Roger Sherman took this risk, his timing was ideal. Even at that, it was a very close call. Delegates talking over the weekend, arguing in small groups at the Indian Queen, all seemed to warm to the idea of just such a compromise. But when a vote was organized during the following week, it was agonizingly close. Of the eleven states represented (because New Hampshire and Rhode Island were not present) five voted affirmatively—Connecticut, New Jersey, Delaware, Maryland, and New York. Five others voted against the Compromise—Virginia, Pennsylvania, Massachusetts, North Carolina, and South Carolina. That left only Georgia as the tie-breaker, and one of its two delegates voted against, leaving the whole outcome to a young man named Abraham

Baldwin, a former Yale College tutor who moved to Georgia only a short time before and became a surprise choice as a delegate to the Constitutional Convention. The vote he was about to cast would be a historic event, and there was a hush as Baldwin's decision was awaited.

Nobody in the room knew much about the serious young man, and he has had little attention since. Yet he may have carried the fate of the Convention—and the future of the United States—in the hand that held the ballot. He was thirty-three years old, the son of a remarkable blacksmith who ran up a huge debt to give his six children educations. Abraham Baldwin became a Yale graduate, a keen student of religion, and served as a chaplain in the Continental Army for five years. Then he took an interest in the backward state of Georgia and made it his residence because he was intrigued by the challenge of bringing higher education to an almost virgin territory. But since Georgia had few educated men, he was first asked to become the state's delegate to the old Congress for a few months, mostly attending meetings in New York City. The state then asked him to come to Philadelphia as a Georgia delegate to the Constitutional Convention. No one there had learned much about his policies, but now this was the main question in all their minds.

Baldwin was almost as unsure as the men watching him. Deeply religious as he was, he did not approve of slavery but he thought each state should be left alone to create policies that suited its situation. And he really saw no future for Georgia unless it had some years of slavery to build up enough wealth for development of cities and institutions, so he was inclined to add another negative vote, which would have meant that Georgia, as a state, voted "no"—breaking the tie and killing the Connecticut Compromise.

But Baldwin knew how close to disaster the Convention had come—and also that its failure could well lead to a Union collapse and the creation of two or more new state groupings. Whatever Georgia's state policy might be, such a breakaway from his beloved New England and Yale and the North's sophisticated cities seemed appalling to him. Yet while he might hold the means to destroy the United States, he had no power to save it, for a positive ballot from him would mean that Georgia's vote was split, counting as no vote at all. He would be accused of wasting Georgia's voice. With Georgia thus excluded, the final vote would still be a five to five tie. But Baldwin reasoned that this, at least, might lead to something. He knew not what—perhaps some tie-breaking procedure that was beyond his own political experience. Better to try the unknown than to stop the action.

He voted "yes" to the compromise. Georgia's vote was split and would not count, yet it was one of the most valuable votes in the nation's history. The five to five tie that prevailed was given a dynamic interpretation by Baldwin's more experienced colleagues.

An early historian said, "All honor to Baldwin's memory," because this did allow the formidable political skills in the hall to go to work, appointing a special committee of eleven men (of whom Baldwin was one) to consider how to deal with the tie. Elbridge Gerry, a favorite son of Massachusetts and a respected leader in national affairs, was named its chairman, which might have seemed to be bad news for the compromise, since Massachusetts had been one of the negative states on this issue. But Gerry was a statesman and ran a fair committee, concluding that New Hampshire and Rhode Island, if present, would surely have voted with the small states in favor of the compromise. On this convenient premise, the Connecticut Compromise was said to pass seven to five, and the new Constitution continued to be built.

Abraham Baldwin went on to be a Convention member who talked little, but who played a great role in the work of planning and rewriting that took so much of the delegates' time. On returning to Georgia, he was admitted to the bar. With a lawyer's income, he began to frame his cherished plan to create a university. He became the first president of the University of Georgia. His half-brother, Henry Baldwin, became a justice of the United States Supreme Court. Together they devoted themselves to helping their siblings pay off their father's very worthwhile debt for the education of his six offspring.

Even after the committee's report and a speech by Madison that summarized all the points favoring the compromise, the delegates seemed reluctant to vote on the bicameral plan that they had not been able to test in actual talks with the people who might now become their constituents. Eleven more days of calmer debate were required before the guidelines for the method of selecting representatives to a lower house was passed on July 16. A number of points that were thought to be minor were settled during this time, but their far-reaching implications would be realized as time went on.

Congressional terms of office did not arouse anywhere near as much emotion as the basic idea of who was to choose the representatives. Strangely, however, Elbridge Gerry, who had ideas about almost everything, exploded when he heard mention of a three-year term for the lower House. "Not one Massachusetts citizen in a thousand would support such a thing," he objected. The people of his state were accustomed to annual elections, and they were suspicious that men who were sure of their jobs for any longer period would begin thinking themselves more important than the voters and levy ruinous taxes. Partly for this reason, the terms were left undecided until the last month of the Convention, then made two years in the lower House and six years in the Senate.

Madison's single greatest objective had been passed—a lower house with proportional representation to be directly elected by the American people. The rule that senators were to be appointed by the state legislatures was only altered in 1913 by the Seventeenth Amendment, finally calling for the people of each state to elect their senators. But even its original form was not considered a great setback for Madison. By achieving one house of Congress that represented the American people and not the American states, he was on a subtle route to reforming the government. The Virginia Plan had been considerably modified, yet Madison's principle of stressing the rights and responsibilities of the people, rather than states, was upheld so far, a great victory for him if that rule could survive the debates and votes that still lay ahead. Up to now, when members of the Congress had spoken in the House, they represented their states, for the states appointed them. Now the new congressmen would be representing individual voters. If they hoped for reelection, it was by pleasing these Americans that they had the best chance of succeeding.

The rule that decisions could be reconsidered and revoked during the life of the Convention was still a threat. But if this one victory could be preserved, even an imperfect constitution might be adaptable enough to allow the newly empowered Americans to keep enhancing their dignity and stature.

Chapter Eleven

A WAVE OF
CONFIDENCE

This radical shift of the true power—from the states to the people—brought a new and positive reaction to the Convention. There was a surge of spirits over the realization that no mere revision of the old Articles would be sufficient to deal with such a fundamental change. The wave of the future suddenly became visible, and it showed that there could be no escape from the creation of a radically different form of government.

The enmity between large and small states seemed to vanish. Like rival lawyers who lunch happily together after a bitter case, delegates who fought like Capulets and Montagues now quickly showed their satisfaction that they had reached an agreeable compromise. Gunning Bedford apologized contritely to several separate individuals for his frightful lapse. And William Paterson had a truly astonishing reversal, for after having been the most convincingly negative debater, he became an equally upbeat advocate for the Virginia Plan and a devoted Federalist from that time forward—just as Cotesworth Pinckney had predicted in jest.

No such sense of change touched the two New York delegates, Lansing and Yates, who perpetually hampered and humiliated Alexander Hamilton by outvoting him on every ballot. Even though they seemed to be lackeys for Governor Clinton, they were intelligent men, so they understood the basic policy swing that had occurred—the very thing their governor had specifically sent them to fight against. They showed signs of losing interest, and some thought they might be about to leave the Convention. This would not have cleared the way for Hamilton to cast New York's ballot according to his own wishes, because his state's rule was that at least two New York delegates had to be present to constitute a quorum. As a lone delegate, he would be as badly shackled as when his rivals were outvoting him.

The moment of uplifted feelings was short-lived. A little over a month since the date of their first formal meeting, sensing the onset of July heat and now more aware of the lengthy work that still lay ahead, the delegates sounded harsher and often sarcastic in their debates. This, though it seemed dismaying at the time, would one day be recognized as a sign of strength in the fabric of young America. If overcoming a single great problem made it seem that all disagreement had vanished, it would have been a false peace. These fifty-five men represented some four million people, many of whom had natural ambitions directly opposed to the aspirations of other Americans. It was time to gird for the next fight. This is how it should be for as long as an active democratic society lasts.

Accordingly, in a matter of days, new rivalries and disputes sprang up. For Madison, the disappointment was particularly acute, for two recent happenings felt like personal defeats to him. For one thing, he had still hoped to achieve proportional representation in both houses—a most impractical hope. The small states were converted into full partners in this Convention by being assured that equality in the Senate would never be taken away from them. Only impaired judgment resulting from overwork and fatigue would seem to explain Madison's brief new attempt to make such a destructive change in the rules for the upper house. He moved from that defeat to a second attempt to gain support for his cherished idea of inserting "a negative on state laws" into the Constitution. Later experience showed that he may have had a point in feeling that it was not enough to call the Constitution the "Supreme Law of the Land." Madison wanted a clear statement that the national government could step in and instantly negate any state law that was out of line with federal policy. But most other delegates refused to burden themselves with a need to go home and defend such an affront to their state's dignity.

Madison was seriously crushed; enough to consider leaving the Convention. His studies of history convinced him that the slightest doubt about a government's ability to put down a challenge to the supremacy of its laws was the worst sign of its impermanence. But his depression did not last long. With something of the same reasoning that led him to accept the dreaded compromise with slavery rather than destroy the chance for a Constitution, he decided to strive hard for workable solutions to other problems, even if he could no longer feel enthused about the end result.

The westward spread was the next great subject talked about as a cause for dread. New Englanders had long feared that any significant population move toward the Mississippi would create major problems. They thought people active enough to be farming near the eastern side of the Mississippi River would be tempted to make trial crossings to the nearly empty western side that was divided by the claims of Spain, France, and Britain. Such adventures, they believed, would certainly create problems, perhaps escalating to war. They foresaw European forces crossing into the American side of the great river as a way of punishing the intruders, and this succession of actions and reactions, some thought, would lead to a call for young men to defend western parts of the United States.

After a churning debate over how to cope with this western problem, no plan of action developed. Instead it morphed into a related subject. Even supposing that there were no such military encounters, how could the original states preserve their own principles and practical power if a spreading population produced many new western states that might become political competitors?

Two New Englanders—Elbridge Gerry and Rufus King—thought they had an answer and mischievously offered a measure that they said was intended to forestall any such antagonism between East and West. The two sons of Massachusetts laid out a plan calculated to keep the East supreme: They proposed that the total number of representatives from new states in the west must never be allowed to exceed the total number from the original thirteen. That would have made new western states, not yet born, into permanent inferiors. (Imagine modern California being limited to two or three congressmen because the comparative East-West numbers would not allow more.) It would have resulted in more sectional politics and aroused continuing antagonism between different parts of the country.

Yet this menace was not immediately apparent to all. Four states—Massachusetts, Connecticut, Delaware, and Maryland—seeming not to see the potential harm, voted for the measure. Or they saw the danger (because some of the finest minds in the room were from those four states) but still preferred to assert their dominance over strangers in states that were not yet born.

Several days of intense debate were required before the newly cooperative New Jersey and the four states south of Maryland added their weight against the unwise idea. This was an example of the many proposals that came up each week, some discussed at length before being discarded.

Madison's assertiveness in these days went beyond anything the public could have predicted. In one case, he talked as if the state—or rather, the public's devotion to the states—was the enemy of progress. He once made a statement that sounded exactly like Hamilton—that there would be no harm done if a republican government swallowed up all the state governments, whereas "Take the reverse supposition that state governments became independent of the General Government, and the gloomy consequences need not be pointed out."

At one point, according to the Convention notes being kept by New York's Judge Robert Yates, Madison was so anxious to scuttle the arguments for states' rights that he made a startling remark about the old question of whether the states had ever really been sovereign. "In fact, they are only political societies," he said. "The States never possessed the essential rights of sovereignty. Their voting in Congress as States is no evidence of sovereignty. The State of Maryland votes by counties. Does this make the counties sovereign?...The States ought to be placed under the control of the general government—at least as much so as they formerly were under the king and British parliament."

This was a clear argument for moving ahead with none of the regard for states' rights that probably a majority of Americans still approved. No one knew of the remark until the Yates notes were published in 1821. Those notes were disputed for a time; Madison disparaged them, for states' rights were still a boiling issue over thirty years later. Then it was shown that even the briefer notes kept by Rufus King quoted Madison in much the same way. Madison was too practical and intellectually honest to dodge the truth any longer. It was clear that under the cloak of Convention secrecy, he had taken a position that would have infuriated many partisans of states' rights. He promptly revised his own notes to come closer to the Yates version.

The issue brought an unusual clash between Madison and Gouverneur Morris. They were opposites in many ways—Morris very conservative and Madison radical in many of his views—but they respected each other and had a common goal in wanting to see a strong general government. Morris, however, definitely favored rules that would keep the westerners in a position inferior to that of the original states. In a dispute over how to apportion the original membership of the new Congress, Morris warned, "If the Western people get the power into their hands they will ruin the Atlantic interests." He thought apportionment should be entrusted to the duty and honor of the House members themselves.

Madison's answer had an unaccustomed jesting tone. He was surprised to hear "this implicit confidence urged by a member who on all occasions had inculcated so strongly the political depravity of men. If the House could be so trusted, what need is there of a Senate? Mr. Morris wants the South to trust the Northern majority, yet exhorts all to distrust the West. To reconcile the gentleman with himself, it must be imagined that he determined the human character by the points of the compass." More seriously, he warned that "all men having power ought to be distrusted to a certain degree." Followers who were uncomfortable when Madison and Hamilton seemed to disagree would have been pleased with such a statement, seeming to reconcile their views in a compromise conclusion about how much to trust popular government.

While this much talk of state and sectional differences dominated the delegates in the State House, it was no surprise that the most aggravated subject of all began to show its threatening face. Misleadingly, it appeared to be merely a new variation of the endless dispute over congressional representation. But representation was based on population, and the southerners thought slaves should be counted as people when it suited their owners, so it was actually another backdoor approach to the North-South difference regarding slavery. The subject was struggling to burst into the open, while those who saw that it could destroy the Convention tried to suppress it. There were gasps of surprise when Madison, in the heated argument over the New Jersey Plan, prophesied that North-South disputes would one day be the severest issue, and the wisest delegates realized that the dreaded specter of secession was making its first eerie appearance. As Professor John Fiske wrote soon after the war between the states, "From this moment down to 1865, the shadow of the coming Civil War would hover over the nation."

This 1787 debate previewed the inevitable. In a muffled way, the private agreement that Madison and Pinckney made to avoid a confrontation about slavery was being carried out, but other questions flowing from slavery were debated. Again, it was as if slavery were being discussed in code.

The disagreement between North and South—another way of saying between slave and free states—became starker every day. As the struggle between the pro-slavery and antislavery parties grew more visible, it resulted in another of the compromises by which the irrepressible conflict was postponed until the North became strong enough to confront the ghost of secession and stop compromising.

A key compromise was deciding the number of representatives that each state would have in the lower house of Congress, which became closely linked with the slavery issue. Some thought congressmen should be chosen according to the wealth of each state while others wanted to base it on population. The distinction caused some aggravated arguments, for at that time it was considered essential that the wealth of a state should be represented as well as its population. In most cases, a state with larger cities, containing manufacturing plants and large commercial ventures, had more people and also more wealth, so it was possible to cover both criteria by simply counting residents, which was easily accomplished.

Massachusetts had somewhat less population than several larger states, but felt that its aggregate wealth was far greater, if manufacturing plants and other productive capacity were counted. Massachusetts was far from happy with having its delegation in the new Congress based on the simplistic approach of simply counting the number of persons who lived there, for it seemed to be getting inadequate representation in relation to its superior quality of life, its far greater trade, in short, its greater contribution to the wealth of the nation. But the Convention struck down the Massachusetts position by determinedly focusing on how much easier it was to count population than literally taking stock of how many cows, sheep, pieces of machinery, and fine homes each state could show. Massachusetts lost this dispute because a majority group was able to rule against any special provisions, pointing out that in most cases, population was a fair enough index of wealth.

But this problem of representation turned out to be much more subtle between northern and southern states because the southerners regarded as wealth a "possession" that they conveniently chose to call "population" in counting heads for the new Congress. The slaves were definitely population, but they were also chattels in the eye of the law. This strange kind of property was the bulk of the wealth in some states. The southerners claimed that slaves should count as wealth and also as a basis for voting rights. Cotesworth Pinckney and Pierce Butler, both of South Carolina, pretended that slaves must certainly be counted in determining the basis of representation because they were definitely part of the population. The very thing that Madison and Charles Pinckney had tried to settle in advance between themselves now exploded into a raging dispute.

South Carolina pretended that it was properly proposing a uniform rule that would apply equally in all the states. But of course this rule would give huge political weight to the South and make hardly any difference at all to the North where the slave population was small and declining. Worse yet, the places where slavery was most deeply entrenched would gain the most representation and the added political power that came with it. The more slaves they imported, the more votes they would have in Congress. The northerners shouted that slaves could no more be included than houses or ships. "If Negroes are not represented in the states to which they belong, why should they be represented in the general government," demanded New Jersey's Paterson, who was not about to be silenced by any prior gentleman's agreement.

And fearlessly outspoken Gouverneur Morris said, "I would sooner submit myself to a tax for paying for all the Negroes in the United States than saddle posterity with such a constitution."

Virginia was in the most difficult position of all. Madison, Washington, and other great Virginians were looking forward to seeing their own state moving away from slavery, so they did not want to see the terrible institution strengthened. But they saw that South Carolina was absolutely determined on its position. If she turned away from the Convention, North Carolina and Georgia would also drop out. And when it came to the hard ratification fight that they could already see shaping up, with New York and Rhode Island opposed, a negative vote by the three southern states would almost certainly rule out any chance of having a new constitution.

Madison—never losing sight of the fact that standing up fearlessly to the slave states would only result in their seceding and continuing to be slave states—now offered a compromise that he had used four years before. He remembered that in 1783, when the old Congress was trying to apportion quotas for how much each state owed to the central treasury, there had been a similar dispute over the counting of slaves. If slaves were counted as population, the southern states would pay more than they thought fair into the treasury; if they were not counted, the North thought the southerners would be paying less than their fair share. Madison haggled to a compromise whereby each slave was figured as three-fifths of a free man. And John Rutledge, of South Carolina, was one of the people who agreed to it. Now Madison walked to Rutledge's desk and placed a note before him, suggesting the same fractional method of getting over the problem of representation. Rutledge looked pensive, then raised his two hands in a signal that seemed to mean, "Wait." Of course he would need to put the idea before his fellow southerners. Soon after the session ended, Rutledge came back to Madison and told him his proposal was acceptable if enough other states agreed.

The following day's debate on the Madison-Rutledge proposal was heated, but most of the furor originated among the northerners. The southern delegates, even though they would face some anger back home, knew that they had much the better of the deal, while Madison's supporters were appalled at his having proposed a solution that they felt forced to accept.

James Wilson angrily cried out that he would go along, even though there was neither rhyme nor reason to it. Many others from a variety of states who were abolitionists at heart—Washington, Madison, Rufus King, and enough more to carry the day—all reluctantly swallowed their distaste. In the context of those times, many Virginian founding fathers were abolitionists at heart, but failed to emancipate their slaves during their lifetimes because they had heavy bank loans and their slaves were part of the collateral they had posted. Some were so deeply in debt that they could not have withdrawn the slaves from the loan arrangement without making a large payment to the bank, and they could not find cash for the purpose.

Washington's situation was even more complicated, and he spent sleepless hours trying to find a solution. Some of his slaves were already part of a legal arrangement that would make them the property of younger relatives after his death, so they were not his to emancipate; some of these slaves or Martha's had intermarried with other Mount Vernon slaves. The Washingtons were firmly against any change of ownership that would separate slaves from their husbands, wives, or children. Some leaders—Jefferson for one—could be faulted for allowing years to pass without considering a plan to free their slaves. But like many bad habits, slavery was a terrible trap. Many of the owners believed no solution was satisfactory. Even releasing slaves and hoping they could make a life of their own might condemn many to a terrifying existence.

One point on which the northerners were determined—and which they won—was that the South must not be allowed to count slaves for the purpose of representation and yet to exempt them for the purpose of taxation. "You cannot have it both ways," Gouverneur Morris told them. "If you count them for votes, you must count them for taxes. Otherwise, don't count them at all. Choose one way or the other." He was rather startled at how quickly the southerners agreed—choosing the voting advantage, while accepting the added taxation.

The odious fraction that made a black individual less than a whole person would be invoked again during the Convention, and it went on serving that purpose for over seventy more years. It meant that a black was "among the voters," but with his white master deciding how his three-fifths of a vote would be cast.

The slave population of the United States according to the census of 1790

North		South	
New Hampshire	158	Delaware	8,887
Vermont	17	Maryland	103,036
Massachusetts	——	Virginia	293,427
Rhode Island	952	North Carolina	100,572
Connecticut	2,759	South Carolina	107,094
New York	21,324	Georgia	29,264
New Jersey	11,423	Kentucky	11,830
Pennsylvania	3,737	Tennessee	3,417

Total 704,897

This table shows that the northern states, except for New York and New Jersey, possessed so few slaves that a simple order to emancipate all their slaves would have posed no problem, beyond the necessity to be sure that the few thousand emancipations did not turn these freed persons into hardship cases. What it fails to show is that states in the right-hand column, with the exception of South Carolina and Georgia, were talking actively about phased emancipation. Plans to declare that new children born to slave couples should be born free were gathering adherents.

Not only were the northern states rejecting slavery, even North Carolina and Virginia showed real signs of wanting to put it behind them. And even in the two bleakest examples, South Carolina and Georgia, many men admitted that slavery was undesirable. Charles Pinckney, the elegant and polished young man whom Jefferson and Madison would later be proud to send abroad as an American ambassador, expressed the hope that South Carolina, "if not too much meddled with," would by and by voluntarily count herself among the emancipating states. Not even his less-advanced relations and colleagues defended slavery on principle. It could not be foreseen that even the great state of Virginia, which appeared to be on an abolitionist path, would shortly revert to greater reliance on slaves.

The abolitionist party of Virginia dwindled and died during the 1790s, so it is quite possible that the compromises agreed to in order to create the Constitution were to blame, making them even costlier in terms of human suffering than the Convention delegates calculated.

At the time of the compromises, George Mason and Edmund Randolph were so appalled by the concessions made to the pro-slavery interests in June—and another that would follow in July—that this was one of the reasons they later refused to sign the Constitution. Randolph worked for its ratification, but even though he had so much to do with its creation, he withheld his signature as a form of protest. Mason made some of the strongest attacks ever heard on the slave trade, calling it "this infernal traffic." "Every master of slaves is born a petty tyrant," he said. "They bring the judgment of heaven on a country. As nations cannot be rewarded or punished in the next world, they must be in this. By an inevitable chain of causes and effects, Providence punishes national sins by national calamities." And in this he was, of course, a prophet.

But even the most inspiring words are wasted unless one can turn them into acts and deeds. The compromises resulted in a Constitution and a government that finally became stronger than "this infernal traffic." Without compromises, without the Constitution, anarchy would have so weakened the new nation that the states would have been torn apart and left the great majority of the slaves as even more hopeless captives of the southern slave owners.

In judging Madison's role in this terrible choice, it is useful to hear his own words when, as a very old man, he thought back to the atmosphere that had prevailed in 1787:

Such was the aspect of things, that in the eyes of the best friends of liberty, a crisis had arrived which was to decide whether the American experiment was to be a blessing to the world, or to blast forever the hopes which the republican cause had inspired.

Chapter Twelve

HAMILTON STUNS THE MEETING

In the very center of the excitement that transpired during these pivotal June days, Alexander Hamilton took the floor and opened another front on June 18, 1787.

No one expected a long speech, for in the slightly more than three weeks of activity Hamilton had not seemed himself at all. There was none of the fire, nor even signs of the leadership that he usually projected. Clearly, everyone thought, he must have been somewhat dissatisfied with the Virginia Plan, but reluctant to create more problems for Madison. Now, however, he gave the impression of a man who was about to say, "Whether anyone likes it or not, I simply must tell you what I think." And essentially, that was just what he did, for hours.

Just how many hours is a mystery. Most accounts have specified "five or six hours," but this seems much too long a time, and it may be that later historians have copied from an early authority's exaggeration. Looking at the points contained in the speech, it is hard to see how anyone could have spent more than half that much time delivering it. The written notes—including Hamilton's own rough notes and Madison's excellent version (which Hamilton pronounced almost perfect) would indicate far less time, even with pauses for emphasis or to drink a glass of water. It could not have been that short, however, for one of the listeners mentioned that delegates did not even break for lunch, yet finished about three o'clock. So perhaps Hamilton, speaking from notes, expanded his remarks greatly. And perhaps even Madison's version, excellent as Hamilton said it was, was a condensed account of a much longer speech. But it has the earmarks of an event in which the element of surprise and excitement caused the listeners to expand the true figure and later writers amplified it further.

This event began when John Dickinson of Pennsylvania appeared to set the stage for Hamilton. Dickinson was highly respected because he had been firmly against the Declaration of Independence and kept trying to arrange for peaceful settlement with Britain up to the last moment. When war came, however, he instantly enlisted in the army. He was the leading writer of the Articles of Confederation, yet he showed no opposition to their overthrow. He was also admired for a gallant fight against his own poor health, as well as for his brilliance and clarity whenever he chose to speak. Now, with his usual attitude of seeking wide agreement, Dickinson asked the Convention to postpone consideration of Paterson's New Jersey Plan and to return to the basic idea of trying to make the government of the United States adequate to the preservation and prosperity of the Union.

This sounded like an invitation for some delegate to come forward with a new idea, and Hamilton rose to say that he had remained silent because of respect for the superior experience of his colleagues. But now he was forced to reveal that he could in no way agree with any plan he had heard. He then moved quickly to demolish the New Jersey Plan for being much too close to the confederate government that was failing so badly. But he went on to say that such an amazingly large nation was very unlikely to hold together under "any general sovereignty that could be substituted." In other words, that a government relying so much on the (presumably fickle) will of the common people as the Virginia Plan could not create the single-minded focus that only "a permanent will"—such as a hereditary monarch—could bring about.

Hamilton made two major points: All people divide themselves into the few and the many—"the wealthy and well born" and "the people." Madison thought much the same thing, but Madison always seemed to make it clear that he wanted to give the people control. Crude as they might be, they were the natural ruling class—if only because they were clearly the vast majority. But what an inferior society they would form, Hamilton seemed to say. He talked as if there were two separate populations—one born to lead, the other limited to hoping that their leaders would be fair and merciful.

"The people are turbulent and changing," he said. "They seldom judge or determine right...Nothing but a permanent body can counter the imprudence of democracy." And he quickly made a second point clear. He considered the British constitution, with aristocrats having the ability to prevent popular excesses, "the best model the world has ever produced."

Startling as Hamilton's statement was, something much more shocking has remained hidden—the wide agreement with his views. The speaker was surrounded by admirers and heavily praised immediately after his talk, though some said to him frankly that they would not dare to bring any such proposal back to their home states. "Hamilton's proposals have been praised by everybody, but supported by none," one delegate said a few days later.

Hamilton's thoughts were expressed in a temperate fashion. But in doing so, he also saddened most of his listeners, for the number who gathered around him after the session and praised him for having perfectly reflected their own views meant that they were left with nowhere to turn. Follow Madison and they were putting the nation into the hands of an incompetent rabble; follow Hamilton and be soundly defeated, in Philadelphia and at home.

Some have tried to brush away the idea that Hamilton had a poor opinion of the people, attempting to explain that his doubts were caused mainly by the familiar fear that this great expanse of territory could not be managed by a single popular government. But his own words and those that are attributed to him in the notes made by listeners do appear to make Hamilton's view of the common man unflattering.

His New York colleague Yates, for example, appeared to be so impressed by Hamilton's presentation that he seemed to forget their political enmity, and quoted him in this accurate way:

> All communities divide themselves into...the rich and well born and the mass of the people. The voice of the people has been said to be the voice of God, but this maxim...is not true in fact. The people are turbulent and changing; they seldom judge or determine right. Can a democratic assembly, who annually revolve in the mass of the people, be supposed steadily to pursue the public good? Nothing but a permanent body can counter the imprudence of democracy. Give therefore to the first class a distinct, permanent share in the government. They will check the unsteadiness of the second, and as they cannot receive any advantage by a change, they therefore will ever maintain good government.

Years after Hamilton's death, John Quincy Adams, whose personal brilliance and independence have never been questioned, carefully restudied Hamilton's original plan and pronounced it superior to the Constitution that was finally created. Hamilton himself, late in his life, still thought well of the theoretical plan he had sketched with no real expectation of seeing it adopted.

He pointed out that in the Convention, five states had shown their agreement with him by favoring an executive who would serve "during good behavior," that is, potentially for a lifetime. And he revealed a belief that Madison himself voted for such an unlimited period at one point, though this is questionable.

Hamilton made it clear that he knew no way to accomplish the form of government that he preferred, but was trying to present "a model which we ought to approach as near as possible." This basically meant that class interests, rather than individuals in the mass, should be represented. Senators would be chosen only indirectly by the people. Voters would choose electors who, in turn, would pick the senators. These last would hold office during good behavior, or essentially for life. State legislatures, he said, should be confined to local concerns. But (apparently to guard against an accusation of monarchism) he did not favor a permanent president, but suggested an executive who would rule for no more than three years.

Hamilton's most forceful prescription was the virtual elimination of the states. He dwelt on the total inadequacy of the Confederation, and felt that the seriousness of the governmental crisis obligated the delegates to do whatever they deemed essential to the country's happiness. He thought both of the main plans submitted dwelt too much on fastening the people to local loyalties and therefore were doomed to failure. (Note that this was a passionate belief of George Washington's.) Hamilton was also deeply worried that the states might start reforming into partial confederacies, falling into European-style wars or even forming alliances with European powers. Apart from a fear of shocking public opinion, he saw no good reason to avoid substituting a single general government in place of the existing state governments. The states, he said, were not necessary for commerce, revenue, or agriculture, but he acknowledged the need for subordinate authorities to handle local matters.

In a wide-ranging look at many examples drawn from other nations, he said,

> Let us examine the federal institutions of Germany. It was initiated upon the laudable principle of securing the independency of the several states of which it was composed and to protect them against foreign invasion. Has it answered these good intentions? Do we not see that their councils are weak and distracted and that it cannot prevent the wars and confusions which the respective electors carry on against each other? The Swiss cantons, or the Helvetic Union, are equally inefficient.
>
> Such are the lessons which the experience of others afford us, and from whence results the evident conclusion that all federal governments are weak and distracted. To avoid the evils deducible from these observations, we must establish a general and national government, completely sovereign, and annihilate the state distinctions and state operations.

Hamilton quoted numerous classic sources to support his arguments. In insisting that "the British government is the best in the world," for example, he invoked Jacques Necker, a brilliant French economist, who said the British constitution united "public strength with individual security." And, Hamilton said, "we should go as far in order to attain stability and permanency as republican principles will permit."

At the end, he left a room that was dazed—full of approval for his views and visceral distress over the impossibility of meeting his standards. It gradually became clear that the majority of delegates longed to say, "Yes, that's exactly what we would like to see." But they knew it to be a political mirage. It was the picture of an aristocratic society full of individuals much like themselves—all gentlemen, more than half of them college graduates—the elite who have risen to the top and who long to merge with others like themselves. Working against this vision was the fact that it was not made for an America that consisted mostly of working-class folk. Such a plan could not be presented to these lower orders as a rulebook for how they should see themselves, behave themselves, and improve themselves over the centuries to come. It had to be immediately acceptable to eighteenth-century Americans and effective in their hands.

Hamilton had not written the speech in full. He used an outline with topic heads as his only guide. But he delivered it with great fluency. Three of the delegates made notes as he spoke, the most important being Madison, who is thought to have recorded nearly the whole of it. Its accuracy was attested to in an odd way, because Hamilton called on Madison just as the latter was completing his draft. Hamilton was asked to check it for accuracy, and he "acknowledged its fidelity, without suggesting more than a very few verbal alterations which were made."

There could be no better evidence of Madison's objectivity and intellectual honesty than this faithful recording of a speech that could have threatened his own cherished plan. Rufus King prepared a shorter version, very similar to Madison's, but far less complete. And, as noted previously, the most surprising was the report of Robert Yates, the New Yorker who was such a confirmed Clinton man and political enemy of Hamilton's. He must have been carried away by his rival's oratory, for his notes appeared to approve heartily of Hamilton's plea for a strong central government—the last thing in the world his New York faction advocated.

The delegates' practical turn of mind was being rigorously tested, for however much they were attracted to Hamilton's vision, they kept uppermost in their minds the need for ratification. Their new Constitution would have to be presented to the people and voted on before it became law. And Hamilton's idea of good government would insist that only persons who owned a respectable amount of property should be qualified voters. Eight of the states had been considering all white men eligible voters for the past several years. If many of these were now suddenly told that they would not be voters under the new government, how much chance was there that they would choose to ratify a plan that denied them a long-held privilege?

Virginia's George Mason put it very sensibly, "What would people say if the ones who have earned the right of suffrage were now told that they should be disenfranchised?"

Hamilton's longing for a benevolent ruler made everyone envision a king, and this always led people to think of George Washington, without considering who would be his heirs or whether anyone named to succeed him would be acceptable. Hamilton was willing to see a lower house of Congress elected by popular vote every three years, but he wanted a senate elected for life, so that the senate would serve the same conservative purpose as the British House of Lords, and the president would be an elected temporary monarch, not hereditary, but with an absolute veto over laws passed by the Congress.

It cannot be proved that Hamilton was sincere in admitting that he knew his dream of approximating the British system was impossible for America. Impossibility was not a normal word in the Hamilton vocabulary. Was it the first or last part of the sentence that he cherished when he said, "It is a thing not attainable by us, but a model which we ought to approach as near as possible"? The sadness it created among the members was not only that they saw how very disruptive it would be to this Convention, but more painfully because it was just what most of them wanted to see and yet had to turn away from.

Months later, Hamilton drew up a modified outline plan for a new government and gave it to Madison. He never presented it publicly, but it was generally considered to be a superior, more mature, plan. It would have called for a longer tenure of office by the executive and members of the legislature, which he called a responsible term, but temporary or defeasible. It was not, however, an approximation of the republican model, as several scholars and even Hamilton's son, John Church Hamilton, later remarked.

When Hamilton left the Convention, more in sorrow than in anger, his dogged New York foes, Yates and Lansing, also left the meeting for good. It is often said that Yates and Lansing left because they were furious about the unfavorable turn the Convention had taken for them. But considering the unusual note-taking by Yates, it is not impossible that his emotions were disturbed by the rare appeal of Hamilton's speech.

It should be recognized, in fact, that these two men were not such buffoons as they have been characterized by some of Hamilton's followers. They took orders from Governor Clinton because he had long been the state's boss. But well before coming into his orbit, in fact ever since their first study of the law, they were both recognized as outstanding barristers. As both built thriving law practices, they were leading jurists. Finally, Yates, the older of the two, moved up to the supreme court of New York, and eventually became chief justice. He also became Hamilton's surprise choice as a candidate for the governorship of New York in 1789. The fact that Yates accepted this nomination to run against Clinton, his longtime patron and benefactor, may have dated back to his positive reaction to Hamilton's speech at the Philadelphia Convention. Clinton won the hotly contested gubernatorial election, but the animosity in New York's state politics increased. Lansing also joined the state's supreme court and took over as chief justice when Yates stepped down. Lansing's life ended mysteriously when, at age seventy-five, he went to mail a letter and disappeared, perhaps a victim of foul play. To the many people who followed Clinton's career—and who saw him become vice president of the United States in James Madison's first administration—Yates and Lansing were admired men.

On July 10, Washington wrote a letter to Hamilton that showed how much he relied on such a trusted friend. It also made clear that Hamilton felt impelled to obey his old commander when he called in such a touching way.

Washington's letter clearly tried to cope with the division that had occurred between two of the men he relied on most. He wrote, "In a word, I *almost* despair of seeing a favorable end to the proceedings of the Convention and do therefore repent having had any agency in the business." And he castigated the men who opposed a strong and energetic government as "in my opinion, narrow-minded politicians or under the influence of local views." Washington said pleadingly and a little reproachfully, "I am sorry you went away. I wish you were back. The crisis is equally important and alarming, and no opposition under such circumstances should discourage exertions till the signature is fixed."

Hamilton was back at the Convention just three days later. He had said it was a waste of time to remain there, and the departure of Yates and Lansing now made it impossible for New York to cast any vote at all because of the New York quorum rule. Washington's plea was almost surely the reason for his return.

Biographer Broadus Mitchell casts an interesting light on the more mature plan for the Constitution that Hamilton showed to Madison three months after his first sketchy presentation. Mitchell pointed out that the Convention itself had an improving effect on most of its members, who appeared to grow and gain wisdom during that time. It is not surprising that Hamilton, just a few months later, already showed great signs of not only maturing but of learning to compromise, because he was sensing the rhythm and mechanics of the meeting. Each member of the body of fifty-five men (or at least the average of forty that were in attendance at any one time) was a superior delegate three months later: The whole convention displayed development of individual and collective thought. Subjects supposedly settled were reopened several times. Threats made in the course of the debates were later withdrawn, and ultimata were retracted on cooler consideration.

Largely unspoken was the fact that most of the delegates felt just as Hamilton did and were determined to suppress their own view. As self-serving individuals, they could not join in a plan that would single them out as elitists. As practical politicians, they could not create a document that was unattainable. And yet, as honest men, they were suddenly stricken with remorse at having to pretend that they approved of this Constitution which was not what they wanted. Madison was neither surprised nor entirely dismayed when he realized that so many of the delegates admired Hamilton's ideas. Very late in his life he spoke of the pressure he had felt from knowing that many Americans had opposed the Convention because they had "a secret dislike of popular government, and a hope that delay would bring it more into disgrace and pave the way for a form of government more congenial with monarchical or aristocratic predilections."

Dickinson, for example, said in June that he hoped members of the upper house would be chosen by the individual state legislatures, in order to give the Senate "distinguished characters...bearing as strong a likeness to the British House of Lords as possible," and there was no reaction. In fact, Connecticut's Roger Sherman seconded the motion, feeling that this mode of election would promote harmony between state and national governments. And Sherman added his own belief that the states and the people should both be represented in the legislature—the people in one branch, the states in the other. Another seconding move followed, this time from Gouverneur Morris, of Pennsylvania.

Those thoughts eventually affected the original selection of the upper house, but they did not immediately prevail, for it was one of the times when the rock-solid James Wilson of Pennsylvania demurred, insisting that, "The British government could not be our model. Our manners, laws, disdain for primogeniture, the whole genius of the people are opposed to it."

More of them thought like Gouverneur Morris. The man who spoke most often and who became a dominant figure of the Convention called Hamilton's speech "the most able and impressive I ever heard." And this was the man who would actually write the Constitution. Morris and

Hamilton were particularly good friends. However much their politics differed, they were very similar in personality and mentality. The outgoing Hamilton made this clear when he wrote, with typical sprightliness, in a May 19, 1788, letter to Morris, "I hope you believe there is no one for whom I have more inclination than yourself—I mean of the male kind." And much later, when Morris had spent years traveling abroad, Hamilton wrote plaintively to Rufus King, "Why does not Gouverneur Morris come home?…Men like him do not superabound."

Chapter Thirteen

A GREAT MAN'S SUPPORT

Paradoxically, George Washington's desire not to participate actively in the discussions and maneuvering at the Constitutional Convention seemed to enhance his role as a leader. He could occasionally be an impressive speaker, but this depended on considerable preparation and something approaching stage management. At other times, a stolid silence was his most impressive tool, as when he had been chosen to head America's first wartime army. He had more of a military background than anyone else who was available, and his silence had enhanced the impression of strength.

What made him an ideal choice for the top leadership role was a trait that would develop in the course of the war: A capacity to adapt. Almost as amazingly as his friend Henry Knox intuitively learned how to use artillery by reading books, Washington quickly developed the multiple capacities of a true supreme commander—strategic planning, intelligence and espionage, guerrilla tactics and other clandestine operations, the difficult art of conducting an orderly retreat, and perhaps most of all, he exuded the "attitude of command" that made other men follow his lead. He was not a "great general," like the few whose tactics are studied by military schools around the world. But he was the perfect commander for Americans fighting in a revolution, because he pinpointed what was essential and made it part of him. Among other specially acquired traits, he was unsurpassed in the delicate skill of integrating many foreign officers into his forces, and this played a large part in American success.

Washington also had the rare gift for remembering the lessons of past defeats and continuing to profit from them. As long ago as 1754, when he was the twenty-two-year-old commander of the Virginia Regiment in what came to be known as the French and Indian War, he had been forced to surrender after heavy losses in the Battle of Fort Necessity, a small stockade in Pennsylvania near the forks of the Ohio River. Forever after that, the date July 3, 1754, seemed to persist in his mind even more strongly than July 4. He spoke of his grateful remembrance for having escaped, and he remembered not only the errors that had caused defeat, but also the helplessness of a loser, which would later make him exceptionally attentive to his own prisoners of war.

Even with all the prestige and aura brought by his great victory, however, he did not develop an easy manner of standing out in a large meeting. On several occasions, with careful preparation for a specific appearance that was deemed to be critical, he prepared and even stage-managed a magic moment. But it was not an ability that he could use at will, and certainly not in an all-day session. This deficiency misled the hot-headed John Adams, who sometimes jumped to premature conclusions, to write in a diary a cutting opinion of Washington's preparation for his task: "He is too illiterate, unread, unlearned for his status and reputation."

Adams was, in a sense, correct in calling Washington "unread," for he had little or no interest in reading for pleasure. Looking through Washington's diary pages over the years, it is clear that his hours were seldom devoted to anything beyond practical reading matter that touched on surveying, farming, or governing. But while he would not have studied ancient history as Madison did, he was not at all unaware of its merits. His way of tapping these benefits was to listen carefully and respectfully to the men who knew them best, and here Madison was at the head of the line.

One facet of the General's great wisdom was that he clearly understood his own shortcomings. He avoided prattling on with extemporaneous talk that would have declined in quality. He was careful not to speak often, and this purposeful silence gave the appearance of depth and penetrating thought.

Washington was also unusual in his willingness to rely on close associates who had the superior abilities needed to accomplish certain objectives. Most men who are hastily thrust into great positions are afraid of seeming inadequate if they surround themselves with individuals who might outshine them. The General recognized the men who possessed the finest minds of his day and had self-confidence enough to solicit their advice at every turn.

Later, Washington's reliance on Hamilton, Madison, and Jefferson turned into an agonizing dilemma because these men fell to warring among themselves. It was Jefferson and Madison on one side and Hamilton on the other when he became president. The conflicting views and advice of the men he trusted most would make the conflict among them a grueling experience for Washington. When the impossibility of reconciling their opposing suggestions angered him beyond bearing, he would, on more than one occasion, stomp around his office literally kicking the furniture.

It may seem surprising that the General was adept at light conversation with women. This may have dated from his youthful attempt to obey simple rules that were laid out for table manners and conversation. Whether that is the case, he mastered the gentle banter that was considered the proper way for a gentleman to play his part at a dinner or other evening event. He was a splendid dance partner and even skillful at the light flirtation that was often thrust upon him. His wife Martha accepted his behavior in social settings, knowing that he was usually doing his best to keep the ladies at bay.

There was one lady, Annis Boudinot Stockton, the sister of a former president of the Continental Congress, Elias Boudinot, whose overtures to Washington were excessive; she not only took part in spreading flower petals at his feet, she also wrote him torrid poems. It did annoy Martha that her husband corresponded with Annis and stopped to visit her in Princeton when he was en route to Yorktown. But his letters always discreetly closed with "Good wishes from Mrs. Washington and myself," and his attentions were probably no more than kindness to a longtime acquaintance who had lost her husband in very sad circumstances.

Some histories, and especially the book *Cincinnatus* by Garry Wills, insist that Washington carried on a determined campaign to perpetuate his power, so his grand gesture of resignation was designed to make Americans ready and indeed insistent that he move on to political leadership. Wills concludes, "He was a virtuoso of resignations. He perfected the art of getting power by giving it away."

Accepting this thought means ignoring the stronger evidence that Washington wanted no such thing. His letters to friends, like those to Lafayette and Jay that have been cited, cannot be called insincere unless one is determined to see them that way. The abundant evidence suggests that he would not have intentionally misled Martha Washington in promising that he was through with public life. And his serious financial shortages made it far preferable for him to remain free to supervise his properties and investments.

Of course, there is always a large gap between even the greatest man's abilities and the public's expectation or willingness to cooperate in his efforts. That is why the usually sour attitude of Virginia congressman William Grayson strikes a useful balance between the two. As the Convention was just getting under way, Grayson wrote to James Monroe on May 29, 1787, saying, "The weight of General Washington is great in America, but hardly sufficient to induce the people to pay money or part with power." And Connecticut congressman Stephen Mitchell wrote on June 6, obviously with tongue in cheek, "I find the wisdom and magnanimity of the Convention are much praised, all our difficulties are at once to be removed, and we are to have almost a new earth. The clergymen begin to omit poor old Congress in their prayers and substitute instead thereof—the Convention. You know many of our ideas in New England have their birth in the pulpit."

Washington had a different relationship with each of his principal advisers—he discussed very high-level subjects with Jefferson, practical politics with Madison, and long-term policies with Hamilton. These are so predictable that they help to confirm purported conversations—or to dismiss them as false. For example, there is an anecdote—unproven, but widely believed—that Jefferson, just after his return from France, asked Washington at breakfast why he had agreed to the establishment of a second chamber in Congress. Washington replied, "Why did you pour that coffee into your saucer?" Jefferson said, "Why, to cool it, Sir."

"Exactly," said Washington. "We pour legislation into the senatorial sauce to cool it."

This would be more credible if two different participants were named. The question could not have been Jefferson's because he had suggested a bicameral legislature to Madison long before this imaginary conversation. Nor would it have been like Jefferson to ask the president a probing question; and certainly not like Washington to give that flippant response. But the anecdote is a useful reminder that Jefferson did, indeed, spend a great deal of time with Washington and discuss a multitude of major subjects, domestic and foreign. As such a longtime associate, and one who was later estranged from him, former president Jefferson wrote a letter on January 2, 1814, responding to a historian's request for information. It said, in part:

> I think I knew General Washington intimately and thoroughly, and were I called on to delineate his character, it should be in terms like these:
>
> His mind was great and powerful, without being of the very first order; his penetration strong, though not so acute as that of a Newton, Bacon, or Locke; and as far as he saw, no judgment was ever sounder. It was slow in operation, being little aided by invention or imagination, but sure in conclusion...He was incapable of fear, meeting personal dangers with the calmest unconcern...His

integrity was the most pure, his justice the most inflexible I have ever known...He was, indeed, in every sense of the words, a wise, a good, and a great man...His heart was not warm in its affections; but he exactly calculated every man's value, and gave him a solid esteem proportioned to it.

Although in the circle of his friends, where he might be unreserved with safety, he took a free share in conversation, his colloquial talents were not above mediocrity, possessing neither copiousness of ideas, nor fluency of words. In public, when called on for a sudden opinion, he was unready, short, and embarrassed.

On the whole, his character was, in its mass, perfect...and it may truly be said that never did nature and fortune combine more perfectly to make a man great...I am satisfied that the great body of republicans think of him as I do...We knew his honesty, the wiles with which he was encompassed [and here Jefferson refers to Hamilton's influence on Washington] for he was no monarchist from preference of his judgment...He has often declared to me that he considered our new Constitution as an experiment on the practicability of republican government, and with what dose of liberty man could be trusted for his own good; that he was determined the experiment should have a fair trial, and would lose the last drop of his blood to support it. And these declarations he repeated to me oftener and more pointedly because he knew my suspicions of Colonel Hamilton's views...I do believe that General Washington had not a firm confidence in the durability of our government.

These are my opinions of General Washington, which I would vouch at the judgment seat of God, having been formed on an acquaintance of thirty years...During the war and after it we corresponded occasionally, and in the last four years of my continuance in the office of Secretary of State, our intercourse was daily, confidential, and cordial. After I retired from that office, great and malignant pains were taken by our federal monarchists, and not entirely without effect, to make him view me as a theorist, holding French principles of government, which would lead infallibly to licentiousness and anarchy…I felt on his death, with my country-men, that "verily a great man hath fallen this day in Israel."

One description of Washington that is interesting to view beside Jefferson's was left by the Hessian sergeant Johann Conrad Dohla who was a war prisoner in America for several years. Precisely because he never met Washington but assembled this vignette from comments given to him by several Americans whom he had come to respect, it has the merit of a composite view. This was written after the sergeant returned home to Germany, so he cannot be suspected of trying to curry favor with the man who controlled his destiny. The similarity to Jefferson's assessment lends great authority to both versions. Here is Sergeant Dohla's summary of what various Americans had told him:

> As so many inaccurate descriptions of the American field com-mander have been made, I will share the following from believable American descriptions of the person and character of Washington.
>
> The great General Washington is of respectable height, has a martial face, and although already old, more than fifty, he is in blooming health. His entire bearing is reserved and careful, not pro-fuse in words and more inclined to loneliness than to great sociabil-ity in order to use the time for thought. Outside the camp he has no more than a single servant, and when he returns to camp, he is accompanied by only a few riders. At New York, he often visits his field and camp posts all by himself and often converses with a sen-try a full quarter of an hour.
>
> When he has something great in his mind, he often sends his suggested plan around to a few others to solicit their advice with-out having superimposed his judgment. He is not the least bit proud or arrogant, and he speaks with a sentry as with a staff offi-cer. He rewards good conduct on the spot. Toward the prisoners who fall into his hands, he is very humane and attentive to their good treatment.

A careful review of Washington's actions in every relationship and circumstance of his life, and especially in the months leading up to and through the Constitutional Convention, match these portraits. When the specifics of Washington's post-war actions are examined, the emptiness of the "monarchical" charges becomes even clearer. His opposition to the aristocratic aspects of the Society of the Cincinnati is one example. A more telling point is his "legacy" letter, with the hard demands it made on the people. An ambitious politician would have begun with a letter that touched very lightly, if at all, on points that he knew to be unpopular. No intelligent person—as Washington unquestionably was—would have insisted on grasping the prickliest part of that day's most important need by telling Americans to "sacrifice local interest to the common good." Not unless ambition were the farthest thing from his mind.

And finally, if one were looking for signs of ambition, what kind of ambition would it become? The world already rated him more highly than kings. He sensed that the presidential office he was later obliged to occupy would be extremely difficult for him, because the tugs of opposing parties were especially upsetting. And the frequent charges that he was strongly attracted to the idea of heading a benevolent monarchy could not have been more totally squashed than Washington did in a letter of August 1786, when the consternation over Shays's Rebellion might have seemed like an opportunity to a man who had monarchical ambitions. Washington's reaction at that time was one of such loathing that he departed from his usually precise language: "I am told that even respectable characters speak of a monarchical form of government without horror...How irrevocable and tremendous! What a triumph for our enemies to verify their predictions! What a triumph for the advocates of despotism to find that we are incapable of governing ourselves."

The simple explanation is that Washington did not really know or envision what an American government should be like. He spelled out in his legacy letter, written when he dismissed his troops in 1783, the wish to see the states somehow harmoniously cooperate. He must have come to realize that the solution, if it could be achieved at all, would require an endless number of compromises—some major, some irritatingly petty.

Such work held no appeal for him. All he knew for sure was an inspiring but unfinished thought for the ages—that Americans must somehow not be proved to be "incapable of governing ourselves."

A reminder of Washington's enormous prestige, setting him apart from anyone else in the hall, would come when a proposal of his, which would surely have caused long debate if suggested by anyone else, was instantly adopted. In September, on the Convention's final morning, Washington espoused a suggestion by Nathaniel Gorham of Massachusetts that the lower house should have one representative for every thirty thousand inhabitants, rather than every forty thousand. Washington spoke out in support of the idea, because, he said, the lower house seemed likely to have too few representatives, and the change would enlarge the chamber appropriately.

It may well be that Madison, with his wish to add to the power of the people, spoke of this both to Gorham and the General before the subject came up on the floor, but having Washington support it brought a response that was unlike any other business transacted during the entire four months. The subject was, after all, substantial enough to have warranted discussion. But after hearing Washington say, "It would give me much satisfaction to see it adopted," the measure carried unanimously without another word.

Two main reasons have been given for this great impact that he had on others: One was his actual presence, which the English historian Trevelyan described as "the outward gift which is seldom despised except by those to whom it is refused." As Robert Morris told a neighbor, "Washington was the only man in whose presence I felt any awe." His large size and powerful body were joined by a masterful bearing that had great appeal. The other trait was character, a thing which is seldom noticeable, but which in Washington was immediately obvious and striking. His self-control was unmistakable, and even after age and dental problems had damaged his good looks, the control was visible and his character stood out as a palpable force.

An unusual portrayal of George Washington, the newly-elected president, as an almost divine figure and clearly named as the "Father of His Country."

Probably the most attractive picture ever made of the young James Madison. This shows him as he probably was early in the Revolutionary War, when he was making his first appearance in Virginia state politics.

Montpelier—Madison's residence in Virginia.

Alexander Hamilton as the first
secretary of the treasury.

James Wilson, the Pennsylvania
delegate who was Madison's firmest
supporter during the Convention.

Gouverneur Morris, the delegate who starred during the debates and who finally wrote the final draft of the Constitution.

Portrait of Abraham Baldwin, the almost unknown Georgia delegate whose courageous vote saved the Convention from collapse.

Thomas Jefferson—a voice from overseas that echoed at the Convention.

An early picture of the State House, Philadelphia, which was to be the site of the Constitutional Convention.

A discussion of strategy in Benjamin Franklin's garden, showing Franklin with Madison, Hamilton, and Wilson.

The signing of the Constitution—one of the best attempts to portray the great event, although even this is historically inaccurate. For example, Benjamin Franklin is clearly portrayed here, even though he was too ill to attend the session.

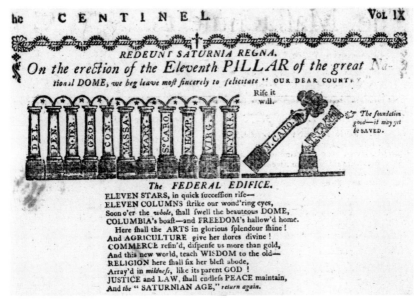

"The Erection of the Eleventh Pillar"—a dramatic newspaper cartoon showing each ratifying state as a separate pillar to support the national arch, with New York as the eleventh and North Carolina on the way.

A famous picture known as Penn's Tree, showing the harbor scene where the founder of Pennsylvania envisioned Philadelphia as a small city, just eight blocks square.

Chapter Fourteen

EXCITING
ASSOCIATES

Entering the latter half of July, seven weeks after the start of the Convention, some of the knowing delegates realized that their work was probably no better than half done. It was a daunting thought. Sitting in the State House for six to eight hours daily through a particularly hot summer was especially punishing, as the windows were kept closed to ensure that no eavesdroppers could overhear the debates. But the wonder of it was the generally good-natured acceptance of the discomfort. More than that, many of the men at the Convention were astonished to find themselves with a sense of awe at the privilege of being there.

Men who had left home somewhat reluctantly because they had personal affairs that needed attention, or who still thought grimly of the long times they had sacrificed to war just a few years ago, suddenly found themselves caught up in the importance of this event. They were determined to do the right thing—as General Washington made them see that they must do. And even though they often agreed among themselves that they would be fortunate to come up with a document that would survive for ten years, they felt that it would be long cherished, perhaps setting the stage for another constitution. The Union was the thing; this thought kept coming to the forefront. Not even during the war to win their freedom had they felt this as deeply as they did now. The attachment to a single state, the regional patriotism that had blotted out thoughts of the Union for the past few years, receded, and their feeling for a United States of America was growing apace.

The quality of the men around them and their willingness to consider ideas proposed by new acquaintances helped to foster this attitude. It was exemplified by the startling admission of Rufus King, an independent-minded man of thirty-three years with ambition to rule over the entire nation, that his "mind was revolutionized" just by talking informally with Hamilton for two hours. A rising political leader would not usually want to admit that anyone else could easily rearrange his thoughts. But the atmosphere of the Convention made it seem natural. It was as if they had joined a club that set them apart from everybody else in the world. Their ideas were as interesting and exciting as if one had discovered new ways of looking at the world.

One of the great surprises of the Convention was a man previously unknown to any of the others, Major William Pierce of Georgia. He once said he had expected to be regarded as a savage, for Georgia was known as one of the most backward states at that time. Certainly it was the least developed, with its plantations just being organized, its slave economy in the process of formation, and its borders under siege from the Native Americans along the Georgia-Florida boundary. Savannah, at that moment, was heavily fortified against attacks by the Creek tribe.

Pierce had only recently been chosen for the old Congress and was entirely new to public affairs. He was presented with a sword by that Congress for gallantry during the Revolution when he was aide de camp to General Nathaniel Greene. In addition to his military background, he became a merchant and served briefly in the Continental Congress. His language, both spoken and written, was plain and sometimes a bit crude, but his words, even some that he invented, were eminently serviceable. Mainly, he turned out to have a rare perceptiveness and his descriptions of fellow delegates provide precious portraits of those unusual days.

For one thing, Pierce, with no previous knowledge of Madison, saw his important traits much sooner than people usually did. In this case, he was guided by the opinions of many others when he wrote of Madison, "Every person seems to acknowledge his greatness...In the management of every great question, he evidently takes the lead in the Convention...He always comes forward as the best informed man of any point that is in debate."

But with little such guidance from others, Pierce drew a word sketch of Roger Sherman that is worthy of a Boswell. He seems not to have known the erroneous common belief that Sherman began life as a poor boy who became a shoemaker, but mysteriously rose to be highly regarded by the founding fathers in 1776 for the valuable ideas he contributed. Pierce made his own perceptive assessment:

> Roger Sherman was the oddest-shaped character I ever remember to have met with. He is awkward, un-meaning, and unaccountably strange in his manner. But in his train of thinking, there is something regular, deep, and comprehensive...The oddity of his address, the vulgarisms that accompany his public speaking, and that strange New England cant...make everything that is connected with him gross and laughable; and yet he deserves infinite praise...No man has a better heart nor a clearer head...He is an able politician, and extremely artful in accomplishing any particular object. It is remarked that he seldom fails.

The truth was that Sherman's father was a successful farmer who learned to make shoes earlier in life. He taught his son some of the rudiments of that craft and let him do some shoemaking for neighbor families during summer vacations from Connecticut's esteemed Stoughton School, sometimes even living with those families as the work progressed. But his father also maintained an excellent library, and the real secret of Sherman's knowledge is that he became an avid reader. Because he knew that Stoughton's mathematics courses were inadequate ("When you had learned fractions, you were considered a mathematician"), he studied on his own and became skillful enough to make the intricate calculations of stars and tides for a first-class almanac. His early records show that most of his allowance money was spent on books, although he liked to jest by quoting a maxim that, "The man who makes shoes is sure of his wages—the man who writes a book is never sure of anything."

Nonetheless, Sherman began to write, first a pamphlet about the evils of paper money based on his own early experience as part owner of a general merchandise store that his older brother started. Other publications, many of them attacking excessive drinking, and the founding of a successful almanac made him both well-known and affluent, so he rose in the political world. By 1776 he was sufficiently esteemed by the Founding Fathers to take a place in history as "the only shoemaker who signed the Declaration of Independence."

Members of his family were delighted by the description, while a cousin said, "Roger never made a whole pair of shoes in his life." But even though he became the subject of several biographies, and a Connecticut colleague said of him, "If he suspects you are trying to take him in, you may as well catch an eel by the tail," he has never been more intriguingly described than in William Pierce's few crisp lines.

William Paterson of New Jersey, who won such a victory for small states, was highly praised by Pierce, briefly, yet with sincerity; "A man of great modesty whose powers break in upon you and create wonder and astonishment." But the brevity of his praise for Rufus King, the aspiring young man from Massachusetts, somehow carried an air of momentary and limited importance, virtually forecasting the failure of his presidential ambition: "Tout en semble he should be ranked among the Luminaries of the Present Age."

One of Pierce's greatest favorites was Gouverneur Morris, in whom he quickly spotted the characteristics that lifted this individual from his reputation as a playboy to a real star of the Convention. This Pennsylvania delegate was not as important as Madison or Hamilton in his contribution to the Constitution's success, but he spoke more times than anyone else, usually at carefully chosen moments that lightheartedly eased the debate, and then was so effective on a final review committee that he was chosen to do the actual writing of the final document.

Pierce saw him this way: "One of those geniuses in whom every species of talents combine to render him conspicuous and flourishing in public debate. He throws around him such a glare that he charms, captivates, and leads away the senses of all who hear him...never pursuing one train of thinking, nor ever regular."

Morris's famous wooden leg, Pierce quipped, was not really caused by leaping from a balcony to escape an outraged husband, though he was sure that would have been a reasonable expectation. But in fact, he recites the truthful account of Morris's carriage accident, so severe that his left leg had to be amputated. When a friend came to console Morris on this terrible event, Pierce remarked, he told Morris at length what a good effect this would have on his morals, keeping him safely free from the dissipations in which young men were apt to engage. Whereupon Morris replied, "You argue the matter so handsomely that I am almost tempted to part with the other."

Gouverneur Morris did not disappoint Pierce or his other admirers, for he delighted almost everyone there. Many had known him only by reputation, and they could not have supposed that he really had the power to charm a whole roomful of people, some of whom may have disagreed with his conservative viewpoints. Morris could appear to speak for all types and conditions of human beings, even when comparing the interests of large landholders like himself, in opposition to John Rutledge, who was speaking for South Carolina slaveholders. "Life and liberty might be the first consideration of savages," he said, "but in civilized conditions, property is the principal object of society."

Pierce, however, had a unique way of doing an about-face and introducing an opposite view of the same person. Of Morris, he said, "But with all these powers he is fickle and inconstant." No matter, for the entire Convention sat entranced when, in a moment of critical disagreement, Morris used his rich voice to say:

I flatter myself I came here in some degree as a representative of the whole human race, for the whole human race will be affected by our proceedings. But now it seems to me that [we act as if] we were assembled to truck and bargain for our particular states. I believe this country must be united. If persuasion does not unite it, the sword will. The stronger party will then make traitors of the weaker…State attachments and state importance have been the bane of this country. We cannot annihilate them; but we can perhaps take out the teeth of the serpents.

Not all of Pierce's little character sketches were complimentary. Luther Martin of Maryland tired all the delegates with his over-long speeches, making them forget that he had once been a brilliant scholar. He had become a blowsy alcoholic. Pierce, gentler than most, left that misfortune out of his description and simply said, "This gentleman possesses a good deal of information, but he has a very bad delivery and is so extremely prolix that he never speaks without tiring the patience of all."

Even his own Georgia colleague, the heavy-set William Houston, received a set-down for both mind and body from Pierce: "Nature had done more for his corporeal than for his mental powers. While he had an amiable temper and honorable principles, I feel obliged to record that he was confused and irregular."

Elbridge Gerry, a delegate who had to be counted as very important because he was such a favorite son of Massachusetts and a signer of the Declaration of Independence, was neatly dispatched by Pierce as "a laborious speaker who was only sometimes clear. He goes into all subjects, speaking on without regard to eloquence or diction." Rufus King would have agreed with Pierce on that score, for he once exploded with frustration when he was trying to keep notes of a talk that Gerry was giving. The notes became more and more confused, and then ended with King's angry words, "I give up!"

But Pierce's lowest rating of all—emphasized by its brevity—was reserved for the disputatious George Read of Delaware: "I find his remarks tiresome to the last degree."

While not nearly as complete as Madison's notes of the proceedings, Pierce's more personal account went beyond humor and touched on incidents that some sober delegates regarded as very significant. He told, for example, of one delegate's having lost his copy of the Virginia Plan on an early June day. Most delegates copied this plan in their own hand, but they were strictly reminded of the importance of keeping this document from public notice. A Pennsylvania delegate found a lost copy and gave it to Washington.

The General held it all that day and then, just before adjournment, he spoke sternly of having this paper, reminding them how damaging it would be if words spoken there should get into the newspapers. Then Washington said, "I know not whose paper this is, but there it is"—and he threw it disgustedly on the table. "Let him who owns it take it."

Pierce was horrified to find his own copy missing, but this didn't prove to be the one lying on the table. His copy turned out to be in a pocket of the coat he had left carelessly at the Indian Queen Tavern— nearly as bad an offense, he moaned, but blissfully free of consequences.

The oldest man at the Convention figured in almost every recollection of the event, so it is a surprise to note that Franklin spoke infrequently—just 31 times in comparison with Gouverneur Morris's 168 and Wilson's 170 appearances. Late in life, Madison told historian Jared Sparks, "Dr. Franklin spoke rather little in the Convention, but with great pertinacity and effect." His words were longer remembered because he waited patiently to speak only when they would stand out or punctuate the debate.

An unknown commentator once said, "Franklin was one of those speakers whom listeners would rather quote than quarrel with." In one case, this led to a letter of his being read aloud in the Maryland house of delegates, which was improper because it came from the secret proceedings of the Convention. Franklin had sent Daniel Carroll, Speaker of that house, a copy of a speech about representation in the new congress that was being debated. This was actually improper of Franklin, but Carroll's publicizing it in this way increased the chance of embarrassment. Carroll wrote to Franklin with a deep apology, explaining that Luther Martin had so badly misrepresented the motives of both Franklin and George Washington that he wanted the truth to be known. No harm was done, and, in fact, it meant that another memorable piece of reasoning by Franklin was made part of the public record.

Far from being embarrassed, as Carroll had feared, it was one of the many times when Franklin refused to take an occasion as seriously as others did. He treated it in the same spirit that he often called his "Principle of Public Service: Never ask, Never refuse, Never resign." This meant that he was always available to take on an additional load of public duties, but he never asked to be appointed to anything, never refused to serve when asked, and never resigned if things disappointed him. The last point is the most telling one. No matter how little he liked the look of things, he always believed in "doubting his own infallibility" and waiting to see how they might turn out.

At times when a change of pace or a refreshing thought was most needed, Franklin would recall an experience or an anecdote that seemed to be of little significance; yet it almost always served a purpose—to illustrate a point he was making or even to interrupt an exchange of angry words and send the talk in a new direction. In most cases, his interjection achieved more than one goal.

An example occurred when the members were debating how judges should be chosen. As he saw the level of frustration rising and the voices in the lawyer-filled room taking on a harsher note, Franklin cleared his throat and softly observed that only two ways of selecting men for the bench had been mentioned; either by the legislature or by the executive branch. "I want to remind this house of a third way, a way that is used very successfully in Scotland, I am told. The lawyers choose the judges. These lawyers"—and here Franklin probably paused to look slowly and meaningfully over a room that was half full of barristers—"always select the ablest members of their profession, in order to get rid of them. That way, they can share all those lucrative practices among themselves." Five men who heard Franklin offer these comments would become Supreme Court justices: Wilson, Rutledge, Paterson, Ellsworth, and Blair.

A related element that gave the Constitutional Convention a special quality and created the atmosphere for success was the degree of exaggeration that prevailed; the frequent use of overstatements or understatements that were not meant to be taken seriously. Considering how much wisdom finally crowned the work of the Convention, it is easy to enjoy and admire much of the apparent nonsense these men dispensed along the way.

The misleading demands that they advanced with serious faces and tones of voice created a facilitating environment. Far from being a distraction, this was a wonderfully new and typically American quality that had not usually been present at public meetings and certainly not under the Articles of Confederation. It had a practical aspect, for the ability to make an exaggerated suggestion without being taken literally opens the way for talk of compromise.

This easy quality was at least partly due to the number of youthful delegates. Five were age thirty or less, with Jonathan Dayton of New Jersey the youngest at twenty-six. But seventeen men—virtually a third of the group—were less than thirty-five years old. The average age of the fifty-five delegates was forty-three, but this was inflated by the presence of Pennsylvania's Benjamin Franklin, eight-one, and Connecticut's Roger Sherman, sixty-six. Without those two, the dozen most active leaders in oratory and debates had an average age of only thirty-nine years. But it is much more significant that the two elderly delegates happened to have the most youthful and flexible approach. Franklin's mind seemed to play hide-and-seek with any thought that might uncover a bright new bauble. And Sherman, while sounding tough and plainspoken, was a champion negotiator, as anxious to reach a workable bargain as any man there.

So fears that the Convention was about to collapse until this or that compromise was reached may sometimes have been exaggerated, even though many delegates thought them real at the time. Like Maryland's Luther Martin, some delegates once thought that "the Convention was on the verge of dissolution, scarce held together by the strength of a hair." This is surely what many believed when they heard Paterson, sounding so ready to quit the Convention if small states were denied equal representation; his game was exposed when he quickly boarded the federal bandwagon as soon as he won a compromise.

There would be more such sudden conversions in the latter half of the Convention. Historians have naturally tended to follow these on-the-spot impressions that each demand signaled a crisis. But it is revealing to note that a considerable number of players had two essential traits: determination to reach a positive conclusion and thespian skill in pretending that they were ready to quit. Because the rather unconventional mood of the meeting gave them great freedom to bargain, it brought about rapid decisions on some difficult issues that would otherwise have taken years to resolve.

One non-member of the Convention who was never in the room figured in the spirit of dash and panache that often pervaded the State House. It was Major General Baron von Steuben. Nothing could have captured the dawning American spirit of delight in mocking pomposity so dramatically as his rise to universal acclaim. He happened to be in Philadelphia during much of the Convention's duration because the city was delighted to have him reviewing its troops and taking part in parades. His review of the Philadelphia armed forces drew a larger and livelier crowd than General Washington's review of the Light Horse a few weeks later. By now, most of the nation knew and could laugh repeatedly at the stories of von Steuben's disastrous attempts, a decade earlier, to convey orders to the troops in a combination of German, French, English, and profanity.

With the Cincinnati members all over town, and several of them in the Convention hall, the repeated tales about von Steuben's misadventures and eventual triumph were on more lips than the surrender of Cornwallis. The first time he assembled a whole battalion of shabby recruits and tried to display the drill routines he was teaching them, the result had been total chaos. His German commands were misunderstood. Some squads suddenly swung into other squads, men kept milling around, some falling to the ground, as their furious instructor shouted:

Nein, nein, goddam, vas ist los? A la gauche, la gauche, ah Mon Dieu. Was machst du, dummkopfen, goddam bitches' sons. Links! Links! A la gauche!

Only the presence of a young soldier named Benjamin Miller, who understood German and French, had saved the day. Together, von

Steuben and Miller got the men back into formation, translated the series of instructions into an English version made up by Miller, and put on a creditable display of what was originally intended.

Miller and von Steuben became lifelong friends, and it was Miller who buried the German soldier years later. But during the war years, two miracles had happened and they still echoed at the Convention: von Steuben's book of instructions for American soldiers and his roughly translated personal commands had actually converted a listless band of soldiers who seemed hopelessly outclassed in battle into fighting units that repeatedly surprised the British with their steadiness and discipline. And the circulating stories about that first chaotic day, gaining new curses with each retelling, made von Steuben into one of America's favorite persons. It was the unlikely success story that gave it such appeal—the epitome of the American dream—an immigrant who succeeds and joins in the laughter while teaching the Americans new tricks.

Von Steuben's appeal was enduring because his character was genuine. One afternoon, while the Benedict Arnold treason was in everyone's mind, von Steuben heard a young recruit say that his name was Jonathan Arnold. "How can you call yourself by such an ugly name?" he asked the man. "You should change it at once!" "But how can I do that?" the soldier asked. "I don't have any other name." "Then I'll let you use mine," the general responded. "In America, you can do anything as long as it is good. Get some paper and write down that you are now Jonathan Steuben, and send it to the state governor's office. That will make it legal." It was not a momentary display for von Steuben. He kept in touch with the soldier after the war, took an interest in his family, and let them move onto a part of his own land. Even in the next generation, the soldier's descendants had Steuben in their names. A state park in New York dedicated to von Steuben's memory has a large boulder near his grave, bearing the inscription: Indispensable to the Achievement of American Independence.

Chapter Fifteen

PRESIDENTIAL QUESTIONS

The method of selecting a chief executive, the term, and the powers of that office came to be the longest debated subject of the entire Convention. It also featured the least thoughtful comments. Questions or remarks sounded haphazard, giving the impression that the speakers were amateurs with little skill in analyzing public affairs. The issue was brought up in July, then discussed sporadically through most of August, and continued to concern and trouble the delegates until the final days in September. In the course of so many sessions, earlier decisions were often reopened or rejected.

On most other subjects, the issues were discussed after some study of precedents, and individuals who made proposals usually buttressed them with reasons supporting each point. In dealing with the presidency, there was little indication that serious thought was given to the issue. A series of suggestions proposed that there be from one to three presidents, that these individuals be chosen directly by the people, popularly elected from a group nominated by state legislatures, or selected by the joint houses of Congress. Many different terms of office were proposed, varying from one year to life. There was one serious proposal that the president be selected by drawing lots, though it had a short life.

Only in retrospect can we understand why the delegates responded so haphazardly. No faction among the delegates seemed to prefer a particular outcome. Unlike the very definite commercial aspirations that applied to trade or commercial subjects, most delegates came into the State House with no plan for the selection of a chief executive. While participants often grow testy at finding that other people in a meeting seem to be promoting selfish interests and pressing their points hard enough to become disagreeable, that kind of pressure—within limits—is more bearable than the unfamiliar feeling that no one has any position.

Unlike the points considered in counting the slaves as part of the population, or in regulating the formation of new states, there was no state or group that seemed to have a vested interest in how a chief executive should be chosen or what kind of advisory staff should help him in decision-making. On the questions of trade, seats in congress, or rights to land ownership, the players were well known, and their positions could be assessed and usually refashioned so that a compromise could be reached. Here men seemed to have little or nothing to say, then finally spoke up because it was expected of them, but they did so without conviction. Most would have been content to see the leader's term doubled—or cut in half. This open-endedness, with no outspoken proponents or positions, made a decision much harder to reach, and some delegates had an uneasy sense that a possible major mistake might be in the offing. The situation had all the tiresome formlessness of young people trying to decide what game to play.

A few delegates did show preferences about a president's term of office and the right to succeed himself. But these were usually based on an underlying interest in monarchy or fear of it. Those who wanted long terms and unlimited rights to reelection were usually indicating an unspoken interest in a royal ruler. But this was not always traditional monarchism. Even some members who firmly opposed having a king were known to feel that the country would sooner or later have to adopt a hereditary monarchy; they were looking for an interim plan that would work well enough to put off the inevitable for as long as possible. This led to improbable ideas, some that were almost humorous. For example, one historian of old said he learned that a triple-headed executive was suggested, meaning a three-man executive team, administering the eastern, middle, and southern states. This was apparently derived from the fact that associated Roman emperors sometimes ran different parts of the empire, in the belief that physical location reasonably close to the people ruled was an essential part of successful governing. The Virginia Plan had not specified whether a single executive or a group was proposed. Madison wanted a single individual, for efficiency, while some of his Virginia colleagues feared this choice would incline toward tyranny.

The delegates would remain silent for such a long time that Washington asked if they would like him to "put the question," meaning to move ahead with taking a vote, even though no specific measure had been proposed. Most delegates looked puzzled. "But what *is* the question?" they obviously wondered. Franklin, in great surprise, signaled and said he would like to hear what members had to say on the subject before any thought of voting came up. John Rutledge, an experienced South Carolinian, reminded the members not to be so shy. "Speak up," he urged them, "for you can always change your remarks later, if you like, and no one will know what you said first." To set an example, the southerner came forth with his own opinion, which was in favor of having a single executive for the sake of efficiency and in order to concentrate responsibility. But he would not give that person war-making powers. After that, others did make suggestions more freely, but not much more usefully.

Roger Sherman, with his typically reasoned approach, reminded that the executive's duty was to carry out the will of the legislature. He proposed that the legislature should select the executive, with the number being left open for that body to decide on the basis of the business that needed to be done. (He may have known this was a concept the British had been exploring for many years, but the delegates apparently did not know of it, so few others followed up on Sherman's remarks, and this idea did not get as much attention as it may have deserved.)

Along the way, there was a move that reinforced the evidence of the Convention's wish for an executive with monarchical overtones. In addition to more and more frequent remarks about the desirability of a life term, it was suggested that a privy council should be set up for the twin purpose of advising the president and restraining his ability to act. One plan proposed that this council consist of eight men—the president of the Senate, Speaker of the House, chief justice of the Supreme Court, and principal officers of five federal departments. These men would have the duty of advising the president on matters that he would lay before them, but without forcing him to change his own plan of action. Madison, Wilson, Dickinson, Mason, and Franklin approved of the idea, but it was voted down. This rejection infuriated Mason, who shouted that having a president without such an advisory body would be the most dangerous experiment on which any government had ever embarked. The outburst was at least refreshing, and the deadly serious Mason must have been apoplectic to hear a low ripple of laughter.

Because of this lack of a council, the Convention decided instead to have the Senate share in more of the president's functions. This was how the Senate came to play a regular role in the appointment of ambassadors and supreme court justices and the approval of treaties.

It was a little later, during Washington's first term, that the heads of certain executive departments began to be called the president's cabinet. It has been noted that these officials, since they do not belong to Congress and are not meant to work on legislation, really constitute a sort of privy council, although not the kind of safeguard against error that Mason had in mind. If an American president who was determined to go to war found members speaking up against him at the next cabinet meeting, he might simply decide to have fewer meetings.

There was never a decision to establish a cabinet, as such, but it was implied in Article II, Section 2, with the words that the president "may require the opinion, in writing, of the principal officer in each of the executive departments upon any subject relating to the duties of their respective offices." The Constitution does not say which or how many executive departments should be created, thus giving presidents great latitude. The term "cabinet" began to be used early in Washington's first term, probably because most of the men who made up the group knew at least some French. But Hamilton, who really knew the language, was probably amused by the demotion that the term implied, because in French, "cabinet" usually means the office or the staff of a minister, not the minister's highest associates. Even more uninvitingly, the French took their word from the Italian term gabbinetto, meaning a small office, but derived from cavea, meaning a cage.

Pennsylvania's Wilson spoke several times about presidential powers and advisers, each time with a powerful plea for a single executive. His logic seemed unassailable, but somehow it failed to gather much support. On top of that came long discussions about whether the executive should be elected by the people or chosen by Congress and how many years he should serve. Rufus King said sarcastically, "Better make it twenty years, for that is the average reign of princes." Hamilton, not at all like himself, appeared badly confused, perhaps by the conflict between his personal wish for a monarchical government and his recognition that this was not possible. Consequently, he went along with Gouverneur Morris's wish to have the executive chosen for life, though subject to removal for bad behavior, apparently forgetting that his own proposal of a three-year presidential term was still pending.

Many delegates said that they need not worry about a president trying to stay on too long, for no one would want to keep working beyond a reasonable point. Wilson rose to disabuse the delegates of that notion. "Where did we learn this curious thought that an elderly president would not wish to stay in office?" he asked. He pointed out that the Roman Catholic Church seemed to have no trouble finding men who were already quite old to serve as popes, that one Venetian Doge was already over eighty when he was chosen, and that the practice was not limited to Italians, for Lord Mansfield, a British chief justice, stayed on thirty more years after reaching the age of fifty.

This comment brought laughter, but still no one rose to speak convincingly on this imprecise subject. A relatively short term was clearly preferred by most delegates, but there was no motion to adopt a set number of years, so the lackluster talk allowed the subject to drift and moved on to another and even more elusive target.

It was time for the agonizing matter called "mode of election," and Wilson, Madison's staunch ally, took the floor again. While admitting to some apprehension, he spoke in favor of election by the people. He mentioned the successful results of this form for electing the first magistrates of both New York and Massachusetts. For years, the citizens of those states had chosen successfully because they were selecting between persons who were already generally known to them. "Why should anything be preferable to this simple and direct method?" Wilson asked. Washington, Madison, Gerry, and Gouverneur Morris spoke in favor of this view, while Sherman, Mason, and Rutledge strongly favored selection by the legislature. Mason, in fact, thought the people so lacking in knowledge of the candidates' characters that the idea of direct election by the people would be "as unnatural as to refer a trial of colors to a blind man."

This struggle over method of election went on, in short bursts, for weeks. One suggestion was that each state should choose its own "favorite son," and then a president might be selected by Congress from those thirteen names. At one point, in desperation or perhaps with sarcasm, Wilson proposed making the choice by blind chance, as ancient Greece had sometimes done; he proposed that fifteen members of Congress should choose a chief executive by lot from among a group of their congressional colleagues. To his credit, he reconsidered and quickly withdrew the suggestion, saying, "This was not a digested idea." Finally, on July 26, a motion made by Mason passed: a single executive chosen by the national legislature would be appointed and called president of the United States for seven years and not eligible for a second term. This ban on reelection was to prevent the president from pandering to Congress in his quest for another term.

The word "finally," however, was transitory, for Rutledge reopened the whole question at the end of August, feeling that the two houses of congress might work against each other if one exerted a strong negative on the choice made by the other house. He proposed that the two houses should proceed by "joint ballot," meaning that a single total would apply. This appeared to have carried, when Gouverneur Morris—in a powerful speech—reminded the Convention of his previous warnings that an election by Congress would result in boundless intrigue. He pointed out that it had already started, and he persuaded the Convention to go back to a device that had been discarded before, namely, an electoral college having votes equal in number to the two houses of Congress put together. These delegates could do their job by sending their votes under seal to the Congress, thus avoiding long trips by that many persons, which was a big consideration at that time.

As finally worked out, the Senate and House together would meet and count the ballots, and the candidate with the highest total would be president if he attained a majority. If no one had a majority, the Senate would choose one person from among the five highest in the ballot count. In either case, the candidate with the next highest total would become vice president.

Almost as an afterthought, an objection was raised about the office of vice president: there seemed to be nothing for him to do. It was decided to make him president of the Senate, and everyone seemed satisfied that this was quite enough.

As late as September 6, alterations were being made in the election scheme, taking the job of counting away from the Senate alone and saying that "The President of the Senate shall, in the presence of the Senate and the House of Representatives, open all the certificates, and the votes shall then be counted." This step was taken to guard against the failure of an election through any disagreement and wrongdoing between the two houses.

As one might expect, arrangements with so many delicate complexities and so much anticipation of dishonest behavior were found to contain several safeguards that were of little use, while failing to guard against some unforeseen problems. For example, there was no thought of possible double returns that might be sent in by rival governments in the same state. This left the door open for a danger greater than some of those that the Convention delegates agonized over. The great majority of historians from then until now who have commented on this intricate mechanism have denounced it as being unnecessarily cumbersome and yet not covering all the potential attempts to achieve perfect electoral results.

James Wilson's powerful plea for simple direct election of the president by the people was hastily dismissed by a large majority of the delegates. They felt that the democratic sentiment in the convention was too weak to justify such a choice. In short, here is additional evidence of how strongly the delegates agreed with Hamilton's doubts about the fitness of the American people to conduct a democratic nation.

But at least two other reasons were cited on that day. First, the distances seemed so great that the prompt arrival via slow coaches and mailbags carried on horseback was deemed too great a chance to take with such important documents. Second, it was also felt that the people would lack sufficient data for judging the merits of public men who were presidential candidates. In contrast, electors, being eminent and well-informed men, "screened from the sophisms of demagogues," could select the best candidates with superior judgment.

From the start, the elector system never lived up to this vision of it. The first great struggle involving parties occurred in the election of 1800, and the eminent electors—showing no sign of the careful selection process expected of them—instantly divided along party lines. The Constitution has had to cope with one fundamental error made by the Convention delegates—an unspoken attempt to borrow from the British system that so many of them considered superior, but without really understanding the changes that had been going on in Britain for many years.

In almost everything else they considered, these delegates were dealing with subjects they really knew first-hand and understood clearly. Their debates and compromises were practical. But on this electoral subject, and especially in their attempt to model it on British lines, they were out of their depth. All the delegates who had studied the law learned from the books of Blackstone, the great British legal authority, and from Montesquieu, the elegant French political writer who also revered the British system. Those authorities wrote about King, Lords, and Commons as being three staunchly separate pillars of power on which a balanced government rested.

But Blackstone and Montesquieu failed to take account of the fact that the Revolution of 1688 began the process of making England's real executive an arm of the legislature. This decision was reinforced in the time of Sir Robert Walpole, from 1715 to 1742, and was completed under Pitt in 1784, when it became clear that no prime minister who was politically strong could be dismissed on the basis of a sovereign's wishes. Even the sovereign's power survives only in theory, for use if a government should act to destroy the democratic or parliamentary bases of the constitution. Unless the sovereign's judgment should be supported by public opinion, the monarchy would be placing itself in jeopardy. Authorities have pointed out that if a prime minister loses support in the House of Commons, attention focuses on his duty to resign or to dissolve Parliament, rather than on the sovereign's right of removal, for the latter is not within the scope of practical politics.

The books the delegates had studied were sadly outdated classics that no longer applied. The supreme power in Great Britain had already been gathered into a single body, the House of Commons, as it is today. The House of Lords only continued to exist by submitting to Commons, as is also true of the monarchy. So if the Convention delegates wanted to copy the true British system, they would have made the president a creature of the Congress, making it an absurdity to think of this executive as a separate power. If he loses control of the Congress, he should be automatically out of power.

If the delegates had been familiar with the updated facts about the British system, they might have recognized that Roger Sherman's suggestion to let Congress select the chief executive, cited earlier in this chapter, might possibly have given a new slant to their decisions on the election, term, and duties of the American president. But perhaps not even the amazingly studious Madison was as well versed in this as Sherman, "The Shoemaker." The only record of precisely what Madison's law studies covered is not promising. It reads: "Studying with Mr. E. Shippen, Blackstone *Commentaries on the Laws of England*."

Oddly enough, while the British system was being radically altered to keep pace with the ongoing march of events, American lawmakers were worriedly asking whether their people could keep step with an outworn and discarded constitution from Britain's past.

There is no way to say whether the Constitution would have been a stronger instrument if Sherman's suggestion had been heeded and the British method of making the president a creature of the Congress had been used. The principle of basing the government on the will of the people would have prevailed, just as it has done in America's present system. But there is much room for argument about the strength and flexibility of the Constitution's only segment that may have been badly handled by the delegates. This is also of special interest because it proves how great Madison's contribution was in all other aspects of the Constitution's creation. If there is one portion of the document that is defective, it resulted from the only occasion when Madison presented no firm plan to guide the others.

Chapter Sixteen

DISTASTE FOR FINANCE

Monetary chaos enveloped the states after the Revolutionary War because there were no punitive laws that could force states to pay what they owed to the central government and they were unable to find compromises that might have created an orderly system for turning people's work into forms of real money that would have lasting value.

Madison remembered from his experience in the Congress that most delegates preferred not to discuss financial issues, and now he saw that this same aversion to the grim subject was persisting at the Philadelphia Convention. Although word from the outside world and from their homes warned the delegates that monetary chaos was worsening during these very days, most leaders preferred not to hear financial discussions. Men with whom he could have an intelligent talk on other topics wanted to turn away and not listen to anything about money. It was not a subject that Madison enjoyed either, but he forced himself to grapple with it because he saw that nothing else would succeed without the establishment of a sound financial system.

The clashing attitudes dated back to the war years, when there had been no reliable circulating currency at all. States issued inconvertible paper money. This consisted of paper bills that were not backed by gold or any other generally accepted substance that was rare and costly to produce. Paper money was sadly misrepresented as a godsend by those who said, "poor people need poor money." The flash of mock prosperity that it could produce was always short-lived and great suffering would follow, as people felt momentarily rich then found their paper was worthless. Working people were tempted into extravagance, then left with nothing of value and often with debt that might put them into prison. Speculators, especially in foodstuffs, infuriated George Washington into abandoning his steady manner. He was angered into making futile remarks that were not typical of him, once saying, "I would like to hang them all on a gallows higher than that of Haman."

Until 1785, there was no national coinage at all, meaning that the only circulating form of exchange was "specie"; English, French, Spanish, German, and other coins of uncertain values that were well-known enough to be accepted by merchants as payment for goods. There were ninepences, bits and half-bits, picayunes and fips; gold pieces, such as doubloons and pistoles; there were pennies issued by local mints in several New England states. The values of these coins varied widely according to the differing demands in each state. The English shilling had sunk from one-fourth of a dollar to only one-sixth in New England but it was only one-eighth in New York and one-tenth in North Carolina.

Such a thing as paying taxes was called "an amiable eccentricity," so by 1782, no trace of money existed in the country's treasury. Robert Morris, who heroically found ways to supply George Washington with funds for one emergency after another during the war, continued to be in charge of the Confederacy's finances until 1784, when he quit in order to rescue his own shaky fortune. (Tragically, considering all he had done for the United States, he failed to correct his tangled accounts and later became a fugitive before being captured and put into debtor's prison. After his release, he was a broken man.)

Thanks to the other Morris—Gouverneur—the first American coinage created in 1785 was based on the decimal system. Morris credited Thomas Jefferson with some of the ideas for it, but he was the chief designer. However, it was a committee of the Congress that controlled the money, and it never succeeded in acquiring enough solid funds to serve as a credible backing for any cash it created.

A young government might borrow from abroad the gold or other hard money to serve as support for money that it planned to issue. But then the interest on that loan would immediately begin to create a deficit that would lessen the value of the new money. The normal way to create a basic fund, without having to borrow, would be to collect substantial taxes from the states year after year; but not even a Hamilton could produce such a miracle without a constitution to force compliance.

This failure to produce a money supply simply hastened the old Congress toward a crisis. By 1786, this situation merged with Shays's Rebellion as a clear reason for moving in some new direction. Now the Convention delegates were receiving daily reports about near-panic financial conditions back home. Still they were slow to develop a plan, because they feared the subject could only damage their standing in their individual home states.

Only Connecticut and Delaware were able to resist the epidemic of paper money crashes, while at least seven states were falling into near disasters over this subject. In the Carolinas and Georgia, what has been called a "Kuklux" society was formed (derived from the ancient Greek term kyklos, meaning a fraternal circle, but now implying the use of terrorist methods). In this case, it was often called the "Hint Club." Planters or merchants were urged to sign a pledge that they would accept paper money, making no price distinction between paper and gold. Government was literally forcing its citizens to become willing victims of robbery. If they hesitated, they were given a "hint," which was recognized as a threat that their house might suddenly burn down or some even more serious result might ensue. In some places, punishment was carried out by unofficial activists, many of whom were leading citizens of their communities.

In Georgia, official coercion of this kind prohibited any planter or merchant from exporting his product unless he signed an affidavit that he had never refused to accept the state's scrip at full face value. Major William Pierce, who was writing his piquant sketches of fellow delegates in Philadelphia, discovered that his merchandise-trading business was now failing, and he was forced to leave the Convention early for his home in Savannah. He never had an opportunity to sign the Constitution, even though he was in favor of it and had planned to affix his signature to it. He went bankrupt soon after reaching home, losing his wife's entire dowry, which had been used to finance his company. Pierce died two years later at age forty-nine, leaving a mountain of debts.

Virginia, followed by Pennsylvania, has been prodded by Madison, Mason, and Washington into taking some sound money measures that gave its paper money a special reputation and meaningful value. But in 1786, even this paper drifted to eighty-eight cents, twelve cents below its original value. And the maritime states, especially Massachusetts and Rhode Island, suffered most severely from British blows at their carrying trade, as shipping was often called. It should be remembered, when Rhode Island's refusal to pay national obligations or to make firm promises seemed so inexcusable, that this state's finances were hurt most by the war and that the occupation by enemy troops lasted the longest time there. Some conservative Rhode Islanders fought hard to regain a sound money, even when they were repeatedly threatened by violent demonstrations for not cooperating with the popular will. (See chapter 23)

Wherever attempts were made to force local merchants to accept paper money, their sufferings merged into what became a national scandal. In one example, a worker from another town tried to buy a joint of meat in Newport, found that the seller refused to take paper money in payment, and brought charges against him for disobeying the "forcing act," which forced businessmen to treat paper as if it were gold on pain of huge fines. The merchant faced a fine of five hundred dollars for violation of the act. In turn, the informer would receive half of the sum for supplying the information, so he could not lose. Huge crowds gathered outside when the court was to consider the case. The majority of people surrounding the courthouse made it plain that they favored the easy-money way and wanted the merchant found guilty, because paper money was all that the people had. They showed no sympathy for the merchant who was being robbed. When an honest and courageous judge declared the forcing act unenforceable and dismissed the case, the furious crowd turned on the judge.

With this travesty being repeated in most of America, the lack of a reliable currency slowed business almost to a standstill, and there were places where near starvation followed as shops preferred to stay closed rather than trading foods for money that was soon to become worthless. Farmers were hit hard, because their products could not be sold for reusable money. In most of the country, farms and homes were being sold for non-payment of foreclosed mortgages; farmers like Shays's men lost literally everything they had and went to debtor's prison to boot. The effects brought on unreasonable behavior. People were increasingly infuriated against the local authorities, the courts, and the confederate government. This was the atmosphere that Henry Knox quite accurately communicated to George Washington in the letter from New England that converted the General from a bystander to a participant.

With all the terrible experiences that some states suffered after issuing paper currency, the Convention delegates found themselves aligning against any more monetary adventures. They decided promptly that states should be firmly barred from producing their own money. Only the national government would have the right to issue money in both coin and paper form, but the paper money must be fully backed by gold, so that a person with a paper bill from the United States Treasury could present it and demand a gold coin of the same amount. Once established, such a system would give a federally issued dollar bill a new level of respect, and very few Americans would even try to convert their convenient paper money into gold.

But an obvious related question soon emerged. Should the federal government be granted the power to create inconvertible paper money? Intense feelings pro and con existed on this subject. Opposition to the idea seemed to be strong at first. Gouverneur Morris urged that the national government should be prohibited from issuing currency, bills of credit, or promissory notes—anything that pretended to be legal tender but was backed by nothing but the government's word. He prophesied that within a few years, if a war or other national emergency erupted, people would quickly back the idea of the government printing easy money, leading to the same disaster that had almost destroyed several states. He said now was the time to end this evil.

Roger Sherman supported Morris, saying, "This is the time to shut and bar the door against paper money." James Wilson was firmly of the same opinion. Hamilton was absent during most of these discussions on a subject in which he had become expert, but they all knew that he would have eloquently opposed paper money that was not fully backed by gold or other hard assets in the nation's treasury. There were a few delegates who reminded the meeting that one could not always foresee every circumstance. The Revolutionary War, they pointed out, could not have been fought without relying temporarily on paper money. So it might be unwise to tie the hands of future legislatures. Both Mason and Randolph joined in this cautionary note.

But when a vote was taken, nine states opted to bar the government from issuing inconvertible paper. The only man present who spoke strongly in favor of paper money was one whose status as a delegate was almost a joke. John Francis Mercer of Maryland had been last to arrive, long after discussions started, because he demanded expense money that the governor of Maryland did not want to provide. He left just a week later and never returned. Other delegates called him verbose, vain, and a man of intrigue. His defense of paper money was ridiculed, but his words on that one subject must have made an impression on a few other delegates: Maryland and New Jersey joined in opposing any firm written rule against paper money, and their opposition had an effect.

It was decided that the Convention was definitely against allowing the national government to create paper money that was not backed by hard metal, but because many thought this was clear, they saw no need to write the ban into law. The delegates believed there was no danger that a future government would turn to paper money if it were not expressly permitted in the Constitution. This view proved to be wrong, because the Legal Tender Act of 1862 enabled President Lincoln to use paper money in financing the Civil War. Many of the country's ablest legal authorities later agreed that this was a massive violation of the clear wishes expressed by the Constitution's creators. Lincoln might not have been able to take this course if it had been expressly forbidden in writing. How badly that restriction might have hampered the North's war effort is not known. But it is intriguing to note that the success of President Lincoln's desperate fight to hold the Union together may have been influenced by the words of the Convention's most derided member, John Francis Mercer.

The issue of government debt—in particular the responsibility for the Revolutionary War debt—was hotly disputed, sent to a special committee made up of one member from each state, and finally put into the new Constitution with this ambiguous wording: "All debts contracted and engagements entered into by or under the authority of Congress shall be as valid against the United States under this constitution as under the confederation." But since there was no certainty about what debts were valid against the Confederation, this was another one of those points, like the location of the federal capital, that really said, "We do not know. To be answered later." Strangely, the two issues of debt and the federal capital that were coupled in this evasive way were destined to become more closely linked in a compromise reached after the Constitution had been ratified.

The delegates to the Philadelphia Convention knew that any form of taxation was universally unpopular. Madison saw that the fear of taxes was so great that a simple 5 percent impost on imported goods in 1781 roused public speakers to excessive heights of oratory. A Rhode Island professor, David Howell, begged his state to refuse the disgraceful calls to pay tax money on demand to the Confederation and to maintain "the noble system under which you are to grant your money like freemen, from time to time, bound only…by your sentiments of justice, of virtue, and by your sacred honor."

Thoughts going back over twenty years were expressed in reminding delegates of the unsavory reputation that all taxation had. Names like Grenville and Townshend were recalled—British ministers who had instituted new taxes that fired Americans to sever relations with the mother country. Taxation was a subject that could spell only trouble to the new breed of politicians who were preparing to represent the voters back home. With such memories, the delegates were slow to take up even the related subjects of money, finance, and trade. Madison knew, too, that when the time for ratification came, he would be facing a furious Patrick Henry, who would attack the new government's taxing power. Henry was already known to have said that federal sheriffs would outdo the ravages of "those unfeeling bloodsuckers, the state sheriffs." While insisting that he had no idea of proposing Virginia's secession from the Union, he planted the idea in every mind by saying that "Virginia and North Carolina could exist separated from the rest of America."

On July 12, a full month and a half into the Convention's life, Gouverneur Morris, referring to the "Great Compromise" that settled the weight given to slaves in determining seats in the lower house, proposed that the matter of taxation be treated in the same way. That is, since representation in the Congress was to include slaves counted as three-fifths of a white person, "I propose to say that direct taxation should also be in proportion to representation." This had already been agreed to in the compromise, but the sheer novelty of hearing a delegate speak openly of taxation startled everyone. With the pervading spirit of compromise and the feeling of progress dominating the room, Morris's smooth voice made his proposal sound legitimate. The motion was soon adopted. Another big step had been taken.

When the Constitution was written, Gouverneur Morris wrote this formula into the very first page, in Article I, just as he said it in the fateful meeting:

> Representatives and direct Taxes shall be apportioned among the several States which may be included within this Union, according to their respective Numbers, which shall be determined by adding to the whole Number of free Persons, including those bound to Service for a Term of Years, and excluding Indians not taxed, three fifths of all other Persons.

In Section 8 of the same Article is the further statement:

> The Congress shall have Power to lay and collect Taxes, Duties, Imposts and Excises, to pay the Debts and provide for the common

Defense and general Welfare of the United States; but all Duties, Imposts, and Excises shall be uniform throughout the United States.

Section 8 reads like a recipe for setting up a country, for it goes on to name a long list of other positive powers granted to the Congress:
- to borrow money and to coin money
- to regulate Commerce with foreign Nations
- to establish rules of Naturalization and laws on the subject of Bank-ruptcies
- to establish Post Offices
- to punish piracies and felonies committed on the high seas
- to declare War, provide and maintain Armies and a Navy, to provide for calling forth the Militia to execute the Laws of the Union

This last phrase, incidentally, adds great clarity to the much-abused Amendment II of the Bill of Rights when the two are read together. This amendment does not deal with a generalized "right of the people to keep and bear Arms," but pointedly stipulates that this right "shall not be infringed," because arms are required for "a well-regulated Militia" which, in turn, is "necessary to the security of a free State." Bearing arms for any other purpose is simply not mentioned.

∾

When hard bargaining on financial subjects surfaced, Madison's group of young members, along with most other delegates, were somewhat outclassed by sixty-six year old Roger Sherman, who could shape a stunning financial compromise with the panache of a Moroccan street vendor. Sherman succeeded—and earned increasing respect—because he was willing to treat a bargain as a two-way arrangement, expecting to give a good bit for the gain he made. As William Pierce said, "It is remarked that he never fails."

So it was that Sherman made a great deal for his and other small states while also allowing a victory in financial power to fall into the laps of larger states when a second major multi-state arrangement was consummated. This one was thought to be a minor part of the "Connecticut Compromise," but it would prove to be more far-reaching than anyone believed at the time.

The bargain was this: The agreement that preserved equal representation for small states in the upper house of Congress was in jeopardy because the large states were still unhappy about the great concession they had made to the small states. Sherman and others who were desperately anxious to hold the arrangement together sweetened it for the large states by further agreeing that "All bills for raising revenue shall originate in the House of Representatives; but the Senate may propose or concur with amendments as on other bills."

It had already been a bill that favored large states by putting great financial force into the chamber where they had the most weight. Now, stipulating that all such money raising must *originate* in the lower house seemed like a minor new benefit, since both houses could then take part in passing, amending, or killing the bill before it became effective; however, it proved to be important in many sessions of Congress, especially at times when the two houses are controlled by different parties. If the House refuses to introduce it, there will be no such bill. The Senate's hands are tied.

A dramatic example of this occurred sixteen years later, when the Louisiana Purchase doubled the nation's size. The treaty that James Monroe and Robert Livingston signed in Paris in April 1803 was approved by the Senate on October 20 of the same year, and ratified by President Jefferson on the following day, making the treaty official. But while the treaty was the Senate's business, the payment of fifteen million dollars to Napoleon Bonaparte's France had to originate in the House of Representatives. There was not really much doubt that this would be accomplished, since the country was wonderfully excited by the movement toward control of almost all the continent.

But a loud and boisterous congressional debate was staged before the appropriation was passed. Some Congressmen clamoring for attention suggested a variety of quite ridiculous objections to the deal, such as the chance that Napoleon Bonaparte might send troops to slaughter the

American color guard that went to New Orleans for a flag-raising ceremony. The stalemate ended within days, but it demonstrated what power the lower house could have whenever the party that controlled it might wish to make a major stand and refuse to originate a financial bill that was urgently needed.

Gouverneur Morris complained that making only the lower house the originator of money bills would lose the benefit of the Senate's superior judgment and ability to devise such bills. But this was one time when Morris was bested by another leading personality. Benjamin Franklin disagreed with Morris's comment and summed up the reason he favored the great gift of power to the lower house by saying that people should know who had disposed of their money and how it was disposed of. "It is a maxim," he said, "that those who feel can best judge. This end would be best attained if money affairs were confined to the immediate representatives of the people." Once again, Franklin, who pretended to be of two minds before the Convention began, gave his approval at the right moment. Although no one mentioned it, getting the wisest old head on his side was one more of the victories that were accumulating for Madison.

Chapter Seventeen

COURTS AND
COMPROMISES

It is unfortunate that one more astute deal originated by Roger Sherman and Gouverneur Morris has come to be known as the Great Compromise, for it was particularly noxious in certain provisions and effects. Morris used a word that had not previously been in vogue to describe a diplomatic compromise. "It was a bargain between New England and the far south," he said. Some of their colleagues used much less favorable terms, for it was an arrangement between New Englanders and southern slavers that would have profound political effects for many years.

The intricate deal originated in the following way: The New England states, including Sherman's own Connecticut, wished to see the new federal government take control of all legislation intended to regulate commerce, so that every state would be treated equally. As things stood, large states made their own rules about trading with other countries, mostly squeezing out smaller states. If a new constitution allowed this to go on, these commercial disputes threatened to pull the Union apart. But the southern states fought against giving Congress the power to regulate trade, for they feared it would use such authority to favor New England's shipping interests, which might then charge ruinous freight rates for carrying the South's rice, indigo, tobacco, and cotton to the North and to Europe. To prevent this from happening, the southerners insisted that legislation governing such trade should require a virtually impossible two-thirds vote in both houses, and they were able to block any agreement that would have simplified the procedure.

Sherman and Morris thought of an enticement they might offer the southerners to make them abandon that requirement. They knew that South Carolina's clever delegation longed for a way to make sure they could continue to import slaves from either Africa or the Caribbean without paying heavy import taxes on their value. This was important to them because the physical conditions of life and work in the rice swamps and the indigo culture were so bad that slaves sickened and died at early ages; the slavers needed to keep bringing in new people from Africa at a rapid rate. It occurred to Sherman that a way existed to link the interests of South Carolina and his own Connecticut, creating benefits for both.

The Convention was stunned when it learned that Sherman and Morris were ready to promise the southerners the right to keep importing slaves with no import duty for twenty years. The deal also appealed to other states, for it promised the entire nation total freedom from export duties—a rule that has continued ever since.

In return, South Carolina and Georgia agreed to add their votes to those of Connecticut, Massachusetts, and New Hampshire in order to make foreign-trade legislation in Congress easily manageable by a simple majority vote. Both sides got what they wanted, and with the freedom from most duties, both the North and South were headed for very profitable trade.

The fact that it would create profits for the slave owners, whom he had no wish to assist, did not dissuade Sherman, because the old realist knew the southerners were out to make maximum use of slaves in any case, so he felt that any deal of his would only change financial figures, not the lives of blacks. His reasoning can be questioned, however. By making it cheaper for the slave owners to import new victims, the cash value of those enslaved was cheapened, meaning that their masters might take less care with their feeding, living conditions, and working demands.

Hideous as the whole subject was, if the South had been made to pay a heavy duty on every new slave who was brought in, the owners might at least have taken more care with the health of slaves.

The worst part was that in order to give the southerners a reason to cooperate in the compromise, they had to grant them a guaranteed number of years for continuing the importation of slaves; otherwise, the deal would have been of no value to them. The New Englanders agreed to vote for the prolonging of the duty-free importation of slaves for two decades, until 1808.

The coalition of states that agreed to this arrangement—against the tough opposition of Virginia's delegates, who were looking forward to an early end of the slave trade—was made up of New Hampshire, Massachusetts, and Connecticut. They joined South Carolina and Georgia on July 16 to pass what many have called the Great Compromise; not for the quality of its principles, but for the curious diversity of its participants.

It was one of several times when George Mason launched furious attacks on the whole subject of slavery and on the particularly egregious approaches to it that his fellow delegates were about to make. "I hold it essential in every point of view that the general government should have power to prevent the increase of slavery," he stormed. Then quietly, and insinuatingly, "I lament that some of our Eastern brethren have from a lust of gain embarked on this nefarious traffic."

New Englanders tried to deny this charge, each insisting that he never owned a slave and had nothing to do with the traffic. And from the southern side, Charles Pinckney bravely pointed to Greece and Rome as examples of great societies that had slaves, and he used the old argument that "if the Southern states were let alone, they would probably of themselves stop the importation."

His cousin, Charles Cotesworth Pinckney, had better luck by saying that if he and all his colleagues here present "agreed to the new government on terms that limited slavery, they would never obtain the consent of their constituents," and most of the assemblage knew this to be true.

At a time when several states were genuinely looking for a diminution and then a complete end to slavery, the delegates in Philadelphia delivered a blow to the antislavery trend. This trend was gathering force in many states. The first serious antislavery society to be organized originated in New York state. In January 1785, two years before the Convention, the New York Society for Promoting the Manumission of Slaves was formed. John Jay, who would become the nation's first chief justice, was the group's first president. Later, his position on the Court prevented him from speaking out, but his two sons, Peter and William, and his grandson and namesake, John Jay, were lifelong workers in the antislavery cause.

A Delaware Society devoted to the same principles was organized in 1788, and it was followed by the first national antislavery organization, which met in Philadelphia in 1794 with delegations from many states. It was called the American Convention for Promoting the Abolition of Slavery and Improving the Condition of the African Race. But although it lasted until 1837, this group was poorly organized with no publications, no agents linking the head office to the states, and few meetings. Meanwhile, the number of slaves in some places, such as Connecticut, Massachusetts, and other northeastern states dwindled yearly. In many of those states, the only remaining slaves were devoted household servants who genuinely wanted to stay with the same family and very elderly persons who would be unable to care for themselves if released.

But exactly the reverse occurred in South Carolina, Georgia, and even Virginia. The enticements offered to slave owners by the Great Compromise surely played a major part in this chilling development.

The southern slavers had tacit assurances that the northern leaders would not prohibit or impose taxes on the importing of more slaves, and this deadly traffic increased substantially as a result. South Carolina soon had more blacks than whites, and—because of the earlier deal that made each slave count as three-fifths of a person in counting a state's population— these promptly raised the voting power in Congress of the white owners. Five southern whites would have the voting strength of eight northern whites. As the number of slaves grew, South Carolina soon had double the voting power that it would normally have deserved in the new Congress.

This same three-fifths fraction would later be put to work in Mississippi and it went on creating a huge bonus of political power for the

South—giving the most voting strength to "the most barbarous parts of the Union," as opponents of the "bargain" said. Before the deal was closed in Philadelphia, the South had to agree to a minor import duty of ten dollars per slave, but even this charge gave them an unexpected bonus for they won another ugly balancing clause—a promise that the other states would help in the recovery of fugitive slaves.

Hamilton had virtually nothing to do with these arrangements. He was spending much of his time in New York. For the sake of civility, he told Yates and Lansing that he would be happy to accompany them back to Philadelphia if they would like to make a better impression for New York by showing a minimal interest in the nation's future; the two opponents did not accept the offer. Hamilton was probably glad to be away during the days of the unpleasant compromise. He could not have liked the arrangement, but his agile mind would have seen the merits of it for New York's neighbor states.

While the men who arranged this deal kept pointing out the benefits for all in empowering the new Congress to regulate trade and reduce interstate tensions, the disgraceful price paid was the twenty-year extension of the slave trade. Until 1808, the antislavery sections of the country lamented the passage of this deadly compromise.

Madison himself began to share this feeling a few years later when he gave serious thought to ways of banishing the slavery problem. He was attracted to the idea of creating "an African sanctuary" that might be used to give ex-slaves a new start in life. But it was a nagging worry to him that this solution would violate the clause allowing the importation of slaves into America until 1808; he wondered whether the Great Compromise contained a pledge that could not be broken.

By making it easier for the new Congress to regulate trade, the compromise did provide other benefits to the states. The agreement allowed the federal government to control all interstate and foreign commerce, stipulating that all parts of the nation would be treated alike. As a result, virtually absolute free trade now existed between the states.

This reminded the states of a lesson they first learned at the very start of the Revolutionary War, but then forgot. In 1775, even before war was declared, the nation planned to create a fighting navy consisting of a dozen new frigates. The first frigate to get her bottom wet was *Warren,* on May 15, 1776. But until it was outfitted and rigged, a frigate was a helpless hulk, "about as mobile and dangerous as a turtle on its back," as one naval historian, William M. Fowler Jr., said. This was the stiffest possible test of cooperation among thirteen members. In addition to hundreds of tons of iron for guns, armaments, and ballast, a frigate swallowed up miles of cordage for rigging, extra-large cable for anchors, heavy canvas, and lighter duck materials. No one state had everything needed to make, float, and equip a ship. The cooperation was far from perfect, but the job did get done.

Now, the Great Compromise showed the way to a new surge of interstate business cooperation. It opened a previously unused door to the central government's control over a great mass of business-related subjects. The extent of this development was breathtaking and wonderful, as described in the previous chapter.

When a great deal of debate was devoted to whether Congress could take the initiative in subduing a rebellion in any state, it was Elbridge Gerry of Massachusetts whose view prevailed, since he had been closest to Shays's Rebellion. Gerry spoke at length on the question of whether such a federal action to restore peace within a state should require an appeal from the governor or the legislature. He was direct in saying that the federal power should guarantee to every state a republican form of government, should safeguard states against invasion, and—on application by the legislature or the governor—should protect them against domestic violence. This is only a sampling of the proliferating federal powers that were set in motion by this one compromise. In that sense, it was great indeed, perhaps the greatest single blow ever struck in the battle between federal and states' rights.

One of the most resistant subjects for compromise was the selection of a location for the new federal capital city. This issue had been under discussion for several years before the Constitutional Convention began. The possibilities were many, with Philadelphia, Boston, and New York all competing but having almost no chance because of an incident some years earlier in which the Pennsylvania militia had threatened to hold a group of political leaders hostage in order to force them to meet demands for back pay. This event had led to a general feeling that the nation's capital should not be located in any state, in order to be safe from any possible use of force.

Despite this, Trenton had considerable support because it had served as a haven during the earlier flight from the Pennsylvania militia. Trenton gathered the backing of six states, which was only one vote short of approval. Madison worked on the question for some time, and he favored the Potomac River area also desired by George Washington. The small city of Georgetown, he thought, could spread out from land offered by both Maryland and Virginia, and this "double jurisdiction on the Potomac" seemed especially appropriate.

None of the preliminary efforts could be brought to a concluding point at the Convention, however. So the issue of location was evaded by burying it in one hazy clause that describes the various powers of Congress. It simply says that the Congress could "exercise exclusive Legislation in all Cases whatsoever, over such District (not exceeding ten miles square) as may, by Cession of particular states, and the Acceptance of Congress, become the Seat of the Government of the United States."

One delegate, still remembering the old military threat to the meeting in Philadelphia, proposed another clause declaring that this national capital, wherever it might be located, was never to be guarded by more than three thousand troops. Hearing this proposal, General Washington called a young delegate over and whispered, "I do not wish to make this additional proposal myself, but I suggest that you add this point: 'Proposed, that no foreign enemy may attack our National Capital with more than three thousand troops.'" This does not appear on any record of Convention proceedings, so Washington's jibe at the foolish proposal was probably an informal jest between him and one of the delegates. In any case, the original proposal was withdrawn.

The capital's location remained undecided until after the ratification process ran its course. The Potomac River site was selected in 1790. It was the place the southern states had hoped for, because it was south of the

Mason-Dixon Line and close to their section of the nation. But once again, the decision was a matter of compromise. Because the powerful state of Virginia desired that a capital city be built in this location, the South had to share equally in the federal government's assumption of state debts. In effect, all the states together were agreeing to join in paying off the cost of the Revolutionary War; since New England states had the largest debts and southern states had the smallest, this meant that the northern states—for a change—had the better of this bargain, and the southerners would be paying more than their actual share.

∞

Interwoven with these semi-finished subjects was the least noticed and the most glorious of the Constitution's innovations—the judiciary system. Although there were many lawyers in the convention hall, they did not burden this subject with excessive rhetoric. In a series of brief but pertinent speeches at various uncluttered moments, they came up with a simple determination to create a Supreme Court, a few subordinate federal courts, including courts of appeals, that would be developed as needed, and a separate system of state courts for keeping control of local matters. This hierarchy would clearly cause many cases to spend years climbing from one court to another. But in most instances, the exercise itself would discourage the participants and end the proceedings.

At the apex, however, were the early words of Chief Justice John Marshall, "We must never forget it is a Constitution we are expounding." This was a reminder that the judges' minds were not to devise theories of their own—nor to base decisions on the old British law from which their learning derived; they were to be interpreters of what the Constitutional fathers would have wished.

Oddly enough, however, this apparently pacific statement hides one of the most bitter hatreds in American history. A great constitutional principle was built on a jagged rock that seemed destined to unsettle and divide Americans. Marshall wanted to aggrandize the Supreme Court; Jefferson, at times, wanted to humble it. Marshall's loathing of Jefferson was personal, as he considered Jefferson a deserter for having fled an attacking British party and a person "totally unfit" for the presidency. He helped to convince Hamilton that Jefferson's head was full of pro-French theories, and Hamilton tried to convince Washington of this. Marshall also insisted that Jefferson was behind the growing states' rights movement, which he thought would destroy the Constitution.

It is one of those miracles of American success that Marshall's embittered attempt to make the Court into a bulwark against all that he thought Jefferson stood for strengthened the Court and prevented states' rights from overwhelming federal power. At the same time, Jefferson's avoidance of the unlimited opportunities when federal force might have crushed the states kept the opposing furies from destroying the union of states that both sides secretly wished for. The great balancing effect of two powerful hatreds made for a stronger Court and a stronger presidency than any of the Constitution's founders intended.

Although Marshall's hatred of Jefferson almost automatically made him an enemy of Madison's, it is curious that Marshall remained an admirer of Madison. This regard lingered in Marshall's mind from the time when, as a young politician, he attended every possible meeting where Patrick Henry was trying to block the ratification of the Constitution. Marshall was fascinated to see that Henry's greater voice, enormous vocabulary of powerful words, and ability to verbally paint pictures of the horrible times that lay ahead for Virginia's citizens would then be countered by the small figure of Madison, possessing none of these talents yet emerging the clear victor because his arguments were so far superior. Before the ratification fight was over, the callow young John Marshall actually dared to challenge Henry using some of Madison's tactics, and scored points for the winning side.

Within the next few years, a new system of juristic thought would be born. Constitutional interpretation was said to incorporate the intention of the framers and also the intention of the people who adopted it in 1788. It was a whole new concept—combining past and present in a unique way that gave every American who took part in the ratification of this document a permanent role in the effect it would have on the future world it would govern.

Years later, in 1842, in the case known as *Prigg v. Pennsylvania*, a justice took an updated practical view, saying it would probably be found that the safest rule of interpretation would be to look to the particular circumstances of the past "with all the lights and aids of contemporary history that might help to secure the fairest conclusions." This might be paraphrased as looking at ancient situations with contemporary faculties. And there was the added reminder that if one form of strict interpretation would result in a shadowy and unsubstantial conclusion while another method would "attain its just end and secure its manifest purpose," the latter ought to prevail.

One thing has never changed: each case is a separate lawsuit, as in any court, not a special constitutional test. It is always made clear that the Supreme Court is there primarily to settle cases fairly, not to pass on constitutionality in every decision. It will not go any deeper into the constitutional question than is necessary to decide it. The Court will not even consider constitutionality if there is some other ground on which the case can be fairly decided. For example, issues dealing with school or employment discrimination may be dismissed without any consideration of a constitutional issue if the Court believes that the complainant was basically unqualified for the position.

Equally important, the Court is not supposed to judge the policy, wisdom, or expediency of legislation. Those matters are for Congress to consider. "The Court's delicate and difficult office...is to ascertain whether the legislation is in accordance with, or in contravention of, the provisions of the Constitution."

This judiciary arrangement was stated in a few simple words in the Constitution itself, but has somehow taken on a life of its own, giving rise to new approaches and interpretations. It is a perfect example of the Constitution's unique genius for giving small instructions that invited others to create whatever additional arrangements might be needed.

Simple as this sounds, the most gripping questions almost invariably take many years to resolve because any proposed solution appears to deny some basic human right or to interfere with the traditional authority of states. In this sense, not even the intense abortion issue is more confounding than a vital question that increasingly interferes with the First Amendment's command that "Congress shall make no law...abridging the freedom of the press." Even the great Abraham Lincoln questioned whether such a rule must be upheld if it put the nation in genuine peril. "Are all the laws but one to go unexecuted, and the government itself go to pieces, lest that one be violated?" he demanded.

A century later, Supreme Court justice Hugo Black, taking the pro-press view, was still demanding the strongest possible defense of the First Amendment with his 1960 declaration that "no law means NO law." But the issue is still livelier than ever in the daunting question of whether journalists should be forced to reveal their sources.

Each threat of jail for a journalist who alerts the public to an important crime is, in effect, an attack on press freedom, for it reduces the intelligence that a free press contributes to the community and nation. Yet twenty-two reporters received federal subpoenas in a single year (2004) for refusing to reveal the names of informers who were promised anonymity. This more than doubled the average number of such cases in the preceding decade. Connecticut senator Christopher Dodd, arguing for a law that would shield reporters from prosecution in such circumstances, pointed out that the Watergate abuses might never have come to light if *Washington Post* writers could not promise anonymity to the informant known as Deep Throat. This was possible because the District of Columbia and thirty-one states have "shield laws" that protect reporters from prosecution when they refuse to reveal sources.

But nineteen states have no such protective laws. Yet Congress is reluctant to impose a federal law because public prosecutors and judges feel that reporters must not be allowed to obstruct the law's normal right to demand all the facts and to know all the persons who have some connection with an illegal activity. Their objection has a logic of its own, but treating news professionals as "criminals," subject to jail sentences for using a standard journalistic technique, mocks the First Amendment.

James Madison, foreseeing this collision between two normal points of view, said, "Popular government without popular information or the means of acquiring it is but a prologue to a farce, or tragedy, or perhaps both." He may have thought his careful stipulation that nothing must be allowed to "abridge" press freedom would cover this kind of tangential attack on his amendment. But as of this writing, the "farce or tragedy" continues.

Chapter Eighteen

SIGNED BUT NOT SEALED

Waves of exhaustion came and went during nearly three months of meetings. Extreme fatigue, which was felt by nearly everyone, first swept over the proceedings in late June. It showed itself in the form of complaints about tiresome debates, but heat was the probable cause. After twenty-five sessions, some lasting up to six hours, delegates first expressed the repeated belief that this Convention was approaching a deadlock. It now seemed months since the first notable display of irritability had been seen on Saturday, June 23, during a session when the talk turned to preventing corruption in the national legislature. Some of the delegates said petulantly that the speakers seemed to intentionally evade the central issue. It was supposed to have focused on equal versus proportional representation in the legislature, but almost every speaker strayed from the subject. After the session, for the first time, there was considerable talk of quitting and going home.

Around that time, too, Rufus King of Massachusetts, the bright young man who interjected many clever sayings throughout the meeting, did not seem like himself when he began to groan about annoyances, such as New Hampshire's delay in sending delegates because it would not pay their travel expenses. He was also irritated about the dead-end debates, saying that too much time was being devoted to the corruption issue. "We refine on it too much," he said, "nor is it possible that we can eradicate the evil."

Unthinkable as it once was, the sense of utter exhaustion that touched most of the delegates made it seem that they might be forced to end the gathering. This fate was narrowly avoided because of one exceptional fortnight in early August when the temperature eased and spirits unexpectedly rose again. Talk of closing ceased, and that earlier sense of euphoria about their mission reemerged.

But the worst of summer had not yet been seen. The delegates' suspicion that more unbearable hot weather was on its way proved to be all too true. A return of warmer August days, coupled with a realization of the harsher questions ahead, lowered everyone's spirits again. William Samuel Johnson of Connecticut, who kept unusually detailed expense accounts and a daily weather log, described thirty-seven days in July and August as "warm," "hot," and "very hot." The last indicated over one-hundred-degree temperatures. With the windows tightly closed and the men always in their woolen jackets, several delegates were often near collapse.

Perhaps this was an explanation for the curious fact that Madison was absolutely opposed to adding some additional time in order to craft a bill of rights. There was strong sentiment for such an addition. No one understood why Madison, who would normally have been at the forefront of the move, was firmly against it. He insisted that the document, as it stood, made ample provision for the rights of the people, which was simply not true. But the combination of fatigue and Madison's opposition made the other delegates accept the suggestion that a statement of rights could be added as an amendment in the course of time.

Madison may have had a secret reason for wanting to avoid a debate on rights. Perhaps he was fearful that a weary group of delegates might begin to have second thoughts about what they had decided on other subjects, possibly leading them to unravel some of the decisions before a signing occurred. This would be a reasonable rationale on Madison's part, yet not one that he would risk by explaining to the delegates. But for the nation's great new document to be without protection on rights brought many cries of dismay and would make the ratification fights in some states more difficult.

The successes in the form of the major compromises, however, were solid accomplishments that were worth protecting. So after another month had passed, on July 26, it was thought to be time to suspend the meetings in order to allow a smaller group to review all the decisions and judge whether it was time to put them on paper. A Committee of Detail was elected by ballot and consisted of Oliver Ellsworth of Connecticut, James Wilson of Pennsylvania, Edmund Randolph of Virginia, Nathaniel Gorham of Massachusetts, and John Rutledge of South Carolina. The Convention was then adjourned until August 6, "to give the committee time to arrange and systematize the materials collected."

The committee had a daunting job, but all the rest were feeling like schoolboys on vacation at being liberated from the long days in the heat of this especially oppressive summer. Even the sedate, fifty-five-year-old Washington gloried in the freedom, as he told of going "in G. Morris's phaeton, but with my horses, to the Valley Forge area to get trout during this recess." On another day, he went to Trenton with Robert Morris and his wife. Washington fished unsuccessfully that time, but made another attempt the next morning and "did get perch."

One of those days, July 31, was made memorable by the fact that twenty-three lively lines appeared in a diary that had been almost bare for over two months. Something far too absorbing to go unrecorded had occurred: "Whilst Mr. Morris was fishing," Washington observed some farmers at work and entered into conversation with them, leading to an entry about all their fascinating "information with respect to the mode of cultivating Buck wheat—the sowing and plowing that is required, the expected yield, and uses of the crop as excellent food for horses and also for fattening beef." Farmer Washington was in his element.

It must have been difficult in these days for Robert Morris to show good spirits in playing host to Washington when his precarious finances teetered at the edge of a precipice. The man who kept producing the funds that financed Washington's forces during the greatest trials had also directed a massive procurement operation in those wartime days. He had headed an eponymous "Congressional Secret Committee on Commerce" that had a network of correspondents in West Indian and European ports, searching out raw materials that were vital to the American manufacture of munitions and other war goods. He had treated the state of Pennsylvania and the Continental Congress as if they were his commercial partners who trusted his results and asked no questions. It was assumed that, as a partner, he made the transactions profitable to himself and some of his associates.

But lately, after Morris no longer had the link to government, there were whispers exchanged among knowledgeable people suggesting that his own risky and excessive investments were bringing urgent demands from creditors. That the highly observant General Washington knew of this was clear from a diary notation about one of the dinners he had with the Morrises, during which a servant surreptitiously approached the host and whispered to him. Morris then excused himself and left the table. Washington clearly interpreted this to be a dunning visit from a creditor. "Most unfortunate that a host should be placed in such a position," he wrote.

When they convened again on August 6, sixty copies of a first draft of a constitution were distributed to the delegates, and there was considerable surprise. It was found that the Committee of Detail had done somewhat more than anyone had expected. Trying to do a conscientious job of smoothing rough points and settling open issues, they went over the Articles of Confederation again, studied various state constitutions, finally looked hard at a plan that Charles Pinckney had produced months earlier, and took points from each of these sources to fill in specifics and firm up passages that seemed vague. They transformed the broad general authority granted to Congress, the courts, and the chief executive, enumerating many powers more specifically. They even wrapped up the powers of Congress with a sweeping right to make all laws "necessary and proper" to carry out the specifically listed powers. Probably most important of all, the committee finally came to grips with the unpopular subject of taxes, albeit in a brisk way. "The Congress shall have power to lay and collect Taxes, Duties, Imposts, and

Excises to pay the Debts and provide for the common Defense and general Welfare of the United States; but all Duties, Imposts and Excises shall be uniform throughout the United States."

No one was openly critical of the committee for having done so much. Knowing that their colleagues had been working slavishly while the others were taking a needed break, they could hardly express anger. But a flood of comments showed how much revising and rewriting was in store. It took five more weeks of tedious work—in the most miserable hot weather of the summer. They even tried to shorten the process by debating for more hours each day, but this was impractical because it created more fatigue and interfered with the dinner hour.

The committee dared to change the stipulation about who was to pay the congressmen. The Convention originally ruled that congressmen should be on the federal payroll. The Committee changed this to stipulate that the states rather than the federal government should bear that burden. By a large majority, the Convention overturned the Committee's risky proposal. The idea of going home to let their neighbors know that—in addition to many increased outlays—they would have to pay these new lawmakers' salaries directly did not appeal to delegates who knew they might be running for office themselves. It was probably the first time congressional hopefuls realized that they would not be looking to their governors or other state officials for appointment to the new Congress, but to those very neighbors who would now be the most important people in their universe.

It was during this period in late August that some of the sharpest attacks were heard from men who were furious at the way the slave states had been accommodated. Even so, the word "slavery" never appeared in the document. Where slaves were referred to, they were called "other persons" and in one case "Person held to Service or Labour." The complainers were listened to politely, only lightly admonished or contradicted by the men who were responsible for the hated compromises, and allowed to have their say—but not their way.

By the end of August, the exhausted delegates, seeing that many unfinished points remained to be decided, appointed a new Committee on Postponed Matters made up of eleven persons, among them Madison and Gouverneur Morris.

Working hastily over the question of the chief executive's term of office, this group found an important difference of opinion concerning the length of time this powerful official should be allowed. They took the time to debate among themselves, then reduced the term sharply from seven years to four. In order to placate those who were disappointed with this reduction, they decided that the president would be free to stand for reelection. There was no limitation on the number of terms he could serve, except for the tradition established by Washington's retirement after his second term. Only since the Twenty-second Amendment was ratified in 1951 has there been a formally imposed two-term limit.

The status of new states became a thorny issue, with Madison firmly wanting them to be admitted as equals while Morris and several others preferred that the original seaboard states should retain the greatest power. It was finally settled with loose wording in Article IV, Section 3 that made each of these men think he had his way. The Section begins: "New States may be admitted by the Congress into this Union." Then, after several sentences that are not relevant to the question of admission, there is the phrase, "and nothing in this Constitution shall be so construed as to Prejudice any Claims of the United States, or of any particular State." This last could potentially serve as a basis for an existing state to bring an action to bar the admission of a new state that it viewed as a threat to its security or commercial interests. But nothing of the kind has ever occurred. Congresses later interpreted the entire Section to mean that an unlimited number of new states could be admitted as equals, and so it has always been.

Up to the end, there were changes in the wording of the process for amending the Constitution and the relatively short Article V is devoted entirely to that subject. This document itself was a piece of statesmanship like none other in world history, a composition that not only created a working, operating nation but that also has its own self-correcting and self-balancing mechanisms. And on top of that, astonishingly, it contains the means to see itself amended without disturbing the smooth functioning of the whole.

By September 8, the document could be passed on to another group of great distinction—the five-man Committee of Style. Under Connecticut's William Samuel Johnson as chairman, Gouverneur Morris was again in the group, along with Madison, Hamilton, and King. It was Morris whose contributions to each of these committees were so marked that he quite naturally slid into the role of writing the final document, as Madison later attested, saying, "A better choice could not have been made."

Also noteworthy was the fact that this committee, selected by a vote of all the members, picked Hamilton even though he had not been a steady contributor to the Convention's work. Coming at such a critical point near the end, it meant two things. First, that many members were still remembering his major speech and hoping his ideas would somehow be represented in the final work. Second, that his late efforts to rally reluctant delegates to agree to sign the document were being recognized. Knowing that he was still dissatisfied with the Constitution's terms, they were increasingly respectful of his serious efforts to maintain a cordial relationship with Madison and to say, in effect, that nothing in the Constitution justified a rejection that would leave the nation without a functioning government.

After hasty work on Saturday, September 15, and even a reprinting job on Sunday, the Convention met again for the signing on Monday, September 17. It was still a work in progress, for its ratification by the American people seemed questionable. But those who signed did it prayerfully, hoping that time would prove them right.

Forty-one men were in the room that morning; fourteen of the original group had left by choice or due to the pressure of personal business. Because Randolph, Mason, and Gerry, though present, had objections that made them refuse to sign, thirty-eight men put their signatures to the Constitution, beginning with George Washington. A thirty-ninth signature was dubbed in for Delaware's John Dickinson, who had been forced to leave because of illness.

Two noteworthy occurrences came just before the actual signing: George Washington's proposal to enlarge the numbers in the lower House of Congress—from one member for every forty thousand inhabitants to one for every thirty thousand—which was instantly acted on as a command from on high (as mentioned in chapter 13), and Benjamin Franklin's memorable phrases.

Franklin was too weak to give the speech he had prepared, so it was read for him by a secretary, ending with those polished words that implored them all to join him in doubting their own infallibility, and saying that he was signing "because I expect no better, and because I am not sure that it is not the best."

It was indeed the best. But like many things that are destined for long distinction and admiration, the Constitution was not immediately seen to be the jewel that it was and is. Only the patina that comes with time tells of its ability to encompass changing situations not referred to in the text and to match the demands that new generations have asked it to accept.

Chapter Nineteen

JEFFERSON REACTS

In the years just after the successful end of the Revolutionary War, Thomas Jefferson survived the darkest period of his life. He lost a wife who was very dear to him, promising her that he would never remarry, and withdrew from active politics under a cloud (as described in chapter 2), making a similar vow to abjure public life. First among the friends who tried to reawaken his old zest for politics was an amazingly dogged James Madison, but even he was fended off until he was able to bring Jefferson the exciting news that Benjamin Franklin was being recalled from his spectacularly successful role as American envoy to Paris, and that Thomas Jefferson was to replace him. This call to duty brought an instant and enthusiastic response. The year was 1785, and Jefferson was still in France at the time of the Constitutional Convention.

This was a totally reinvigorated Jefferson, who took to French styles of clothing, French tastes in food and wines, and all his old absorption in every bit of art and architecture and philosophy that caught his attention. Even his weakness for feminine charm bloomed again, causing a lengthy flirtation with a married Italian beauty and, some firmly believe, a close relationship with an attractive young black woman who came to France to care for his daughter.

The latter part of Jefferson's Parisian stay coincided with the rising Terror that led to the death of the king and queen. Jefferson's comments about the end of the monarchy—soon after his return to America—did not show him at his best, for he made simplistic remarks that seemed to blame Marie Antoinette for France's intricate and multiple problems and also cheered the news that King Louis was dead, as if that had been a healthy political event. John Adams, whose crusty manner often hid a superior judgment, was much closer to the mark when he said, "Mankind will in time discover that unbridled majorities are as tyrannical and cruel as unlimited despots."

As the Convention in Philadelphia neared a close, a torrent of Jeffersonian correspondence was floating across the Atlantic. Mail written in France five or six weeks earlier was just reaching some of the leading delegates. They realized then that nobody who could write as much or as well as Jefferson was absent from the nation's work simply because he was in Paris.

He refused to enlist in either of the parties that were beginning to form, telling one correspondent, Francis Hopkinson, a Pennsylvania judge, "I protest to you that I am not of the party of the federalists. But I am much further from that of the antifederalists." This appeared to be a way of refusing to become simply a member of someone else's party, and leaving the way open to form a party of his own.

Jefferson did not meet Alexander Hamilton, the man who later became his dedicated enemy, until he returned home in 1790. Their early meetings as members of Washington's first cabinet were entirely cordial, despite the fact that Hamilton privately thought Jefferson's performance as a wartime governor of Virginia had been slack and perhaps even cowardly. But there was no sign of the antipathy that would later force George Washington to choose between these two key advisers.

From any collection of Jefferson's letters, a half-dozen can be taken almost at random and their variety and interest will dazzle the eye and mind. The letters he wrote while he was America's envoy in Paris are illustrative of this and of his active role in helping to judge the proposed Constitution, with the idea of possibly contributing to the eventual shape of the new government.

Eager to keep up relationships with home, Jefferson had exchanges with James Monroe, a protege who had become a great friend; with John Jay, who was considered one of America's shrewdest diplomatic negotiators; with George Wythe, a celebrated jurist with whom Jefferson studied law before developing a close friendship; with John Adams, whose friendship with Jefferson was marred by political clashes; and with scores of others whom he had reason to know.

But most of all, he corresponded with James Madison, who first began political cooperation with him when Jefferson was Virginia's governor and Madison was a member of the state legislature. Madison seemed to be simply a friendly subordinate at first, but Jefferson quickly recognized his remarkable mind and began to consider the younger man's thoughts seriously in his own deliberations. Indeed, it often appeared that whenever their opinions differed, Madison's clear and reasoned thoughts became the last word on that particular subject. Even while correspondence between the two men took two to three months for a complete exchange of their views, each was eager to learn the other's thoughts.

Some of these letters concerned the great variety of books Jefferson sent to Madison. One letter written on July 31, 1788, mentions "a book by Du Pont about the Commercial Treaty with England." The author was probably Pierre Samuel Du Pont, patriarch of the great Franco-American family, whose son founded the well-known company. Pierre Samuel, who was a far better philosopher than a businessman, became a close friend of Jefferson's and later played an important role as intermediary in Jefferson's dealings with Napoleon Bonaparte over the fate of the Louisiana Territory.

Other letters were about botanical and biological subjects that were a prime interest of Madison's. There were also pamphlets on the future of the French monarchy by the Marquis de Condorcet, a nobleman whose name Jefferson liked to use to spice up his correspondence. And some letters were on gadgets that Jefferson found for his friend Madison, like the correspondence about a new pedometer, sent on May 3, 1788, complete with exact directions for attachment and use.

Jefferson wrote: "To the loop at the bottom of it, you must sew a tape, and at the other end of the tape a small hook (such as we use under the name of hooks and eyes). Cut a little hole in the bottom of your left watch pocket, pass the hook and tape through it, and down between the britches and drawers."

Before a Convention or a Virginia Plan had been conceived, Jefferson wrote to Madison of the need for legislative, executive, and judiciary branches as a basic requirement for a balanced and functioning government. Writing in Paris on December 16, 1786, he went further and suggested to Madison how duties within these branches might be subdivided and especially how the executive could be made more effective. He was especially concerned because the Congress still operating at that time had meddled in what should have been an executive matter. Even though the old Confederation had no separate executive, members had proposed to make any new western states fewer and larger. Jefferson stated a conviction that would form the basis of a firm policy in the years of his own presidency. "This is reversing the natural order of things," Jefferson wrote, saying:

A tractable people may be governed in large bodies; but in proportion as they depart from this character, the extent of their government must be less…This measure, with the disposition to shut up the Mississippi, gives me serious apprehensions of the severance of the eastern and western parts of our confederacy. It might have been made the interest of the western states to remain united with us, by managing their interests honestly, and for their own good. But the moment we sacrifice their interests to our own, they will see it better to govern themselves. The moment they resolve to do so, the point is settled. A forced connection is neither our interest, nor within our power.

Here we see Jefferson suggesting thoughts that not only were useful to Madison in the course of the upcoming Convention, but that Jefferson and Madison together, as president and secretary of state, would be putting into effect in the eventual Louisiana Purchase, seventeen years later in 1803.

The separate and conflicting interests of easterners and westerners caused Napoleon Bonaparte to believe he might divide the new nation in order to "create a new empire" in North America. Jefferson and Madison were able to rid him of that idea by their strategy of transmitting huge amounts of misinformation to Napoleon—intentionally misleading him—through the French envoy in Washington.

Some of the most revealing Jefferson letters touched on the Convention's key issue that the 91 percent of Americans who lived from farming were regarded as inferior beings by many of the men who led the nation. It was not the specific individuals who were despised, but the nature of the calling—as if a person who is content with tilling the soil is automatically disinclined to think clearly about complicated subjects. This being so, many delegates felt that entrusting them with the country's greatest decisions would be an act of folly.

But Jefferson's known tendency to favor the farmers and especially the "westerners" who pushed on toward the Mississippi River was more than just a political calculation. It was almost a sacred duty. When he had a thought about groups of people, their varied callings, or various geographical locations, he was ready to suggest ways of moving them around, altering their living arrangements in Jeffersonian style. A letter of August 23, 1785, sent from Paris to John Jay, the leading American negotiator, exemplifies this. Like most of Jefferson's letters, it moved from subject to subject, usually forming a chain of connected and formidable ideas. This one said, in part:

> We have now lands enough to employ an infinite number of people in their cultivation. Cultivators of the earth are the most valuable citizens [this comment made to a man who thought New England bankers deserved that title]. They are the most vigorous, the most independent, the most virtuous, and they are tied to their country, and wedded to its liberty and interests, by the most lasting bonds. As long, therefore, as they can find employment in this line, I would not convert them into mariners, artisans, or anything else. But our citizens will find employment in this line, till their numbers, and of course their

productions, become too great for the demand...This is not the case yet, and probably will not be for a considerable time...I should then, perhaps, wish to turn them to the sea in preference to manufactures.

After discussing how inevitable it is that the greater amount of maritime business will lead to violation of America's ships and men by foreign powers, Jefferson added, "I think it is to our interest to punish the first insult [that is, to strike back whenever a foreign power acts against us], because an insult unpunished is the parent of many others. We are not, at this moment, in a position to do it, but we should put ourselves into it, as soon as possible."

Distant as he was from the gathering in Philadelphia, Jefferson not only presented his own ideas about beauty in city planning or in great statuary, he also took the trouble to make many side trips (at a time when traveling off the main road was an uncomfortable adventure) and to procure costly maps and drawings to prove his points. In offering his views, he risked angering officials who often resented his interference with plans already begun and sometimes were at a loss to know how his proposals were to be funded. The following letter to James Madison, written in Paris on September 20, 1785, begged Madison to interfere on his behalf in the construction of a new capital building for Richmond, Virginia. Just a small portion of the pages he took to plead his cause will show the absorption and drive he devoted to the subject:

I received this summer a letter from Messrs Buchanan and Hay, as Directors of the public buildings, desiring I would have drawn for them plans of sundry buildings, and, in the first place, of a capital...Much time was required after the external form was agreed on, to make the internal distribution convenient for the three branches of government. The time was much lengthened by my other avocations, and the other plan was already settled. The one agreed on here is more convenient, more beautiful, gives more room, and will not cost more than two-thirds of what that would. We took our model from what is called the Maison Quarree [sic, ancient spelling of

Maison Carree] one of the most beautiful if not the most beautiful and precious morsel of architecture left to us by antiquity. It was built by Caius and Lucius Caesar, and repaired by Louis XIV…It is very simple, but it is noble beyond expression, and would have done honor to our country, as presenting to travelers a specimen of taste in our infancy…I have been much mortified with information, which I received two days ago from Virginia, that the first brick of the capital would be laid within a few days…Pray try if you can to effect the stopping of this work…The loss will be only of the laying of the bricks already laid. The bricks themselves will do again for the interior walls, and one side wall and one end wall may remain, as they will answer equally well for our plan…If the undertakers are afraid to undo what they have done, encourage them to it by a recommendation from the Assembly. You see I am an enthusiast on the subject of the arts. But it is an enthusiasm of which I am not ashamed, as its object is to improve the tastes of my countrymen, to increase their reputation.

Anyone who wondered, as some of his contemporaries (and especially his political rivals) did, why it was that Jefferson always attracted followers without seeming to be making an effort in that direction need only read a letter he wrote from Paris on August 13, 1786, to George Wythe, the celebrated jurist who was his professor at William and Mary, then became his close friend.

His emphasis on universal education was a most significant innovation. And the praise that Jefferson heaps on the American people here, putting them on a pedestal that stands so far above all others and yet calling for more to be done for these most fortunate children of happiness, would seem to be excessive flattery if addressed to a person who could be easily fooled. But in telling his views to an esteemed professor, he clearly expects his opinion to be taken seriously. When he said such things to the people of Kentucky or Tennessee, it is no wonder at all that they worshipped him. Only a small portion of this letter will suffice, especially when read in the light of what so many of the Convention delegates were thinking as they pondered the warning words of Hamilton about the danger of entrusting political power to the common people:

> If all the sovereigns of Europe were to set themselves to work, to emancipate the minds of their subjects from their present ignorance and prejudices...a thousand years would not place them on that high ground, on which our common people are now setting out. Ours could not have been so fairly placed under the control of the common sense of the people, had they not been separated from their parent stock, and kept from contamination...by the intervention of so wide an ocean...I think by far the most important bill in our whole code is that for the diffusion of knowledge among the people...the tax which will be paid for this purpose is not more than the thousandth part of what will be paid to kings, priests, and nobles who will rise up among us if we leave the people in ignorance. Nobility, wealth, and pomp are the objects of their [the Europeans'] admiration. They are by no means the free-minded people we suppose them in America. Their learned men, too, are few in number and are less learned and infinitely less emancipated from prejudice than those of this country.

Bear in mind that this was almost a year before his friend Madison would find himself struggling to convince a convention of skeptical men to base a new federal government on how well the common people could choose the best politicians to lead them, forming their opinions on the basis of a few words heard on the street or sometimes only on hearsay. "A ridiculous way of selecting leaders," Hamilton would have said. "Like entrusting a choice of colors to a blind man," as George Mason put it. But if these Americans had "the most benevolent, the most gay and amiable character of which the human form is susceptible," as Jefferson went on to say, would it not be well worth investing in the great education program—the "crusade against ignorance"—that Jefferson was also proposing, and then prove that "the people alone can protect us from all the evils"?

Jefferson saw everyone he met as a potential messenger to carry the ideas he wanted to project. Fifteen years later, as president, he would enlist Pierre Samuel Du Pont, then a flawed and failing businessman, as a messenger to warn Napoleon Bonaparte that America would fight rather than see French troops and colonists in Louisiana. At the same time, Jefferson and Madison were using a young French envoy as a conduit for reporting their crafty falsehoods to the French dictator. These men and others poured such a barrage of Jeffersonian threats into Paris that Bonaparte began to see the sale of Louisiana as something of a winning strategy for him—and, in a sense, it did prove to be, for once freed of his American adventure, he went on to years of victories in Europe and the rule of France as its emperor.

The excitement set in motion by Jefferson's mind and interests can be felt by noting just a few of the hundreds of subjects he took up and wrote painstakingly by hand about in the few years immediately preceding and following the Convention. Despite the overwhelming importance of that single subject, it will be noted that he attacked every other item in his letters with equal zest, making it clear that the range and intensity of his interests were unique. Not all the letters, however, are equally forthcoming. The first example below shows Jefferson giving an evasive excuse for not taking part in an antislavery group.

On February 11, 1788, from Paris, he wrote to Jean Pierre Brissot de Warville:

> I am deeply sensible of the honor you propose to me of becoming a member of the society for the abolition of the slave trade. You know that nobody wishes more ardently to see an abolition not only of the trade but of the conditions of slavery...But I am here as a public servant; and those whom I serve having never yet been able to give their voice against this practice, it is decent for me to avoid too public a demonstration of my wishes to see it abolished...Be assured of my wishes for the success of your undertaking.

There is not a word about the fact that he was a slave owner himself.

That such a communicator also fired great salvos of words with exceptional energy when he was in love is no surprise. But it is necessary to balance his great successes in writing of politics and artistic subjects with certain deficiencies in romantic writing. While sending elevated thoughts to men like Wythe and Madison, he was writing a painfully long love letter to Maria Cosway, the Italian-English beauty whom he met in Parisian society. That she was married to a small man who was usually nearby did not deter Jefferson's flirtation. He and the lady spent long hours together, apparently without ever consummating the relationship, but creating a mountain of memories with long walks and idyllic picnics in beautiful Parisian surroundings. On October 12, 1786, Jefferson saw the Cosways off on a trip to London, then sent Maria a letter clearly intended to intensify their affection at the time of her return.

He employed the unoriginal device of sending Maria a dialogue that took place between his Head and his Heart. Soon, he has the Heart saying, "I am indeed the most wretched of all earthly beings. Overwhelmed with grief, every fibre of my frame distended beyond its natural powers to bear," and much more. The Head is equally wordy in warning that it is about to give some strong admonitions like, "Harsh as the medicine may be, it is my office to administer it...I never ceased whispering to you that we have no occasion for this new acquaintance." At incredible length, the Head keeps telling the Heart how often it has preached against this practice of falling in love, even saying, "This is one of the scrapes into which you are forever leading us." So instead of feeling like a cherished object, Maria was bound to see herself as one of a crowd.

The fact is that Jefferson, in dealings with anyone of the female sex, seems always to be interested primarily in himself and not in the other person. His many letters to his eldest daughter Martha (Patsy), for example, are always tiresome lectures about the importance of learning to be a better wife and reminders that the ability to make a husband happy is a woman's only true calling. He seems to assume that she will be overjoyed to hear these words of paternal wisdom repeated, with no effort to inject the lively variety of thoughts that he offers in almost every letter to men of all ranks.

And it is not only Patsy who experienced this kind of treatment. Mrs. William Bingham, wife of a Philadelphia banker and leader of the aristocratic set there, was known to be ahead of her time in believing that women should take more interest in politics. Jefferson could not have been ignorant of this, but he either chose to ignore it or intentionally tried to reform her, for a letter he wrote from Paris, on May 11, 1788, sent her some fashion prints and sentences like these that indicated where her true interests should lie:

> Dear Madam—A gentleman going to Philadelphia furnishes me the occasion of sending you some numbers of the Cabinet des Modes and some new theatrical pieces. We now have need of something to make us gay, for the topics of the times are sad and eventful. All the world is now politically mad. Men, women, children talk nothing else…Our good ladies, I trust, have been too wise to wrinkle their heads with politics. They are contented to soothe and calm the minds of their husbands returned ruffled from political debate. As for potential news of battles and sieges, Turks and Russians, I will not detail them to you, because you would be less handsome after reading them.

But from the moment of receiving Madison's package with the first copy of the new Constitution, Jefferson set about writing a massive number of letters to men about strictly male affairs, despite the difficulty of doing everything with a painful right hand. (His wrist was badly injured during a country walk with Maria, when he had unwisely tried to impress her by jumping a fence for the first time in years.)

These letters seem to show Jefferson's wish to be a part of the Constitutional event, and to make it clear that he would have opted for many changes, although a long, careful letter to Madison very thoughtfully avoided some of the sharp criticisms that he wrote to others.

To John Adams, for instance, Jefferson wrote on November 13, 1787,

How do you like our new Constitution? I confess there are things in it which stagger all my disposition to subscribe to what such an Assembly has proposed. The house of federal representatives will not be adequate to the management of affairs, either foreign or federal. Their President seems a bad edition of a Polish King. He may be elected from four years to four years, for life. Reason and experience prove to us that a chief magistrate, so continuable, is an office for life...worthy of intrigue, bribery, of force, even of foreign interference. It will be of great consequence to France and England to have America governed by [a man favorable to one or the other].

These fears proved to be totally unfounded. But in fairness, they need to be considered from the standpoint that no one could have known what a standard for the presidential office would be established when George Washington agreed to be president. Even disliking the office as he did, Washington gave it an enduring dignity and correctness that no one could have envisioned.

To Madison, on December 20, 1787, he wrote at great length and detail, starting with more than half a dozen points he liked about the new document:

I like the organization of the government into the three branches. I like the power given the legislature to levy taxes, and for that reason solely I approve of the greater House being chosen by the people directly [other than that point, he thought a directly-elected house would be inferior to the Congress of the Confederacy and ill qualified to legislate on several other matters]. I am captivated by the compromise of the opposite claims of great and little states. I am much pleased by the method of voting by person, instead of by states. And I like the veto power given to the Executive.

The list of things he did not like began with the lack of a bill of rights and he was particularly distressed that the right to trial by jury was not as clearly defined in civil cases as in criminal cases, being removable in civil cases where an amount of less than twenty dollars was involved. He said, "I have a right to nothing which another has the right to take away." He also strongly disliked the abandonment of rotation in office, especially in the presidency. In general, he said, "I am not a friend to a very energetic government. It is always oppressive." This is why, as president, he was so distressed to find himself acquiring a territory that doubled the nation's size. If a president could do such a thing with no authority for it specifically granted in the Constitution, was it not certain that a federal government would turn into a monster that would suck away all state powers?

Jefferson asked Madison to compare again in his mind

> whether peace is preserved best by giving energy to the government or information to the people? To educate and inform the people is the most certain and the most legitimate engine of government. Educate and inform the whole mass of the people...This reliance cannot deceive us, as long as we remain virtuous, and I think we shall be so, as long as agriculture is our principle object, which will be the case, while there remain vacant lands in any part of America.

Also from Paris on May 2, 1788, Jefferson wrote to George Washington, cleverly giving first place to a local subject that Washington was bound to view favorably, while putting the greater subject of the Constitution in second place because he was not yet sure what the General really thought of it. He began with comments on the possibility of connecting two bodies of water in Virginia, which he knew to be a favorite project of the General's. Clearly he preferred to delay praising the Constitution until he had put Washington in a receptive mood, which tends to show that Jefferson was anxious to be in the General's good graces and to have a high position in his government. Jefferson wrote:

Sir—I am honored by Your Excellency's letter by the last packet and thank you for the information it contains on the connection between the Cayahoga and Big Beaver. I have ever considered the opening of a canal between those two water courses as the most important work in that line which the state of Virginia could undertake…Having in the spring of last year taken a journey through the southern parts of France and particularly having examined the canal of Languedoc through its whole course, I have taken the liberty of sending you the note I made on the spot, as you may find in this something perhaps which may be turned to account…in the prosecution of the Patowmack canal.

I had considered to have written a word to Your Excellency on the subject of the new Constitution. I will just observe that according to my ideas there is a great deal of good in it. There are two things however which I dislike strongly:

1. The want of a declaration of rights…2. The perpetual re-eligibility of the President. This, I fear, will make an office for life, first, and then hereditary.

I was much an enemy to monarchy before I came to Europe. I am ten thousand times more so since I have seen what they are here. There is scarcely an evil known in these countries which may not be traced to their king as its source…I can further say with safety there is not a crowned head whose talents or merits would entitle him to be elected a vestryman by the people of any parish in America.

By December 4, 1788, when he was sure that Washington favored the Constitution, he wrote to him in a much stronger tone: "Sir—I have seen with infinite pleasure our new Constitution accepted by eleven states, not rejected by the twelfth, and that the thirteenth happens to be a state of least importance." New York had been the eleventh state to ratify. North Carolina, still pending, would be the twelfth. And Rhode Island took the brunt of Jefferson's contempt as the state of least importance.

Chapter Twenty

REJECTING
EUROPE'S WAYS

In the last chapter, we saw what seemed to be greatly exaggerated words of Thomas Jefferson's comparing Europeans most unfavorably to Americans. Although Convention delegates seemed to doubt the ability of Americans to conduct a democratic government, there are reasons to believe that Jefferson's undoubtedly overstated remarks were closer to the truth.

European society was taught to depend on church, army, aristocracy, and monarchy for safety and stability. America downplayed all of these in favor of a risky trust in the average human being. And this was not done only for America's sake; many of the leaders thought they were doing it for all mankind. Jefferson said, "We are acting under obligations not confined to the limits of our own society." It was called a "bold, sublime experiment."

Often during the Convention, comparisons with Europe were made—observations on how their states operated—and almost always the object was to point out European ways that must be avoided. Somehow, no one seemed to remark on the odd mismatch between the delegates' desire to avoid a long catalogue of European mistakes and their doubts that Americans could rule themselves as well as the Europeans did. If asked to explain, they undoubtedly would have said that European life was held in line by the four ancient institutions that could prevent excesses by the masses.

Europe at the time was consumed by a movement called Romanticism; a view of life which gained no foothold in America. If anything, the America of that day could have been called distinctly anti-Romantic. This may help to explain why Madison's belief in popular government for America may have been more correct than most of his fellow delegates thought.

Romanticism seems to have originated in Germany at the very time that an American constitution was being considered. It was best analyzed by the late Isaiah Berlin, a brilliant Russian-born philosopher who became a leading Oxford University professor. He believed the root cause may have been that Germany "failed to achieve centralized statehood, as England, France, and Holland achieved it." In the seventeenth and even the early eighteenth century, he notes, the Germans were "as progressive and dynamic and generous in their contribution to culture as anyone in European history."

Berlin cited examples of early German cultural leadership, such as Durer as one of the greatest painters and Luther a towering religious figure, but after that, "it is difficult to find anyone among the Germans of that time who affected the thought or even the art of the world in any significant fashion." Among the reasons for this was the Germans' strange existence under scores of princes and sub-princes, and above all, the violent dislocation of the Thirty Years War that killed a very large section of the German population and drowned what might have been a cultural development in seas of blood. It crushed Germany's spirit to a very high degree. A huge national inferiority complex began in Germany, particularly vis-a-vis the French.

Oddly, perhaps, this contrast gave Germany a new kind of importance in the world. Berlin went on to explain the sense of sadness that it implanted in the German soul, infused German ballads and popular literature in an appealing way that made German music greatly exceed anything produced by the English, Dutch, or French. Even more directly, the pietist movement, which was a branch of Lutheranism, put great stress on the sufferings of the human soul. The very word "romanticism" seemed to glorify its practitioners. This brought a certain comfort to socially and politically crushed human beings, even in neighboring countries. By making them retreat into themselves, it created an intense inner life. People began to echo Luther: Reason is a whore and must be avoided. All the highly educated French aristocrats who glittered in the salons of Paris glorified reason, but their poses infuriated and alienated the Germans.

In a sense, these saddened Germans declared intellectual war on the rest of Europe—and conquered for a time. Rationalism, which flourished as part of the earlier intellectual period called the Enlightenment, came to seem shallow and empty compared to the great spirit of the Romantics who thought it far better to die in defense of a wrong cause than to live in a correct one. It was not a matter of logic but of mood. Romanticism became the prevailing mood in much of central Europe.

American thinking went in exactly the opposite direction. Even though it was the thinking of a thin layer of elite individuals, the great miracle was that it touched and affected the mentality of Americans who would not have cared or understood a word about European philosophy. Americans, observing the benevolence of nature and what Jefferson called "the unbounded liberality" of the universe, saw no limits to what could be achieved. But it would certainly not be by sorrowful yearnings. The old words "progressive" and dynamic" suited them better than Romantic terms.

"Nature existed to be put to use," writes Russel Blaine Nye, in his early-nineteenth-century book *The Cultural Life of the New Nation.* "The prevailing eighteenth-century European concept of nature underwent modifications, of course, in an American environment." He points out that even American poets give the impression of being doers, quoting poet-philosopher Joel Barlow (a close friend of Thomas Jefferson) who thought man could attain a perfect state of society if he would just

Look through earth and meditate the skies,
and find some general laws in every breast,
Where ethics, faith, and politics may rest.

This airy generalization articulated by the poets and philosophers was viewed differently by settlers pushing westward, encountering dangers that could kill in an unguarded moment. Dying for wrong causes had no place in this new world. As Nye writes, "In the New World, where nature was much less domesticated, one very practical, urgent problem was to find out about it, tame it, and use it—for food, shelter, wealth, security—on a quite unphilosophical basis."

A Convention delegate, Benjamin Franklin, personified Nye's observation. He not only discovered the relationship of lightning to electricity, but promptly created the lightning rod to tame it. This image of a lone man actually using direct methods to protect mankind against one of nature's most mysterious forces made him the toast of France, where there were no inferiority feelings and Romanticism was tempered with a more practical attitude.

Another view of nature's effect on "the American soul" was related by Emerson scholar Richard Geldard, who observes that Ralph Waldo Emerson's reverence for nature and philosophy of a personal relationship with God resonate in a country founded on individualism. "The essential American soul," he writes, "comes from our founders and is an unusual combination of the sovereignty of the individual and our principle of religious freedom. There is no other country that was founded on those two principles side by side. Emerson was born in the year we made the Louisiana Purchase, and we became enamored of the wilderness."

However much truth there may have been in Hamilton's fear that American voters would not measure up to the quality of the English, the fact that the Americans would evolve more vigorously because of different surroundings and challenges was almost certain to have a bearing on how well the document under discussion was going to perform over the years.

It has generally been thought, for example, that the Americans had an easier road to the development of a thriving society. But just the opposite may have been the case. Instead of being an easy, accommodating road provided by the abundance of space and nature, the early years of the Union's existence were actually a harsher test than Europeans experienced in the same era because most Americans were forced to analyze, learn, and adapt to new challenges unknown to older countries. In this case, the forced self-education that molded Americans into greater citizens and nation builders may have contributed to the success of Madison's determination to make ordinary Americans the masters of their own fate.

It should be noted, however, that although Madison made mention of philosophical thoughts, he did not rely simply on philosophy as his reason for optimism about the result. His basic reasoning was, in fact, rather simplistic. Madison based his optimism about America's future on something exactly opposite of Montesquieu's widely-accepted belief that a republic (meaning a nation in which the supreme power rests in all the voting citizens and is exercised by their elected representatives) could never survive in a large country. Madison thought the opposite: Greater size was an advantage. He writes:

> No common interest or passion will be likely to unite a majority of the whole number in an unjust pursuit. *In a large society, the people are broken into so many interests and parties that a common sentiment is less likely to be felt...*Divide et impera [divide and conquer], the reprobated axiom of tyranny, is under certain qualifications the only policy by which a republic can be administered on just principles.

Note the added emphasis, for that sentence is the core of Madison's reasoning. It is like saying that a few strong voices in a small town may make it hard for others to express opposition, but where one finds a large number of individuals, they are likelier to produce enough varied opinions to lessen the probability that any one clique will be able to dominate.

While others thought agreement was the way to stable government, Madison had the radical notion that only a benignly tolerated disagreement could produce stability without forcing everybody into lock step.

At every stage in America's growth, the fear of great size resurfaced. Some of the concerns—about getting people to feel connected to a distant capital city, for example—have created passing problems. But the Madisonian principle that size lessens the danger of "a common sentiment" and so makes a virtue of dissent has withstood every test.

Chapter Twenty-one

FORMIDABLE
OPPOSITION

The farewells in Philadelphia were said on September 17, 1787. The alternating euphoria and despair that had enveloped many of the delegates were being replaced by dread: they were going back to face the people at home.

If the new Constitution failed to win ratification in a delegate's own state, he would be like a soldier returning from a war that he and his comrades lost; the impression of failure would attach itself to each man who endured those sweltering months in Philadelphia to produce an unacceptable and faulty document. Even if the Convention's work was ratified by a man's home state but then failed to gain approval of at least nine states to make it effective, the hurt would be almost as great. It would still be true that "our work went for nought. It wasn't good enough."

To the people at home it might be just a question of not having the expected change in government after all. But most of the delegates believed the inability to gain approval of a new constitution would spell chaos. They knew the Articles of Confederation were incapable of governing. The states would stumble and break up. Some people might say, "Thank God we have the Articles of Confederation." But that was the emptiest of consolations, fit only for the ignorant. The delegates knew that those Articles had lost all power to govern or to maintain a partnership. The states would be adrift. The fear of seeing separate little confederations, each consisting of three or four states, might soon become a reality.

George Washington's image, moreover, would suffer if the Constitution failed to be approved. Years ago, he won a war; now, it would appear, he had lost a political fight. He was president of the Convention and therefore appeared to be more of a partisan than he actually was. He wanted to see ratification because it would produce more of a government than they had and also because it would give the appearance of success. Washington was careful about his image; not out of vanity, but because he knew that the image of a victorious leader might enable him to achieve things that could never be won by an ordinary man. A Cincinnatus who went home of his own volition was different from one who was sent home in defeat. Madison and Hamilton were alert to this point, too, and, at that critical time, were almost as thoughtful about Washington's future as about their own.

Even before the draft of the Constitution, accompanied by a letter from Washington, was laid before the old Continental Congress on September 26, 1787, it was heard that the anti-Constitution forces were already girding for battle. And very tough, significant forces they were. Richard Henry Lee of Virginia was their leader. Eleven years earlier, he made the motion in Congress for the adoption of the Declaration of Independence. His firmness made it hard for others to back out. Lee was a fighter, backed by Nathan Dane, a strong Massachusetts Anti-Federalist, and by a determined New York delegation. That was just the core of the opposition. There would be many other good men in the opposing camp—Virginia's Patrick Henry, New York's George Clinton and Melancton Smith, South Carolina's Rawlins Lowndes, and Thomas Sumter as the heads of powerful Anti-Federalists all along the Appalachian mountain chain from Pennsylvania to its southern extremity. Within less than ten days, the word began to spread—word that the opposition to ratification was successfully broadcasting its message before anything much was said in favor of the Constitution.

Fortunately, a majority in the Congress seemed to be against these Anti-Federalists. They seemed to relish the idea of change. It would have made things much harder if the Congress had tried to hold onto its waning life. But now again, as in its amazing action on the Northwest Ordinance, the Congress appeared to have more zest in the face of death than it showed in its dubious prime.

The opposing forces quickly jumped on this very point as an argument—the life or death of the old Congress. Was it right to destroy the Continental Congress that kept them all together through the war and beyond? Was it proper for Congress to sign its own death warrant?

James Madison came rushing back to Congress from Philadelphia, assisted by a group that included another Lee—Henry Lee, the war hero popularly known as Light-Horse Harry—and they succeeded in rousing the congressmen in favor of the Constitution. They received the new document with George Washington's own letter of transmittal, asking that it be "transmitted to the several legislatures, in order to be submitted to a gathering of delegates in each state by the people thereof, in conformity to the resolves of the Convention."

The Congress did just what Washington asked and submitted the Constitution to each state for consideration. In many states the people witnessed the emergence of the first real political parties to address a national issue. There were Tories and Whigs before, but they took up old wartime issues; the Tories were overridden, destined to lose. Now new political parties were in a real, forward-looking battle against each other. In this new day, people began to assemble for the purpose of debating in Boston, New York, Richmond, Baltimore, and even in smaller towns— too loudly and raucously in many cases—but talking or shouting, not fighting. This was heartening. It appeared at first that people were showing enough maturity to realize that this document, after all, must be supported or attacked only after studying what it said, not in blind anger.

In short order, during that autumn of 1787, two basic parties formed. Supporters of the Constitution were formally called Federalists, as the people who wanted a stronger national government had been informally known for some time. Those who opposed stronger bonds between states were called Anti-Federalists, which emphasized the fact that their program was mainly negative. (This was to be a short-lived party.)

From Jefferson in Paris came encouraging words. After having been a bit negative about the Convention and especially about its policy of secrecy, he gladdened Madison's heart by quickly writing that "the Constitution is a good canvas, on which some strokes only want retouching." For example, as many other essentially approving men already said, the failure to include a bill of rights must be corrected promptly. Jefferson also added again that although he could not be called a Federalist, he was much further removed from the Anti-Federalist view. His failure to join either party soon made it apparent that Jefferson was planning to have a party of his own; considering his talent for gathering followers with almost no visible effort, this new political step was destined to occur soon after he returned to America.

For the time, Jefferson and Madison had to think and act as Federalists in order to encourage ratification of the Constitution. Later, Jefferson's followers would begin to call themselves Republicans—partly to stress that the Federalists were not republicans and therefore could be monarchists. The main emphasis of Jefferson's party was on strict construction of the Constitution and strong support for the nation's westward expansion.

The Federalists began by being too optimistic about their chances of winning ratifications. Delaware and Pennsylvania, the first states to take up the issue, quickly ratified the new form of government. But their way of doing it and the cause of success was not typical of what would be faced in other states. Nor did it reflect careful examination of the issues.

Delaware gave a demonstration of how relieved the small states were to have won equal representation in the Senate. Their long pretense of indifference and insistence on total equality was shown to have been simply a canny bargaining technique. Now this small state with a population of less than sixty thousand showed that it knew it might never see another central government giving it equality in the upper house. Anxious to speed the process of adoption, delegates Read, Bedford, Bassett, and Broom, who were so fruitfully active in Philadelphia, headed a special meeting of the state legislature on December 7, 1787, and it voted—unanimously—to accept the Constitution.

The usually sedate and proper Pennsylvanians were next to ratify. But they did so in a strangely rowdy fashion. The Federalists were numerous there, and they had organized well. Also, the reasons some other states opposed the new Constitution were lacking in Pennsylvania. Federalists there had no objection to a federal government's control over commerce. They had very few citizens who wanted to see more use of paper money. They had little slavery to protect. Especially in the eastern counties and in Philadelphia, the Federalists maintained a substantial majority. The Anti-Federalists were laying plans for a great campaign of opposition anyway.

But George Clymer, who was one of the state's delegates to the Constitutional Convention, was also in the Pennsylvania legislature and he stunned the opposition party by suddenly making a motion to move right ahead with a convention to consider the proposed new form of government. It was improper, because the old Congress had not even sent out copies of the new Constitution, and the rule calling for three separate readings in the legislature had not yet been obeyed. The move was out of order. But the Federalists were in the majority and determined to shout down their foes. The question was put to a vote, and carried by forty-eight to nineteen, whereupon they adjourned until four o'clock, when the necessary formalities were to be concluded.

The Anti-Federalists were not through, however. It took forty-seven to make a quorum. The opposition realized that if it stayed away, the other side could not complete its coup with only forty-five persons present. They went home, refused to heed the sergeant-at-arms who was sent to force them back, and were determined to remain absent in future days. The next morning, however, a crowd of Federalists broke into the lodgings of two of these holdouts and dragged them to the State House by force, holding them down in their seats to make a quorum. The formalities were accomplished in short order, and a favorable ratifying vote was concluded on December 12. It was not the best example of Pennsylvania civility, but effective nonetheless.

With New Jersey, Georgia, and Connecticut promptly adding positive votes, five states ratified within five weeks. But four of these were small states, fully expected to ratify because they knew they might never again come as close to equality in a federal congress as this Constitution provided. And the Pennsylvania victory was snatched somewhat by force. Madison and Hamilton saw signs that the ratification process ahead was going to be more inflamed and dangerous to their cause than they had imagined. Their two states—Virginia and New York—which were scarred with internal irregularities even before the Philadelphia meeting, were now obviously going to indulge in fierce fighting over that Convention's product. Patrick Henry and Richard Henry Lee were not inclined to wait for the facts to be studied. They began preparing the Virginia battleground even before anyone knew what the disputed document contained. And in New York, George Clinton, with inside information from the two delegates who left Philadelphia early, had a real party organization in gear to savage the hated Constitution.

It was in this atmosphere that the fabled *Federalist Papers* were born. Since so many pamphlets and other publications were already flooding the cities, many of them carrying irresponsible and even fantastic accounts of what the new Constitution would do, Madison and Hamilton agreed to write explanatory essays to counter these misimpressions. It was agreed that the two of them, along with John Jay, whose extensive diplomatic experience provided expertise on foreign affairs, should begin composing their responses as soon as possible. As things turned out, Jay became ill and was able to complete only five, at most, of the *Federalist Papers*. Rather than being mere campaign pamphlets, all these *Papers* have come to be regarded as masterpieces of explanatory writing.

The need for them can be judged from the words of the ebullient Henry Knox, who wrote to John Sullivan of New Hampshire about what he was finding in New York City:

The new Constitution! The new Constitution! It is the general cry this way. Much paper is spoilt on the subject, and many essays are written, which perhaps are never read by either side. It is a stubborn fact however, that the...confederation has run down...the springs have utterly lost their tone; and the machine cannot be wound up again. But something must be done speedily, or we shall be involved in...the horrors of anarchy.

Against this chaotic state, the *Federalist Papers* brought calm and a wonderful tone of common sense. Their most attractive element was a lack of blatant salesmanship. Most do not even give a sense of trying to convince the reader, but simply lay out every fact and angle with the greatest clarity. Broadus Mitchell, one of Hamilton's biographers, writes, "Most would-be guides did not enter beyond the anterooms, while these penetrated to every hall and corridor, cellar to attic, of the proposed political edifice."

Most of these *Papers* appeared in the *Independent Journal* of New York, starting with the October 27, 1787, issue. Hamilton had a book-length set of the *Federalist Papers* specially bound for Washington and sent them with a note, saying, "I presume you have understood that the writers...are chiefly Mr. Madison and myself, with some aid from Mr. Jay." One of the amazing things about the whole project is that haste prevented the writers from checking the work with each other to prevent overlaps and redundancies (and they seldom had time to reread their own papers, as the printer was always pushing them for the next essay), yet the works read as smoothly as if they were edited at leisure by a single mind.

As a result, it is recognized that the very close ratification proceedings would almost surely have had a rougher course and may well have failed altogether had there been no *Federalist Papers*. And because Madison found himself pulled away from the project by Congressional duties and because he had to campaign in Virginia's very touchy ratification struggle, Hamilton wrote at least fifty-three of the papers (many signed as Publius), Madison between twenty-four and twenty-seven, and Jay three to five.

Although all three of these contributors have been pictured as scribbling hastily while a printer's messenger waited to whisk away the latest *Federalist Paper*, it was Hamilton's law office that repeatedly served as the setting for such a drama. The miracle is that Hamilton could have written essays of the highest quality at a time when he was forced to put in full days of work in his heavy law practice and also fight on a second front in the tumultuous ratification struggle in his own state of New York. The amount and quality of work that he did and the great results he achieved on a project that he admittedly had grave doubts about truly make him, if not another father of the Constitution along with Madison, at least its heroic godfather.

Madison himself gave great credit to Hamilton, adding that the enormous effort "in a cause that was not entirely his own" deserves the highest praise. Were these two men partners or enemies? It was a question since their first meetings, and it would never be answerable by any single word.

Meanwhile, the Federalists had no monopoly on strong arguments in the battle that was about to be joined. Worthy opponents, some almost as skilled as the *Federalist* writers, were appearing with their own persuasive arguments. As bold as the immortal players in this drama were and as lavishly as their accomplishment is praised today, some of their opponents had arguments that deserve to be heard in retrospect, for not all their alternate plans can be dismissed as hopeless.

One opponent who wrote in a measured way, using the name "Brutus," said that he (or she) did not mean

> to unnecessarily alarm the fears of the people by suggesting that the federal legislature would be more likely to pass the limits assigned to them...than that of an individual state...but they may so exercise this power as to annihilate all the state governments and reduce this country to one single government. And if they may do it, it is pretty certain that they will; for it will be found that the power retained by individual states, small as it is, will be a clog upon the wheels of the government of the United States; the latter therefore will be naturally inclined to move it out of the way.

To give these opponents their due, what Brutus was being asked to accept in 1787 can reasonably be compared with the enormity of modern Americans suddenly learning that fifty of their fellow citizens have secretly arranged to merge the United States with the European Union, indicating that some new city, probably Brussels, will become its capital and the seat of all major decisions. The people would be told that "some small degree of power is left to the states, but a little attention...will convince every candid man that all that is reserved for the individual states must very soon be annihilated."

Those are some of the words that Brutus wrote plaintively to the citizens of New York in 1787 and 1788. He or she apparently was not one of the blindly conservative who saw no need to change the Articles of Confederation, but one of the thoughtful persons who hoped for renovation of the world he knew, without seeing it changed it beyond recognition.

Was it unreasonable for Brutus to suspect that the power of individual states would tend to be moved out of the way in order to rid the federal government of "the clog upon its wheels"? This objection cannot be dismissed without admitting that the federal government did, in fact, quickly begin to "move the power retained by the individual states out of the way." The near-inevitability of this tectonic change is demonstrated by the fact that two men—John Marshall and Thomas Jefferson—who took exactly opposite positions on the issue of federal expansionism nonetheless soon found themselves playing a major part in this triumphant march of big national government.

In 1803, Chief Justice John Marshall, in the famous case of *Marbury v. Madison*, managed to slap his enemy Jefferson while simultaneously establishing the principle of judicial review, which empowered the Court to declare acts of Congress unconstitutional. The case was relatively minor—wherein an interim appointee, William Marbury, sued the secretary of state, Madison, for the right to be seated as a District of Columbia justice of the peace even against the will of the president. Without mentioning Jefferson, Marshall's reasoning in favor of Marbury showed the view that the Constitution should be construed in a most liberal fashion—even saying at one point: "Though it be not law, could it be as operative as if it were law?" It was virtually a celebration of the use of implied powers, opening the way to courses of action and federal supremacy that only a radical thinker like Hamilton had imagined before.

But it is even more significant that a leader of the strict construc-tionists, exactly opposite to Marshall's position, found himself almost forced to take part in a move as "loose" as one could imagine. For in that same year, 1803, Jefferson realized that his astonishing achieve-ment of winning the entire Louisiana Territory and doubling the nation's size would inevitably be ascribed to some "implied power," because he certainly had no specific authority for a land purchase in the Constitution. Knowing that this could be used by later presidents to perform more great federal works that dwarfed the states, Jefferson thought it might be necessary to seek a Constitutional amendment in order to prove that the purchase was made in accordance with a specific provision and not an implied power. It was Madison, then his secretary of state, who convinced him that the delay involved in seeking an amendment would cause Napoleon Bonaparte to slip out of the deal; Jefferson coveted the land enough to go ahead on the "implied" basis that he supposedly deplored.

People who were passionately anxious to see a large, strong national government were inclined to unfairly ridicule or attack the very term "states' rights" as if it were an immoral ambition. In the case where emphasis on states' rights was actually a sly way of insisting on the right to conduct slavery, there was good reason to deplore it. But many Amer-icans who detested slavery still loved their own states and preferred not to see them drained of all power.

Madison's aging father, still very alert to public affairs, wrote to his son immediately after a first reading of the Constitution, expressing deep dislike of the provision for the president's term and veto powers: "A sole executive, who may be for life," he wrote, "with almost a negative upon the legislature."

This was an astute observation, thoughtfully held by many others, pointing out that a president who solidified his position might well be reelected endlessly and that his power to veto bills could virtually dominate the legislature. It may seem astonishing that the presidential role was vir-tually ignored by more critics. The reason was simply George Washington. Almost everyone's assumption that he would become president seemed to make this excessive power acceptable. And although Washington served only eight years, his voluntary departure after two terms and the definition that he gave to the office did, in fact, create a substantial barrier to future misuse of the presidency.

As the ratification struggle went on, there was not quite the groundswell that the pro-Constitution forces had hoped for, but neither did the opposition gather any great momentum. If anything, the mood shift seemed to be slightly in favor of the Constitution. Those who believe the *Federalist Papers* should be credited with the victory point out the small but steady increase in strength that appeared to match the public sentiment as thoughtful readers became more and more respectful of the surprisingly restrained arguments the *Papers* introduced.

Not only America, but the whole modern world took an increasing interest in this gathering debate. Intellectuals abroad felt like more than mere observers. Many Europeans behaved like participants and often weighed in on the much-discussed subject of what makes the Constitution unique. Among the wide variety of opinions, one suggested the American presidency has the perfect attributes for success: He cannot in the normal course of business be removed by the legislature, as the British prime minister can be. He is more like an old-fashioned king, except that his short term of office forestalls his power for mischief. But while in office, his power to act and even to veto the actions of the Congress give him enough authority to carry out meaningful endeavors.

The almost supreme power of the judiciary branch is another feature that is much admired by foreign observers. While it is less noticed than the presidency, the federal court system is noteworthy as the only branch that is not chosen by the people, the only one that has life terms, and the only one that regularly uses its judgments to regulate and discipline the other two branches.

The fact that the Supreme Court is even charged with interpreting the general principles of the Constitution itself has led to its being called "the most remarkable and original of all the creations of that wonderful Convention" and even "the most noble, most distinctive feature in the United States government."

This should not detract from the truly monumental personal contribution of John Marshall in his three decades of mastery that helped to shape the court system. As the Constitution wrote it, the Court might have taken any number of forms. Marshall strengthened not only the Court but also the presidency. He was not at all immune from the politics of his day, and it is known that he sometimes had to think politically in order to defend himself. But he was dedicated to the principle that law, and not men, should rule. And his wish to make decisions comply with the intent of the framers was an overriding consideration.

Not until 1924 did a new principle called "linguistic indeterminacy" invade the fortress that Marshall built. By constantly shifting the definition of words in order to approve legislation that would have failed to meet the test of constitutionality at an earlier time, the Court was seeming to say that one interpretation was as good as another. Even Marshall would have agreed that the Founding Fathers did not speak with absolute clarity on all points. He did believe that a natural tradition of laws dating back to the seventeenth and eighteenth centuries gave a certain amount of permanent guidance. And he believed that the Constitution was imposed on a culture that was essentially local, so that it had to be stretched and shaped to fit the new demands of a national society. In the end, he might have come around, as the modern judges did, to the view that nineteenth-century situations so pleadingly cried for new decisions that the framers might well have accepted the modern language of the Court. Remembering the delegates we met in the foregoing pages, it is challenging to wonder how each might have reacted: James Madison? Alexander Hamilton? Gouverneur Morris? The Shoemaker? But there's no need to ask about the ever-youthful Benjamin Franklin.

The Constitution's opponents who thought the federal government was certain to obliterate the state governments were wide of the mark. The federal tendency to dominate has been unmistakable, but it has not prevailed. The reasons are more sentimental than specific, but any form of patriotism has a sentimental component. In part, the lack of a total federal takeover exists because states, even when they disagree with the complaint of another state, usually tend to support the rights of that sister state; they see their own future rights as part of the dispute, even when the issue is not relevant to them.

There is also considerable residual patriotic feeling about one's state of origin. Most Americans are comfortable with their right to move their residence at will, but nonetheless they like feeling assured that their original state will retain its individuality. Consequently, while states' rights declined sharply over most of two centuries, they have had substantial rebounds, often affecting human rights issues and the related electoral politics. Especially in Florida and Texas, they have also affected limited areas of foreign policy.

Foreign scholars and other observers have been known to marvel at the conception of a nation in which every citizen lives under two complete and well-rounded systems of laws—the state law and the federal law—each with its legislature, its executive, and its judiciary moving one within the other: it has been called one of the longest reaches of constructive statesmanship ever known in the world. There never was anything quite like it before.

❧

But ratification still had to be achieved before the gloating could begin. Not all the opposition was worthy or high-minded. When South Carolina's ratification convention met in May, 1788, a most active Anti-Federalist, Rawlins Lowndes, who had opposed the Declaration of Independence, declared that they were "already living under a wonderful government that had withstood the test of time. Why are we impatient to pull it down? And why are the northerners so jealous of our importing Negroes? Why limit us to only twenty years more?"

The Pinckneys knew when they struggled to win a compromise in Philadelphia that they would encounter this kind of attack when they returned home. It was Cotesworth Pinckney who now replied to Lowndes:

> By this settlement we have secured an unlimited importation of
> Negroes for twenty years. The general government can never

emancipate them, for no such authority is granted, and it is admitted on all hands that the general government has no powers but what are expressly granted by the Constitution. We have a right to recover our slaves in whatever part of the country they may take refuge, which is a right we had not before. In short, we have made the best terms in our power.

It is probably one of history's twists that the two Pinckneys and John Rutledge of South Carolina are largely and unfairly remembered as simply three of the southern slavers who were in Philadelphia. In fact, these three men managed—before, during, and after the Convention—to defeat the arguments of a southern party that favored the establishment of a separate southern confederacy and regarded the three with suspicion. Many Virginians, too, were somewhat attracted to the idea of separation because they were still infuriated over a shocking treaty that John Jay had made with Spain two years before. He had actually recommended to Congress that the Union should give up the right to navigate the Mississippi for twenty-five years—a clear gift to the New England shipping interests at the expense of the South and West. Since Virginia's Kentucky County touched the Mississippi, the thought of such an incredible gift of its rights to Spain seemed to confirm that there was no limit to the perfidy of the New Englanders. It was a strong influence on Patrick Henry's wish to break up the Union into separate confederations. The threat was greater than modern readers think.

The absence of a bill of rights was also a factor in the ratification fight, seen everywhere as a potentially crippling defect in the new Constitution. While Madison probably had good reason for resisting the creation of such a section during the Convention, he had promised to take care of this in the form of an amendment to the Constitution as soon as the new government began to operate. He eventually, and reluctantly, kept his word, but the delaying tactic very nearly jeopardized the ratification process, for it raised undue suspicions and created a real disadvantage that the pro-Constitution team had to overcome in order to win ratification.

Like so many things that people regard affectionately, the Constitution is often chided with unworthy remarks. Some were tasteless enough to say, "It took forty-two well-bred, well-fed, well-read, and well-wed white men from twelve of the thirteen states to create our national government."

Even Alexander Hamilton, who worked prodigiously to win ratification for the Constitution, belittled it with the term, "a bundle of compromises." And this set of parchment pages that is regarded almost as a sacred relic has had over ten thousand bullets fired at it—in the form of proposed amendments. But only thirty-three of these were taken seriously enough to be sent to the states for consideration, and only twenty-seven have actually been adopted, including the first ten in the Bill of Rights.

Chapter Twenty-two

NARROWEST OF VICTORIES

A constitution had been delivered, but its survival still trembled in the balance. The fight over its ratification was by far the most arduous part of the process.

In a remarkably short time, political parties formed, seemingly more determined to prove their own power than to ensure the nation's viability. Among the infuriating factors was the stand taken by esteemed men who were active delegates at the Convention but who refused to support its work because of disagreement with just one point. Since they knew how much the newborn document meant to America, their willingness to risk a stillbirth was incomprehensible. Maryland's Luther Martin might be excused on grounds of alcoholism. But a trusted statesman like Gerry of Massachusetts? A Virginian of genius like Mason? They could have expressed disapproval of the submission to pro-slavery forces by refusing to sign, but then gone on to support ratification, as Virginia's Governor Edmund Randolph did. Nothing could excuse their disruptive behavior.

Reaching for reasons to oppose the new order of things, logical or theoretical, opponents headed by such leaders as Henry and Lee opined that the Constitution itself was unconstitutional, because the Convention clearly exceeded the authority it received from the Congress. This objection came as no surprise, but the Constitution's supporters were helped by the fact that ratification was being practiced openly in each state, making it clear that each state's favorable vote would mean the people were, indeed, choosing the Constitution. In order to get the maximum benefits from these public discussions, the defenders had to allow their opponents every opportunity to challenge the validity of the document. In standing up to this ordeal, the battle for ratification had many heroes.

Massachusetts was a special case, for it was a close contest that was complicated by local customs and by the elusive subject of religion. It was generally agreed that a Constitution without Massachusetts's approval would be of little value, because the state was so respected that the others would think poorly of any union made without her. At the same time, there were several obstacles in the way of a favorable vote.

The Massachusetts district called Maine had a strong wish to separate and form a new state. For that reason, half the Maine delegates planned to vote "no" simply because they feared that the Constitution would cause complexities and prevent their separation.

Massachusetts was more concerned about states' rights than almost any other state. Town meetings had always flourished in that state's cities and hamlets; citizens there were strong defenders of local and accessible government. It was said that the towns of Massachusetts were like little semi-independent republics and that the state was a league of such republics. The idea of being governed by officials in a remote capital seemed like delegating their precious rights to leaders they did not know. And there was fear that some form of oppression would grow from it. There was also common talk that the admired Samuel Adams was secretly opposed to the Constitution, that Governor John Hancock was half-hearted in his support of it, and that Elbridge Gerry's refusal to sign the document was because he feared it would lead to tyranny.

Massachusetts took notice that young revolutionaries were responsible for the Constitution's creation, and Richard Henry Lee, a leader against ratification, warned that it was the product of "visionary young men." Although most of the well-to-do people were in favor of Federalism because they were still shaken by Shays's insurrection, Massachusetts was a state where the common people were unusually active in politics and they feared tyrants more than they feared discontented men like Shays.

The Massachusetts ratifying convention, attended by members of the legislature and by the state's regional leaders on January 9, 1788, was noisy and boisterous. Gorham, Strong, and King, who had taken part in the Constitutional Convention, sat listening to loud objections from the many participants. Other famous men on hand were Samuel Adams, Revolutionary generals Heath and Lincoln, and several rising statesmen, including Fisher Ames, destined to have a short life because of a consumptive disease, but to win fame as one of the greatest speakers of all time.

Everyone noted that there were twenty-four clergymen of various denominations, some renowned for their scholarship.

All these dignitaries, presided over by Governor Hancock—magnificent in crimson velvet and fine laces—listened patiently to the negative rumblings of browned and weather-beaten farmers, some of whom had marched under the banner of Shays only a year ago. Three hundred fifty-five delegates were present—more than at any other state convention. All were allowed to have their say, and all were politely heard, for it was a Massachusetts principle that the air was sooner cleared of discontent and disease, and was more likely to heal itself, when men spoke their minds.

Just as Gerry predicted at the Philadelphia Convention, these country people who never delegated power to others for more than a few months at a time thought it dangerous to give terms as long as two years to congressmen who, sitting in some distant federal city, might grow so accustomed to their seats that they would contrive to make their sittings perpetual—and sit there taxing the people without their consent as long as they pleased. Questioners kept coming up with unexpected oddities, such as complaints about the "huge size" of ten miles square for the federal city. Why not one mile square? they asked.

The fact that Congress had the right to establish a standing army with the president as commander-in-chief was another red flag. A delegate from the Maine district cried, "Had I an arm like Jove, I would hurl from the globe those villains that would dare attempt to establish in our country a standing army!"

A more serious complaint seemed to be the charge that "the Constitution did not recognize the existence of God" and did not set up any religious tests for federal office-holders. The place of religion in American life had been exceptionally complicated with arrival of independence. American Catholics, in particular, had been put into a curious position. At the war's end, in 1781, there were about twenty-five Catholic priests in the country, and the Church of Rome provided them with little guidance. Every state but Rhode Island passed laws depriving Catholics of full civil and religious rights. Some states even disarmed Catholics, denying them the right to carry their own weapons as most others were allowed to do.

Since American ties to British Catholicism ended with the American Revolution, French Catholics hoped to take over the role of advising and guiding the priests in America. In response to this intrusion, Father John Carroll of Maryland sent a petition to the Pope requesting the formation of an American Catholic Church, headed by an American bishop. In response, Father Carroll was first appointed Head of American Missions and later made the first Catholic bishop in America.

At the start of the Revolution, all the colonies established official state churches. But these colonies also had a strong tradition of religious freedom, dating from dissidents like Anne Hutchinson, Roger Williams, and William Penn. This tradition continued with the immigration of non-conformist Germans, Swiss, French, Dutch, and Swedes. The Great Awakening of the 1740s, a revivalist movement mostly among Protestant groups that held long outdoor prayer weekends, often featuring spasms and other involuntary body movements, also weakened religious authoritarianism in New England.

By 1776, most legislatures strongly affirmed "free enjoyment of the rights of conscience," as New York's did in 1775. And the Declaration of Independence seemed to free all churches from any parliamentary or legislative authority. To the revolutionary generation, it seemed obvious that the right to the pursuit of happiness must include the right to worship in one's own way, for had it not been included among the "inalienable rights"?

It was also clear that no one church could satisfy this sprawling, diverse, scattered population which, in 1776, already had seventeen different creeds. By the close of the war (1781), the separation of church and state was virtually complete, and subsequent legislation was little more than a summary of existing practices. But the churches themselves were battling a variety of internal complexities, ranging from personnel problems and the management of growth to ethnic and color problems and doctrinal differences. After Yorktown, most churches were involved in similarly varied reorganizations, and these were proving to be great challenges. In New England and in the South, the bonds of church and state were traditionally strong, but not so in the other states. As each colony had its own religious history and the traditions were mixed, each had to cope with a separate set of ecclesiastical problems.

The ties between white churches and slaves were also in flux. During the seventeenth and eighteenth centuries, about twenty percent of the population consisted of humans living in servitude, and both the slave population and black freedmen regularly attended white services. Some even were considered members of white congregations, especially by the Baptists. By the time of the Revolution, black ministers and parishes had appeared, but usually were sponsored by whites. Baptist and Methodist missionaries became active among blacks in the slave states at that time, and both religions soon organized Negro churches in Virginia and North Carolina. At the time of the fight over ratification of the Constitution, black clergymen held a convention to found the African Methodist Episcopal Church. Soon thereafter thriving black churches were established in New York, Philadelphia, Baltimore, and Boston.

The Articles of Confederation and the Continental Congress left church–state relations to the states. Pennsylvania, Maryland, Rhode Island, North Carolina, New York, and Delaware had already inserted a clear separation of civil and ecclesiastical authority into their constitutions or bills of rights. Virginia's law requiring non-Anglicans to pay church taxes was repealed. But Thomas Jefferson's 1779 bill for officially separating church and state was defeated. He was finally able to secure passage of a Statute of Religious Freedom in 1786, after "the hardest struggle of [his] life." New York (with more sects than any other state) put separation into its constitution in 1777, as Maryland and New Jersey had done a year earlier.

But the Congregational Church successfully resisted disestablishment for many years. Many New Englanders opposed it as "a daring affront to Heaven." The Reverend Samuel West, of New Bedford, insisted that "laws for maintaining public worship were absolutely necessary for the well-being of society." So it appeared to be more a matter of civic duty than of religious faith. Three states continued to support their established Congregational churches by public taxes (from which Anglicans and Quakers were exempted)—Connecticut until 1818, New Hampshire until 1819, and Massachusetts until 1833. But these were clearly exceptions to a widely accepted abandonment of such support.

The Constitutional Convention had no great problem in maintaining the principle of non-interference in religious affairs. Along with Madison, it was almost unanimously believed that "religion must be left to the conviction and conscience of every man." And the Constitution simply abolished religious qualifications for any office or public trust in the United States.

But when it came to the huge task of ratification, the religious issue intensified. The idea that individuals could assume positions of great trust without indicating that they possessed any religious beliefs at all had met with great shock among many of the people of Massachusetts. Their complaints in the ratification meeting were so aggressive that a separate meeting was held to consider this subject alone. It was open to all those who had attended the main meeting; the attendance this time was somewhat smaller, but just as determined.

To the great credit of the twenty eminent clergymen who were present on this second occasion, however, they spoke out with finality against the objection. Although Massachusetts began as a theocracy, where only church members could vote or hold office, the reversal of feelings was so complete that several of the clergy now spoke firmly against religious tests for public office. "Such a test would have been a great blemish on the Constitution," said one. Another added, "The imposing of religious tests hath been the greatest engine of tyranny in the world."

And the Reverend Samuel West, who showed such conservatism on an earlier issue, now made a great impression on this special assemblage by asking why it seemed to be taken for granted that the federal government was going to be put in the hands of crafty knaves. "I wish the gentlemen who have stated so many possible objections would try to show us that what they deprecate is probable...Because power may be abused, shall we be reduced to anarchy? May we not suppose that the persons we shall choose to administer the government will be, in general, good men?"

The accumulated words of most of the clergymen present were convincing, and the religious issue faded. But the farmers from the mountain districts took the occasion to switch subjects from religion to their distrust of lawyers and moneyed men who talked so finely and "make us poor illiterate people swallow the pill." Whereupon a plain farmer who had not been known before and is only identified as Mr. Smith surprised the meeting by saying, "I am not used to speak in public, but I am going to show the effects of anarchy, so that you may see why I wish for good government." He went on at length to describe times when people had had their property damaged, or set on fire, and their families attacked, simply because there was no effective government where they lived. "These lawyers, these moneyed men, these men of learning, are all embarked in the same cause with us, and we must all sink or swim together. Suppose we had a piece of rough land and we could not all agree on what kind of fence to put around it. Would we let it lie waste because you did not all want the same kind of fence? Would it not be better that it did not please everyone's fancy, rather than wait until the wild beasts came and devoured the crop?"

These words quieted the meeting, but the situation in Massachusetts took an ominous turn when Richard Henry Lee convinced the ubiquitous Elbridge Gerry that he should insist on another federal convention to take up a variety of amendments. Madison and Hamilton convinced Washington that only his intervention might prevent such a catastrophe.

The General announced: "If another Federal Convention is attempted, its members will be more discordant and will agree upon no general plan...The Constitution or disunion are before us to choose from...A constitutional door is open for amendments, and they may be adopted in a peaceable manner, without tumult or disorder." This worked magically, and Massachusetts became the sixth state to ratify by a slim majority, 187 to 168.

None of the ratification heroes equaled Hamilton's performance in the exhausting months of fighting New York's dogged Governor Clinton. In a period when his legal practice was demanding almost all his time so that he could preserve the financial safety he sought for his family, Hamilton literally worked day and night in order to do a superior job on both fronts.

Hamilton's role in the vital New York battle proved decisive. New York state was only fifth in total population. However, geographical location and all the commercial activities that had formed in and around the state made it the nation's center in many ways. Hamilton's successful attempt to overcome Governor Clinton's powerful hold on many of the delegates to the state convention and prevent New York from destroying the whole Constitutional effort was his greatest contribution and finest moment. As Professor Fiske describes it:

> In nothing could the flexibleness of Hamilton's intellect, or the genuineness of his patriotism, have been more finely shown than in the hearty zeal and transcendent ability with which he now wrote in defense of a plan of government so different from what he would himself have proposed. He made Madison's thoughts his own, until he set them forth with even greater force than Madison himself could command. Yet no arguments could be less chargeable with partisanship than the arguments of the *Federalist*. The judgment is as dispassionate as could be shown in a philosophical treatise. The tone is one of grave and lofty elegance, apt to move even to tears the reader who is fully alive to the stupendous issues that were involved in the discussion.

When it was time to defend the Constitution before an unfriendly assemblage at Poughkeepsie, Hamilton faced a daunting task. The opposition was too great to be silenced. His opponents had to be converted. A letter he wrote to Madison on May 10, 1788, showed him to be pessimistic about winning in New York unless Virginia, where Madison was preparing to fight for ratification, voted to ratify first. Hamilton writes:

> I mentioned that the question of a majority for or against the Constitution would depend upon the County of Albany. By the later accounts from that quarter, I fear much that the issue there has been against us. As Clinton is truly the leader of his party, and is inflexibly obstinate, I count little on overcoming opposition by reason. Our only chance will be the previous ratification by nine states, which may shake the firmness of his followers...
>
> We think here that the situation of your State is critical. Let me know what you think of it...It will be of vast importance that an exact communication should be kept up between us...I request you to dispatch an express to me, with pointed orders to make all possible diligence, by changing horses, etc. The expense of this should not concern you. We will fully cover all costs.

With stunning eloquence, Hamilton ignored his own pessimism and argued for weeks. The reeling Governor Clinton tried to stall by asking whether New York could ratify the Constitution conditionally, reserving the right to withdraw from the Union in case certain amendments the state demanded should not be adopted. On this point, Hamilton consulted urgently with Madison, who had just returned to New York. Could a state adopt the Constitution, and then withdraw from the Union if not satisfied?

Here it was Madison's turn to be heroic. Governor Clinton, in a rearguard action, was offering to give his approval on a provisional basis, thus giving the document's defenders credit for a tentative victory, while still leaving himself an eventual way out. Madison answered decisively—no. The Constitution could not provide for nor contemplate its own overthrow. There could be no such thing as the Constitutional right of secession. Hamilton went back into the fray to argue that issue brilliantly. When Melancton Smith, the strongest debater on Clinton's team, dramatized his desertion of the Anti-Federalists on this point by walking across the room and taking a chair at Hamilton's side, the victory was won. On July 26, New York ratified the Constitution by the bare majority of thirty to twenty-seven. A float representing the ship of state was drawn through the streets with Hamilton's name emblazoned on the side.

The apparent victory in New York was followed by one more brief moment of suspense. Clinton had an afterthought; he wished to call a second federal convention to consider amendments that various states wanted to make. The Virginia legislature supported the move, causing real fear that very unsettling arguments would be reopened, spoiling the great feeling that a massive change had been accomplished. But when Massachusetts and Pennsylvania both opposed the idea, it crumbled.

It should be noted that Hamilton was not disavowing his own principles when he fought for the Constitution. His return to the Convention, determination to be a signer, enormous effort to write most of the *Federalist Papers*, and his brilliant ratification effort—all could be seen as a circuitous route to his real goal. He once hinted that any federal government with controlling financial force—which he hoped to control—would eventually take over more and more power from the state governments, bringing about the kind of truly national government he wished to see, and leaving little power to the states. Such a government might not contain the aristocratic element he preferred, but it would be a major and entirely legitimate step toward one of his main objectives. If that was his chief purpose, he had won a different kind of victory.

One of the most dramatic struggles took place in Virginia, the largest state. Virginia seemed set to be the ninth ratifying state—appropriately the state that would make the Constitution officially effective. Some of the state's most powerful leaders were dedicated opponents of the plan—Patrick Henry, Richard Henry Lee, and George Mason among them. But Madison, of course, was most determined to defeat them. He was joined by the spirited Light-Horse Harry Lee, and notably by Governor Randolph, who refused to sign because of points he disagreed with, but who worked relentlessly for ratification.

Patrick Henry made this struggle into one of the most exciting battles in the entire ratification drama. He took the floor, he said, as a servant of the people—a sentinel over their rights, liberty, and happiness. "Give me leave to ask," he thundered, "what right had they to command 'We the people' instead of 'We the states'?" A great many persons, hearing these challenges, nodded in agreement.

But at one point, another voice was heard, one that would come to stand for interpretation of the Constitution—John Marshall, a young lawyer who had both the militia background that Henry could not boast and an astonishing command of the law that had not been suspected. Listening to Madison's carefully reasoned arguments (and "How Madison slew Goliath," as one hearer put it) had inspired the future great chief justice of the Supreme Court to respond with a withering logic. Marshall had a great regard for Henry, who expected a great future for the younger man. But when Henry objected that the new Constitution said nothing of a right to challenge jurors, Marshall pointed out that neither did the Virginia constitution, nor the English constitution, both of which Henry praised so highly. But the new United States Constitution Marshall was defending allowed for interpretation that would make this right a possibility.

In another of his booming speeches that lasted almost an entire day, Henry said the Constitution was as radical as the resolution that separated America from Britain. Another time, he hinted that Governor Randolph had some discreditable reason for having changed from a non-signer into a supporter. On June 24, he shouted that a great deal of the property of the Virginians was in jeopardy.

Madison came back with shining logic and clarity on these occasions, which triggered an even fiercer response from Henry. Amid all his thunder, a real thunderstorm erupted. Henry was obliged to conclude, but since "interpretation" was in the air, some saw this working in the orator's favor, as if the heavens were in league with him, while others interpreted it as a signal for Henry to subside.

This struggle was still going on when New Hampshire, suddenly seeing its chance for glory as the state that made the Constitution official, generated enough enthusiasm to create a fifty-seven to forty-seven positive vote, winning the accolade as the ninth state to ratify. So twelve years after the Declaration of Independence, June 21, 1788, became the birthday of the Constitution.

Four days later, on June 25, Virginia accepted the Constitution on a close vote, and a remarkably spirited reception followed. Edmund Randolph spoke, attempting to justify his failure to sign the Constitution, but not making himself very clear. The real surprise was that Patrick Henry, ever the great thespian, responded with considerable grace, perhaps because he sensed that his cause was lost.

Just before the vote was taken, Henry said that if the numbers went against him, he would not cease to believe that he had been "overpowered in a good cause," but would dedicate himself to being a peaceful citizen, "working toward the safety, liberty, and happiness of the people." This was a wise decision, as the vote that was taken immediately after his remarks showed that he had lost by eighty-nine to seventy-nine.

Madison may have spent time in the celebratory proceedings before he set about preparing the express message that Hamilton had begged him to send. It would be July 2 before the dispatch Hamilton was waiting for arrived at the Poughkeepsie courthouse. He gave it a quick glance, then rose to read aloud Madison's announcement that Virginia had ratified the Constitution seven days earlier, on July 25. As Ron Chernow's excellent biography of Hamilton notes, "It must have been a deeply moving moment for Hamilton, the climax of his partnership with Madison."

Still, the fight in Poughkeepsie went on for three more weeks. It was July 26 before Madison and Jay helped Hamilton to pound through the thirty to twenty-seven vote that made New York the eleventh state, whereupon the old Continental Congress—with its newfound spirit—decided not to wait for North Carolina and Rhode Island. It called for elections to the new Congress—to be known from then on as the First

Congress. The United States had a blueprint for government that would actually improve with time, its unique genius being that the American people whom the leaders hardly dared to entrust with such responsibilities grew in stature to be worthy of their Constitution.

Ratification problems were still going on after this and, in fact, even after Washington was elected and inaugurated. Sadly, the process of making Washington president brought out some of the worst traits among the men he trusted to help him handle a task he approached with serious doubts.

Chapter Twenty-three

"LONG LIVE GEORGE WASHINGTON"

Washington's overwhelming prestige and victory has left many with the impression that he was the only man considered for the presidency. He was, in fact, one of twelve candidates, and Alexander Hamilton was sufficiently concerned about the outcome to engage in a scandalous—though entirely unnecessary—bit of tampering with the election.

Hamilton's own vision of the nation's future and his personal ambition both depended entirely on a Washington presidency. He lost no opportunity to remind his old commander that no one else could match the stability and confidence that Washington could give it. He was doubtless sincere in saying this, but he was also working toward his own dream: that the first president would then name him secretary of the treasury and allow him to create financial machinery that would drive a dominating federal government.

Hamilton, even as an island youth, was always able to sense just how older men thought and to impress them by seeming to have similar ideas. In his ability to mesh his thoughts with Washington's, this trait reached an astonishing peak. This was why, when he was little more than a boy, Hamilton could write and sign letters that exactly suited what the General meant to say. Now he repeatedly drew word pictures for Washington—examples of what might go wrong if anyone else were the chief executive—and these made certain the General would accept the job he dreaded.

There was never any serious doubt that Washington would agree to let himself be nominated for the presidency, even though he had the daunting task of explaining to Martha why he felt a compelling duty to give the new government the best possible start if the people wanted him to become their first president. It is clear that Washington, although uneasy about the stress of the presidential office, was pleased by the younger man's confidence in him. Washington and Hamilton became closer than they had ever been. During these decisive months of 1788, Washington's well-known apprehensions about possibly failing in this new political calling filled only a part of his mind. He could sometimes think of and write about the greater happiness that this new government might be able to create for Americans who had suddenly become "his people" in an almost mystical way—"when the seeds of happiness which are sown here shall begin to expand themselves and when every one (under his own vine and fig tree) shall begin to taste the fruits of freedom," as he once wrote in his diary.

But once Hamilton had Washington's agreement that he would stand for president, he was seized by a new concern. The defects in the electoral college system were already being discussed by the small coterie of political thinkers who understood it at all. Article II, Section 1 of the Constitution left it up to each state to decide how their electors would be chosen. Based on each state's total number of congressmen and senators, there were seventy-two electors at that time. Some of these were elected by the people (in five states), while others were appointed by state legislatures or by a governor and privy council. But no one could know whether these men would cast their votes exactly as they had indicated during the selection process or would make new choices that would alter the outcome.

One of the flaws in the original system was that the electors were to cast two votes each (at least one of which had to be for a person outside their state), but without specifying separate choices for president and vice president. The likeliest prospect was that all or almost all the electors would cast one of their votes for Washington, and that John Adams, who had heavy support from New England, would come in second with perhaps forty-five or fifty votes. But no one really knew how these electors would act. The fact that electors could—and were originally expected to—think for themselves was the wild card in the game.

The Constitutional Convention approved this system because delegates believed electors would be politically knowledgeable persons, acquainted with the records of the candidates, and therefore likely to make wiser choices than the common people. But because these men were given the freedom to make their own selections without regard to the wishes of the people, Hamilton fretted that a few electors with their own ideas or a sudden change of heart might withhold a few votes from Washington, while voting heavily for Adams. He might suddenly find that the unpredictable Adams was to be president, obliterating all the Hamiltonian plans for the future.

Hamilton's behavior became highly improper, bordering on criminal. Unwilling to risk the slim chance of seeing John Adams become president, Hamilton intervened by urging seven electors in three states to avoid voting for Adams, thus ensuring a Washington victory. The unnecessary action not only infuriated Adams when he learned of it, it made the unanimous Washington victory seem to have been a messy affair, which was not in the least true. It also started a torrent of anonymous "poison-pen" letters that a great many leaders began using indiscriminately to attack each other. Hamilton became the most aggressive practitioner of this outrage.

The old Constitutional Congress was still in power up to this point, and this was the organ that passed the Election Ordinance on September 13, 1788, providing for the selection of presidential electors in the states on January 7, 1789. It also proclaimed that next February 4 would be the date for electors to cast their ballots in the states. In all, sixty-nine electors voted in the first presidential election (because two Maryland electors and one Virginia elector failed to cast ballots). The New York legislature failed to choose its allotted eight electors by January 7, so it cast no electoral votes. Because of the different methods of elector selection and lack of records in some states, the total popular vote count is unknown. But of the 138 electoral votes cast, it was clear that Washington had one of the votes cast by each elector, for a total of sixty-nine votes (the maximum possible), making it appropriate to call him a unanimous choice, and that John Adams, even after the reduction created by Hamilton's tampering, was clearly elected vice president with thirty-four votes.

The other candidates had the following totals: John Jay, 9; Robert H. Harrison, 6; John Rutledge, 6; John Hancock, 4; George Clinton, 3; Samuel Huntington, 2; John Milton, 2; James Armstrong, 1; Edward Telfair, 1; and Benjamin Lincoln, 1.

General Washington was told on April 14, 1789, that he had been unanimously elected as the nation's first president. He arrived in New York on April 23, was entertained at dinner by Governor Clinton, and on Inauguration Day, April 30, was sworn in by Chancellor Robert Livingston. All the onlookers cried "Long Live George Washington, President of the United States!"

Not even his most optimistic moments could have summoned, nor could anyone there have believed, that exactly fourteen years later to the day (April 30, 1803), these United States would double their land area in one stroke when this same Robert Livingston became a co-signer of the Paris treaty for the purchase of Louisiana.

And yet, the people were prepared to believe a great deal, for the mere fact that George Washington was to lead the nation again had lifted the spirits of all Americans. Sensing this, an unaccustomed fear of failure came over Washington, and he told his friend Henry Knox,

> My movements to the chair of government will be accompanied by feelings not unlike those of a culprit who is going to the place of execution. I greatly apprehend that my countrymen will expect too much from me...and I without that competency of political skill, abilities, and inclination which is necessary to manage the helm.

His apprehension was well founded, for he genuinely disliked the nature of the presidential office and especially resented the friends and advisers who later convinced him that it was his duty to continue through a second term. His wife, who abhorred this decision for her own sake was even more appalled at the realization that he must go on with a life that was aging and sickening him. Nonetheless, Washington's terms as president were stamped with an image of character and judgment that left the office ennobled from that time forward.

These early days of his presidency were brightened for Washington by his reliance on two young men who had his entire confidence—and who had not yet become each other's enemies. Hamilton went forward brilliantly with his financial planning, and Madison, at this time, was being used as a one-man cabinet by Washington, advising him whom to select for the various posts. Madison himself was not eligible to head any department, because a rule he had planted in the Constitution disallowed members of Congress from filling offices that were created during the period of their congressional terms. But this made him Washington's favorite source of advice on the subject of appointments.

Madison was so close to Washington at this time that the latter once wrote him, "I am very troublesome, but you must excuse me. Ascribe it to friendship and confidence and you will do justice to my motives." The president even asked him, "Would it be safe to nominate Jefferson for Secretary of State without his consent?" Madison wrote to Jefferson that he had "not ventured on an answer" because he was not sure of Jefferson's mind.

Many accounts have said that Jefferson knew nothing of this appointment until his ship arrived in America. This cannot be true. Washington definitely went ahead with the nomination, for from Thomas Jefferson, who was in England on his way home from France, Washington received one of the first letters addressed to "THE PRESIDENT OF THE UNITED STATES." Jefferson protested that he did not really feel qualified to become the nation's first secretary of state, but assured George Washington that he would accept his judgment and serve in whatever capacity the new chief executive wished.

With his appointment to head the Treasury assured, Hamilton began expanding the department with extreme rapidity. The amount of office space it required and the number of employees were both growing by the week. When the War Department had just two employees and the State Department five, the Treasury Department had thirty-nine and was looking for more. As Hamilton also managed the Customs Service, which provided the government's greatest source of income, his own duties in setting up scores of new management systems almost overwhelmed his ability to keep working without let-up and with hardly time for sleep.

Hamilton imagined that others must see and appreciate what a heavy burden he was bearing for the nation, and he became short-tempered whenever he sensed the slightest disagreement with his views. Having reached the pinnacle to which he had so long aspired, he seemed unwilling to let any time pass in making further progress toward goals that were never openly stated. It was not surprising that critics circulated rumors that Hamilton wanted to make Washington king—and then become his heir. Most such wild theories, including the stories of his alleged secret bank accounts abroad and other repositories for the millions he was said to have stolen were totally false. If Hamilton was impatient, it was probably because he was an immigrant who had been climbing so long that it became oppressive to realize there were no more rungs to the ladder.

But having always succeeded in using his skillful letter writing to get what he wanted, Hamilton started the practice of writing anonymous letters that undercut other political leaders who blocked some of his plans. He attacked the motives and behavior of Jefferson, Madison, and Adams (even though this last was in Hamilton's own Federalist party). The issues of contention among these leaders almost always concerned money—credit, public debt, taxation. There were endless interpretations of how the Constitution treated these items and what the Treasury should be doing.

Hamilton's most earnest wish was to design every move the government made as a symbol of perfect trust, so that the country's money and its credit would be unquestioned. But the task of doing this was mind numbing. The total debt of $79 million was not a single debt, but a melange of about two-thirds national debt and one-third state debts. The government bonds covering these debts were at different interest rates. And the most contentious fact was that many of the bonds were no longer held by their first owners; many of them had been sold at a small fraction of their original value to other persons who hoped to be the ones reaping large profits if a sound government ever moved to pay them off.

The clash between Hamilton's clear and direct plan to pay the full value of every government debt to the present holders and Madison's bizarre idea that original holders had to be sought and found in order to divide the pay-off was the central point in a financial dispute that covered innumerable debts with a variety of dates and interest rates that would have taken a decade to untangle.

An open break between Hamilton and Madison became discernible on February 8, 1790, when the House of Representatives started to review Hamilton's Report on Public Credit. Hamilton was in an insecure position before the Congress when he came to defend his report. Despite the harsh anonymous letters that he and the Jefferson-Madison team had begun to launch at each other, Hamilton expected Madison to continue their old practice of supporting each other at critical moments. Madison, unquestionably the leading man in the lower house, could have made a huge difference for Hamilton. But after a three-day silence, Madison spoke out against Hamilton's key funding plan, which would pay any and every holder of a bond at full face value, while those who had sold them at fifteen or twenty cents on the dollar were simply out of luck.

Madison and Jefferson wanted the original holders to receive a substantial profit, even if they had sold their securities long ago. For, they insisted, most of those old holders had sold in desperation to clever speculators. The truth was, of course, that every bond was a case unto itself— some had been dumped because the original holders lost confidence in America, some because of a family's desperate need. The sales were at a variety of prices.

This time Madison's usual keen judgment appears to have been wrong. In the first place, he was making a rare about-face, contradicting a point he made publicly seven years earlier. In 1783, in his own report to the old Congress, he had written, "To discriminate the merits of these several descriptions of creditors would be a task equally unnecessary and invidious." In other words, no discrimination. Now it was just what he insisted on, and he was not at all clear about the ways he would determine all the facts about each bond and each investor. Hamilton was right—and George Washington was on his side.

Madison's approach would have been like giving the United States government the right to interfere in business transactions of the past, changing the distribution of profits as it saw fit. It was little wonder that Washington, who thought "a deal is a deal," supported Hamilton's position and was disturbed by Madison's apparent departure from the logic that Washington had always found in his views. Washington really wanted nothing so much as for both sides to stop what he was appalled to see: allowing a personal vendetta to interfere with their devotion to the nation.

Although the president correctly blamed both sides for such behavior, there is no doubt that Hamilton's arguments gradually prevailed. As Washington usually sided with Hamilton on specific issues, he was less attracted to arguments put forth by Madison and Jefferson and inevitably less trusting of their judgment.

Chapter Twenty-four

THE TRUTH ABOUT RHODE ISLAND

Washington's government had been operating for five months before North Carolina, the twelfth state, ratified the Constitution on November 21, 1789. There was still one to go: Rhode Island.

Jefferson had dismissed that state as the one "of least importance." While Rhode Island heard many angry insults from the rest of the nation, the truth was that many good citizens there were struggling to dislodge a bad state government.

After all that has been painfully reported about Rhode Island's refusal to pay its debts to the Union and the sneering attitude toward this state that was taken by the other twelve, a number of balancing facts should be recorded. Many of them appear in a plucky little volume that was written by a student of that day—another young patriot—who went on to become a prominent citizen.

Theodore Foster was studying American history in a Brown University seminar when he began to record events that he hoped would become better known. His very slim book was titled *Minutes of the Convention Held at South Kingstown, Rhode Island, in March, 1790, Which Failed to Adopt the Constitution of the United States.* Not surprisingly, this title did not propel the book to early fame. But Foster himself was destined to be a success.

It was clear that Rhode Island was among the worst sufferers from the Revolutionary War. It was last to be evacuated by the departing British troops, and its seaports' reliance on the shipping trade meant that all the dangers and ills of this form of commerce blighted its income to an extent that other states sampled in a less virulent form.

It was also quite true, however, that Rhode Island, as a state, had to be held responsible for a period when unsavory leaders virtually drowned their people in a sea of worthless paper money. When a state failed to meet its obligations, the others were bound to regard it as one great problem, making little allowance for its internal differences. All the while, the courageous citizens who urged sound—if painful—policies tried gallantly to gain the political power that would allow them to chart a new course. The subject is of broader importance because Rhode Island's problems were simply an extreme version of issues that touched nearly all the states.

In his book, Foster made it plain that he was proud of his state and hoped to portray the "evolution of the commercial republic of Rhode Island in the second century after its founding by bands of exiles for conscience's sake."

As Foster told it, Rhode Island's inability to obtain credits abroad, as some other states were doing, became a central part of its financial problem. Rhode Island could hardly hope to find lenders in Europe when it had such a lowly standing in its own country. The nation's richest states were just barely credit-worthy, so there was no way for its poorest state to borrow funds and start rebuilding its shattered economy. Rhode Island's inability to stabilize its paper currency made it impossible to pay its share of the Continental debt, and its reputation as a delinquent made any form of borrowing impossible.

Foster admitted that there seemed to be some hope in 1785, when the Continental Congress exerted limited power to regulate importations and interstate commerce. But while this encouraged states to move in the right direction of sound monetary principles, each state was still free to make decisions of its own about the infusion of paper money. This depended on each state's internal politics. A few states—Virginia, Pennsylvania, and Connecticut—tried hard to keep their currency sound. Rhode Island's government, at the other extreme, was the worst offender.

So this moment of opportunity in 1785 only raised false hopes in Theodore Foster's state. Any hope of salvation was quickly ruined by an election in February, 1786. The state's Paper Money Party grew in strength, meaning that many towns were crying for a new issue of paper currency—which Foster recognized as being poisonous to the health of any economy. The new party in power responded to the apparent popular demand and quickly issued £100,000 of paper money, which was to be apportioned to the people.

Inevitably, merchants began refusing to sell their goods for the worthless paper. The government countered with special laws called "force bills"—they forced shopkeepers to accept the state's paper money or face heavy penalties. Shopkeepers refused, even closed their doors. As a result, people who thought themselves richer because of the paper currency found themselves poorer than ever, unable to buy even basic necessities.

Numerous towns—Providence, Bristol, Newport, and others—tried hard to work out political compromises, but the state assembly continued to pass ruinous laws that worsened the bitterness between classes. Judges who gallantly tried to bring moderation in the war between desperate shoppers and besieged shopkeepers were brought before the unfriendly legislature, charged with attempting to take the law into their own hands.

In June 1787, Foster recorded, the fight to repudiate these wrong policies showed signs of hope. Reformers managed to repeal the force bill that made life so difficult and dangerous for both businessmen and their customers. Once again, this proved to be a false signal. By the following March, an ominous turn saw the reformers under heavy attack. Newport's charter was withdrawn because it had sided with the reformers. The state refused to carry out its obligation to Massachusetts to return certain offenders of Shays's Rebellion. In effect, the lawbreakers were the ones being honored and protected. A state was in league with the rebels against another state.

Several leading citizens of Rhode Island did their best to be heard by the nation when they regretted their state's absence from the Philadelphia convention. On May 11, 1787, thirteen individuals signed a letter expressing regret that their state should not be represented on so momentous an occasion. But, says the letter, "the result of your deliberations...we still hope may finally be approved and adopted by this state, for which we pledge our influence and best exertions." The letter was read to the Convention on May 28 by Gouverneur Morris, and, "being read, was ordered to lie on the table for further consideration."

Meanwhile, the other states in the Union were not shining examples of empathy and understanding. Even the most knowledgeable leaders showed no visible signs of conferring with the Rhode Islanders who were reform-minded or offering useful suggestions. They took part in the general sport of calling the state "Rogue's Island." The usually sedate *Connecticut Magazine* addressed the offending state with this rhyming couplet:

Hail realm of rogues, renown'd for fraud and guile.
All hail, ye knav'ries of yon little isle.

And the *Providence Gazette,* in its April 14, 1787 issue, turned on its own state by contributing a clumsy quatrain that pretended to find Rhode Island's name unmentionable:

Each weekly print new lists of cheats proclaims,
proud to enroll their knav'ries and their names;
The wiser race, the snares of law to shun
Like Lot from Sodom, from R——e I——d run.

But blaming an entire state for the misdeeds of a despicable leadership that deliberately chose hopeless policies as a way of holding power was pointless and unfair. Young Foster showed that determined reformers were fighting to be heard at every turn. And later, when other states were considering whether to adopt the new Constitution, these challengers tried seven times to call a ratification convention. They were blocked each time, even in March 1790, when they seemed to have a chance of success.

Undaunted, they promptly set a new date for the following May. The press in other states taunted them, seeming to consider Rhode Island unwelcome in any case. And the governments of other states cut off all commercial intercourse, announcing heavy penalties for anyone who traded with the Rhode Islanders.

But the next attempt to take back the state government told a new story. On May 29, 1790, a full six months after all the other entrants had crossed the line, the group of determined Rhode Island citizens rammed through a takeover of power from the government that had dominated with wrong policies and made it an outcast among the states. The reformers joyously ratified the Constitution, making the Union of thirteen states whole again. It did not take a week or even a day: the national disapproval and the insults vanished like smoke in a fresh wind.

So wholeheartedly did the already-functioning Washington administration welcome these last ratifiers that the first president and his secretary of state, Thomas Jefferson, waited only two days after Congress adjourned on August 12, 1790, to leave together on a ten-day trip, partly by water, to rejoice with the people of Rhode Island.

Few of the excitements of this historic period were as great as the genuine joy with which the entire nation welcomed back the state that seemed lost. Like the emotion always attached to the parable of the prodigal son, the nation realized how much it had missed the completeness of the original thirteen. The states had never felt so truly united.

Theodore Foster, of course, was not only the chronicler of this triumph. As the state's internal struggle went on, he became one of the reformers. As such, he joined the new national government as a United States congressman from 1790 to 1803. He also went on to earn a Dartmouth University degree and became a Brown University trustee.

Chapter Twenty-five

FIRST FRUITS

The great document these leaders took part in creating contained more wisdom than the men who assembled it displayed. While the creators of the Constitution became their own political creatures subject to the forces around them, the document containing their thoughts put the country's needs and interests first.

With remarkable speed, the election of new congressmen and senators was completed, and the two houses of Congress went to work with a will. Only male voters made the selections, of course, and state laws determined whether all white men were eligible to vote or had to meet property requirements as well. The new members would not be paid for months, because the federal government had no money. But most were men of substance, even though property ownership was not federally required for membership. And most of the members knew each other from having been in the old Congress or in other forms of political life for many years. Yet each morning, it was as if the sun were rising on a new nation. The hastily assembled new Congress began to act.

James Madison was elected to the House of Representatives and not to the Senate, which had been his first intention. This outcome was due to another piece of cruel political work—on Patrick Henry's part in this case.

Madison would have run for a Senate seat, but Henry, his old nemesis, tried to undermine Madison's place in politics. Before Madison realized the threat, Henry had arranged for James Monroe, Madison's friend and a protege of Jefferson's, to seek the seat in the new Senate. Henry even circulated a damaging untrue story about Madison's willingness to give up shipping rights on the Mississippi. With Monroe running for the seat that Madison had sought, both men found themselves ill at ease with each other and their friendship briefly turned contentious. Madison, however, easily gained support when he sought a seat in the lower house, the house he created, where he could most readily introduce new legislation. Yet he was strangely lax about keeping a promise he made at the Convention. He was still unconvinced that there was real need for a bill of rights.

It seemed that Madison was one of those who had a bored reaction to the subject of rights, as if these amendments only assured citizens that they would be safe from persecutions that no one thought of imposing. Alexander Hamilton, in writing *Federalist Paper* number eighty-four, said exactly that, even calling it potentially hazardous to bring such subjects into popular discussion. "Why declare that things shall not be done which there is no power to do?" he asked. "Why should it be said that the liberty of the press shall not be restrained when no power is given by which restrictions may be imposed?"

Others thought the bills of rights that already existed in the constitutions of most states were adequate and that it was a new insult to the states to imply that the federal government had to be invoked to confirm the existing rights of all Americans.

Even when he heard that George Mason and Patrick Henry had joined in saying that "nothing would quiet the fears of the people," and Henry was talking about "the tyranny of Philadelphia," Madison insisted that he "never thought the omission of a bill of rights a material defect." Those who agreed with him, as Hamilton did, said such a bill would prove to be "a mere parchment barrier when worst needed." The minority of

political persons who took this position argued that in a popular government, it is the people who can most easily endanger liberty, so that a bill
to protect the people was meaningless.

Jefferson, on the contrary, not only favored such a bill, but wanted to
see it expanded to ban standing armies, apparently agreeing with Elbridge
Gerry's outrageous remark at the Convention that such armies were "like
a tumescent penis; An excellent assurance of domestic tranquillity, but a
dangerous temptation to foreign adventure."

Madison was impressed, however, when Jefferson wrote again on
March 15, 1789, that the strength of a bill of rights "is the legal check
which it puts into the hands of the judiciary." In other words, the courts
would have no practical means of acting against an injustice unless there
were a law that victims could cite when they asked for relief.

This, plus evidence that his own political standing seemed to be hurt
by his resistance to the issue, brought a sudden decision. Madison's mind
was made up. Because he had clearly been preparing for many months,
he made short work of framing his proposed ten amendments that were
to become probably the best known and most-often mentioned portion
of the Constitution—the Bill of Rights with its famous First Amendment
which guarantees freedom of religion, speech, press, and the right to
assemble and to petition for a redress of grievances.

By June 8 Madison was ready to make a long speech and to present
a complete list of rights proposals. He spoke more determinedly than
usual, even though the House seemed apathetic, saying that all power is
subject to abuse and should be guarded against by constitutionally securing "the great rights of mankind." Even if they were paper barriers, he
argued, they might educate the majority against acts to which they might
be inclined.

Spirited debate arose before passage. A few opponents, such as South
Carolina's Aedanus Burke, thought the whole process was just froth and
that they were wasting their time. But in the end, few changes were made
in Madison's language. A committee dropped the important principle
against unreasonable searches and seizures at one point, but the House
restored it.

The inevitable process of hearing objections to these proposed amendments and then sending the text to all the states for approval seemed endless at the time. The House members who opposed Madison argued that the bills of rights enacted by most states were ineffectual. It was widely said that the states often trampled on the rights of their citizens without regard to their own state bills of rights. Madison nevertheless insisted that the federal context would alter this, and he proved to be more right than he knew. The amendments he drew up riveted the attention of federal officials and jurists to the rights issues that had been neglected.

In the months of the state-by-state ratification efforts, inevitable new opposition arose. For example, Virginia was the last state to ratify—at one point rejecting the First, Sixth, Ninth, and Tenth Amendments—but the opponents' tactics backfired. On December 15, 1791, the process of state ratification was completed, making the Bill of Rights a part of the Constitution. And as George Mason had said, it did "give quiet to the people."

In the course of time, most legal authorities and most citizens have come around to believing that specific guarantees of this kind do create a defensive wall of confidence that they would not wish to dispense with. Even Hamilton's example about press freedom was clearly wrong, for without the First Amendment's specific guarantee of this right, one could easily imagine a panicked Congress, in time of great alien threats, crafting "temporary" legislation to stifle discussion that an insecure administration wished to prevent. At such a time, it would be made to seem unpatriotic to oppose the urgent action. Having the amendment to stand against such an act would undoubtedly stiffen the determination to uphold the cherished principle.

The ten amendments were adopted virtually just as Madison wrote them. Not one was radically changed in form or reduced in force. Madison wished for the amendments to be incorporated into the body of the Constitution, but at the last moment Roger Sherman insisted that they be shown as later additions. Irving Brant, a leading Madison biographer, says that although Madison didn't realize it, this actually "added dignity and force to the collective mandates."

Here are the first ten amendments, known as the Bill of Rights, that Madison created. It should be noted that the numbers shown are only for ease of reading. Numbers were not specifically assigned in the resolution proposing the amendments. The first ten amendments, along with two others that failed to be ratified, were proposed by Congress on September 25, 1789, when they passed the Senate, having previously passed the House on September 24. Ratification was completed on December 15, 1791, when the eleventh state, Virginia, approved these amendments, as there were fourteen states in the Union by that time. (The two proposed amendments that failed to be ratified dealt with the ratio of representation to population in the House and with the compensation of members of Congress.)

First, Congress shall make no law respecting an establishment of religion, or prohibiting the free exercise thereof; or abridging the freedom of speech, or of the press; or the right of the people peaceably to assemble, and to petition the Government for a redress of grievances.

Second, a well-regulated Militia, being necessary to the security of a free people, the right of the people to keep and bear Arms, shall not be infringed.

Third, no Soldier shall in time of peace be quartered in any house, without the consent of the Owner, nor in time of war, but in a manner prescribed by law.

Fourth, the right of the people to be secure in their persons, houses, papers, and effects against unreasonable searches and seizures shall not be violated, and no Warrants shall issue but upon probable cause, supported by Oath or affirmation, and particularly describing the place to be searched, and the persons or things to be seized.

Fifth, no person shall be held to answer for a capital, or otherwise infamous crime, unless on a presentment or indictment of a Grand Jury, except in cases arising in the land or naval forces, or in the Militia, when in actual service in time of War or public danger; nor shall any person be subject for the same offence to be twice put in jeopardy of life or limb; nor shall be compelled in any criminal case to be a witness against himself, nor be deprived of life, liberty, or property without due process of law; nor shall private property be taken for public use without just compensation.

Sixth, in all criminal prosecutions, the accused shall enjoy the right to a speedy and public trial, by an impartial jury of the State and district wherein the crime shall have been committed, which district shall have been previously ascertained by law, and to be informed of the nature and cause of the accusation; to be confronted with the witnesses against him; to have compulsory process for obtaining witnesses in his favor, and to have the Assistance of Counsel for his defense.

Seventh, in suits at common law, where the value in controversy shall exceed twenty dollars, the right of trial by jury shall be preserved, and no fact tried by a jury shall be otherwise re-examined in any Court of the United States than according to the rules of the common law.

Eighth, Excessive bail shall not be required, nor excessive fines imposed, nor cruel and unusual punishments inflicted.

Ninth, the enumeration in the Constitution of certain rights shall not be construed to deny or disparage others retained by the people. [That is, the fact that some rights are enumerated herein does not mean that no other rights may also be retained by the people.]

Tenth and finally, the powers not delegated to the United States by the Constitution, nor prohibited by it to the States, are reserved to the States respectively, or to the people. [This means that "No State shall violate rights which the federal government guarantees to the people in the Constitution, such as the equal rights of conscience, or the freedom of the press, or the trial by jury in criminal cases, etc. Because the first nine were to protect the people from having their rights abused by the Congress, this last is to assure that the people are protected from having their most essential rights abused by a state.]

The brevity of these amendments retained the style of the original document, and most of them were based on long-established common-law rights. More important, each amendment possessed the same rare power to serve as a small pool from which a fountain of rights or exceptions might spring. For example, the Sixth Amendment requires that in a criminal case, the prosecution not only produce witnesses who might help the accused, but that it engage in an active process, compelling witnesses to testify when they are needed. In the case of *Mattox v. United States* (1895), however, it was held that the testimony of a witness sworn upon a former trial and since deceased is admissible against the accused in the present case when a copy of a stenographic report of the former testimony is supported by an oath of the stenographer that it is a correct transcript of the notes and of the testimony of the deceased witness.

Madison found himself a changed person from the one who had been a member of the old Continental Congress. Although inconvenienced, he was undaunted by the fact that he and all the other congressmen were beginning their work as "volunteers," waiting for the new government to collect money for their salaries. But his zeal was redoubled. Apart from his work on the Bill of Rights, Madison's anxiety about getting the nation on the road to solvency was so great that he fretted when other members leisurely took their time to eat breakfast and read their morning paper while he wanted to get started. It was the financial discussions that he was especially anxious to begin. He knew that sound financial structure alone could set this government apart from the ineffectual Confederation. Even if his colleagues continued to start their days in their own way, the results of his leadership were spectacular and instantly noticeable.

In December 1790, the disagreements between Jefferson and Madison on one side and Hamilton on the other, even on the latter's key subject of finance, reached their boiling point when Hamilton proposed that Congress establish a national bank. The Senate voted for this Bank of the United

States at once, and a House committee easily approved it, but Madison attacked it on constitutional grounds. He called it unnecessary, but more than that, completely unauthorized by the Constitution. In his role as a key congressional voice who so often spoke on finance, Madison was now a fierce opponent of the man who helped him to create the Constitution.

After a great debate, the House passed the bill thirty-nine to twenty, but Jefferson made a strong stand against it, while Hamilton gave Washington his own positive view. Washington sided with the latter and signed the bill. It made no sense to him that one could not establish a national bank simply because no one had inserted those exact words into the Constitution. It was another part of the great divide that has existed ever since between those who wish to limit action to what is strictly permitted by the Constitution and those who find a myriad "implied powers" necessary in order to round out the effective functioning of government, with the latter most often victorious.

Hamilton was genuine in his wish to make America's word a symbol of absolute reliability; he was also an over-aggressive politician who, soon after ratification, began to show no resemblance to the Publius who worked so closely with Madison and made an almost superhuman effort to save the Constitution that had been created. The competition between the two bitter political parties would cut across a wide swath of issues. Dominance in New England was mainly in the hands of the Federalists, who made the old word used by the pro-Constitution forces into a party name.

Hamilton was the most forceful man in this party, though the emphasis on his law practice prevented him from being the formal party leader. Jefferson's adherents were strongest in the South and West, and they were called the Republicans, implying that they were true believers in republican government and not secret monarchists as they believed the Federalists to be. The intensifying contest between these two forces, like many political enmities, would tend to contribute energy to the nation's development, although the negative aspects often seemed needlessly painful.

As a notable example, Jefferson and Madison, with their greater concern for the interests of farmers and expansion to the west, created a huge leap forward in 1803 when the Louisiana Purchase doubled the country's land area. Jefferson agonized about having acted as an unwilling "loose constructionist" in acquiring property that was not foreseen in the Constitution. But he wanted the land and kept it, regardless of principle. Hamilton's forces, for their part, saw that the acquisition was hugely popular; they promptly forgot their opposition to westward expansion and cheered the purchase in an attempt to win a western following. Each side clearly showed that opportunism trumped other considerations.

Over the years most political thinkers have felt that, on balance, the nation has grown stronger by following the Hamiltonian approach. Dating back to 1791, when Hamilton's argument won the important permission to create a Bank of the United States, its new system of coinage, highly respected dollar, and instantly admired currency control combined to empower the country's business class as Hamilton predicted. These wealthier Americans, who were mainly creditors, never again had to fear that they would be forced to take worthless paper money in payment of sales they made or debts they were paid for. The rural population—consisting mainly of debtors and less spectacularly prosperous persons—has usually had enough voting power and, hence, political might, to demand assistance whenever its ability to pay has faltered. The confidence this balance of power has built on both sides has been a tonic to development.

So Madison and Hamilton, who swung from being allies to becoming opponents throughout their troubled acquaintance, went on leading the nation's forward march. But now they disagreed again, exchanging blows as they marched. They were far different from the young men who, only three years prior, conferred in Mann's Tavern, Annapolis, where they planned the overthrow of the Confederate government. But Madison, at least, never forgot that the Constitution owed much of its existence to Hamilton.

The nation, too, was different. It set about developing ways to cope with its vast territory—adopting a combination of laws and practical methods that facilitated the management of such a huge domain. The country that had been unable to improve its connecting roads suddenly began sprouting throughways as a healthy plant puts out new branches. By April 1791, the first toll road (patterned on Britain's turnpikes) was inaugurated when a sixty-two mile stretch was opened between Philadelphia and Lancaster. While highways existed within a single state, the idea was soon given interstate status, so that by 1810 three hundred turnpike corporations were operating in New England alone.

In these feverish moments, the Industrial Revolution came to America, indirectly aided by the new feeling of change and development that facilitated everything. Samuel Slater arrived from England with methods he learned there for using steam engines to power weaving machines. He set up the first powered factory in Pawtucket, Rhode Island, in 1790.

The next three decades saw the onset of America's unique ability to send people and merchandise to distant parts. First came canals and steamboats, then the expansion of railroads that did much of the selling of the West. The railroads' ads enticed people to settle in western areas and served to knit the continent together.

America's brilliant beginning that seemed to be in such deep trouble only five years earlier was suddenly greater than any of the Constitution makers could have dreamed. The ordinary people in whom Madison so passionately believed accepted the principles and guidance of the Constitution he helped create for them. In each of more than twenty decades since the Philadelphia Convention, some part of the growing population has seemed to lose its bearings, but it cannot be mere good fortune that a majority has managed to right itself every time and hold fast to the basic course that preserved democratic government for the benefit of all. It is a close call, requiring great restraint in every instance, and one can only hope that future Americans will not slacken.

Madison's foresight was astonishing. At the time of the first census, in 1790, when the inhabitants numbered 3,929,214 people and almost the entire population lived in the countryside—with only one-thirtieth residing in cities—Madison looked ahead more than a century and estimated that in 1929 the Union would have 192 million souls. This huge overestimate was a mere guess that mainly showed what a torrent of growth he expected (the actual number in 1929 was 121,767,000). But very accurately, Madison foresaw a republic where farmers would be outnumbered and outvoted by laborers in teeming cities. This shift in proportion of farmers and city workers qualifies as an inspired forecast of the highest order. The 1930 census showed that the nation had ninety-three cities with over one hundred thousand population, and the official "Center of Population" was in Indiana and drifting steadily westward.

Among all the leaders, it was Madison whose qualities and contributions were lauded by his fellow Americans. Delegates rated Madison's role in creating the Constitution much greater than he saw himself. The brilliant Albert Gallatin, an outstanding cabinet officer who would almost certainly have been one of America's presidents if he had not been foreign-born, called Madison "the ablest man that ever sat in the American Congress." The towering John Marshall, a political rival, defining true eloquence as the ability to convince said, "Mr. Madison was the most eloquent man I ever heard." And nearly everyone who knew both friends well insisted that Madison was definitely Jefferson's superior in soundness and judgment. His Virginia Plan gave the basic structure of the eventual Constitution. The concepts of direct elections and majority rule, the presidential office, and the national judiciary were his creations. He arranged for the powers of the Congress to be enumerated. He foresaw the admission of new states, the need for federal regulation of trade, and even provided for federal officers to be bound by oath. Among a half-dozen key leaders, Madison was unquestionably the one indispensable man.

He did achieve his heart's desire, for his spreading national fame gave him an advantage in the unusual competition for the hand of Dolley Todd. Despite having seen two husbands die prematurely, one in despair over a burden of debt and one with yellow fever, Dolley's beauty, striking figure, and delightful personality caused almost every single man who met her to become a suitor. Having heard of this marvel, and knowing Aaron Burr to be a friend of Dolley's, he asked Burr to arrange an introduction. Dolley wrote to her cousin, Eliza Collins, in great excitement: "Thou must come to me. Aaron Burr says that the great little Madison has asked to be brought to see me this evening." Their reaction on meeting has been described as "adoration on his part, admiration or more on hers."

Madison made his courtship clear from the first meeting. At age forty-one, after almost a decade of living in the shadow of a mindless romance with a girl half his age, he had a Madisonian determination not to lose this time.

But there was no sign of the calculating Madison mind as he and Dolley corresponded while being quarantined and kept apart by waves of malaria in the Virginia homes they were visiting. In August, when Dolley wrote that she was finally on her way to him, Madison answered: "I received some days ago your precious favor from Fredericksburg. I cannot express, but hope you will conceive the joy it gave me."

He and Dolley began their married life on September 15, 1794. After eleven years of marriage, the letters they exchanged have been described as "more like puppy love than grown married people." When Dolley had a terribly painful ulcerated leg and was fearful of letting anyone touch it, Secretary of State Madison declared that he would be her nurse. For three months, while President Jefferson agonized because he relied so much on Madison to keep major issues in order, Secretary Madison handled the nation's affairs by mail, because Dolley came first.

◌◯◌

Caught up as Madison was in the crude politics of the day, he may be at least partially excused for having fired back when Hamilton's blatantly harsh tactics accumulated. But to his eternal credit, when Hamilton was no longer alive to raise objection, Madison chose to remember only the most favorable part of their convoluted relationship. In 1831, when there could have been no fear of a rejoinder, he went farther than before in recalling the man who was his only equal as a hero in the fight to make the Constitution the supreme law of the land. Said Madison, "If his theory of government deviated from the Republican standard, he had the candour to avow it, and the greater merit of cooperating faithfully in maturing and supporting a system which was not his choice."

Fairness to a fallen rival may be expected in a man of honor, but there is something far more unusual in Madison's attitude toward his brainchild, the Constitution itself. What he wanted it to mean to every American, living and yet to come, is shown in a simple remark he wrote to

George Washington on February 3, 1788, for it reveals how genuinely he respected each person's right to choose or to reject this document. He was reporting on the agonizingly close ratification fight that was expected in New York, where the intensity of the debates made it hard to be open-minded about the other side. In giving Washington his assessment of the chances for success, he mentioned some of the opposition voters who had dishonest motives (such as squatters who feared that the new Constitution would threaten their improper occupation of land that was not theirs). But then he described the bulk of the opposing group that they were facing with these words that show his complete generosity to appropriate opposition: "Add to these the honest doubting people, and they make a powerful host." Not "a formidable threat," as he might have been expected to say about the opposition. The word "host" implies respect. His most intense enemies of that very moment were honored as a great and respected assemblage. Such an insistence on according each person an equal right to his own contrary opinion on a seriously contested issue is not only rare, in the political arena it is singular.

The man who always arrived early worked slavishly to make sure his Constitution would have this precious right woven into its fabric. It is as if there is an unseen line in almost every clause: "On this subject, the nation's policy will ultimately be determined by the combined opinion of all the honest doubting people."

Epilogue

A NEW PLACE IN WORLD HISTORY

To the Greeks before the Christian era, a constitution expressed the whole of the national life. It was the expression of a particular life that the state was now electing to live, a certain theory of existence it had determined to put into force.

Even if not written or graven in stone, the constitution existed—like a living thing. Isocrates, an Athenian orator and rhetorician who lived from 436 to 338 BC, was thought to have summed it up when he said, "The Constitution is the soul of the state." But half a century later, Aristotle refined this by saying, "The Constitution is the state."

James Madison had gone to Philadelphia with ancient scholars as his steady companions. He knew not only what the school of Aristotle put into the Athenian Constitution in 350 BC, he also knew the words on broken pieces of stone found in the Athens place of assembly dating back at least to Archbishop Kreon in 683 BC. He reviewed the thoughts of these savants in the candle-lit hours of his sleepless nights, and he held them in a pocket, literally close to his heart, when he rose to address the Philadelphia Convention. At those moments, he was more like the ancient Greeks in his pocket than he was like the Americans who surrounded him. He felt able to predict what ways would endure for a time, what might make for more stable human security and happiness.

Some of the fascinating discoveries about an even earlier period in Greece that would be made by German archaeologist Heinrich Schliemann came nearly a century after this, so Madison could not have known that there had been fine Minoan palaces, a complex economy, and a sophisticated Sumerian religion as far back as 1600 BC. Madison would have loved to know of these achievements and to theorize why they fell.

But Madison studied the thoughts of Thucydides and his theories of a time when the Greeks were not a fixed population at all. The area that came to be called Hellas probably saw frequent movement of races, with families and tribes gradually establishing enough security to imagine a choice of policies for their future. But nothing appeared in "writing" until the Athenians began keeping an "Archon-List"—a record of names of succeeding archbishops. Some three hundred sixty names have been found carved on stone and left in the Athenian Agora or Place of Assembly. There are also inscriptions that pay great compliments to certain persons and later, highly negative inscriptions, even ugly stories about a corrupt Spartan who is called an adulterer and wife-snatcher. These imply the likelihood that active political clashes were common, perhaps revealing examples of constitutions or—most important of all—showing what mistakes they might have made. What Madison knew for sure was that by the time of the fourth century BC, a constitution was thought of as a necessity for any nation or city-state.

In a sense, Aristotle and Madison can be called more alike than they were like other men of their own time, for they were dreaming and pretending more than they wanted to admit. Aristotle dreamt because he defined a citizen as one who is capable of ruling and is ruled in turn. But he recognized that most of Greek history did not bear this out. Even some great Greek leaders, from whom much was expected, betrayed and disappointed their people. And Aristotle's aspirations were pitched much too high for the many poor communities that had to find a way of governing themselves.

The Americans who prevailed in Philadelphia pitched their dreams even higher, expecting to open a new way of life to people all over the planet. Even as they sweltered in August heat, many of the delegates kept themselves going with the thought that this nation must endure because the entire world was looking to the new American concept of freedom. And because of the bounteous lands and good fortune the United States enjoyed, these new dreamers came closer to their aspirations than the old ones did, though these are still early days.

Looking at constitutions from the beginnings of civilization to the present moment, there is nothing that compares with the document that was produced in Philadelphia. Although James Madison studied so many works that were available from the past, he seemed to have no thought of copying what others had learned, but rather preferred to draw on the history of what happened to them, even to profit from their oversights, and to reach firm conclusions of his own.

Madison went far beyond the Greek examples in researching foreign constitutions. The Roman Empire was an obvious model to study, since no other nation ever maintained peaceful control over so great an area or so large a population. With an estimated territory of five million square kilometers and a population of sixty million inhabitants, Rome's long-term stability was almost beyond belief. Facing the skepticism of a general public and a roomful of fellow delegates who doubted that such a huge expanse as the United States and an increasingly mixed population could be shaped into a unified republic, Madison recalled the three main elements that had worked for Rome:

- A system of taxation dependent on the active cooperation of the local elite
- A social order underpinned by criminal and civil justice systems that also depended on the local elite's cooperation with Roman agents
- Political regulation linking each civic community to the Roman State as represented by the discretionary power of the provincial governors

Madison could not be sure how the United States would fare on the first two points. He was certain it would fall far short of Rome in point number three. There would be no area leaders like Pontius Pilate to enforce the capital's wishes.

This helps to explain why Madison was so set on getting a provision into the Constitution on the absolute primacy of United States laws over any possibly conflicting state law. The other delegates thought it was enough to say that the Constitution was the supreme law of the land. Madison wanted an added statement making it plain that there must never be any state law or act that clashed with the Constitution. He even thought of a clause threatening military action in case this rule were violated. He always feared the lack of this provision was a weakness, for he knew the absence of it caused many older federations to collapse.

Madison's studies went even beyond Greece and Rome. There has been speculation that he may have read an admired ancient Japanese constitution, for its seventeen paragraphs are beautifully clear and elegant. And since he was a Freemason, it is even likelier that he studied constitutions dealing with the rules that working masons had created for members of their craft, such as the admired Constitution of the Masons of Strasbourg, dated 1459. This contained items such as, "If any of the articles in these statutes should prove to be too strict and severe, or others too light and mild, then may those who are of the fraternity, by a majority, modify, decrease, or increase such articles," and, "Two masters shall not share in the same work or building, unless it be a small one, which can be finished in the course of a year."

In the end, the Constitution that Madison fathered was a new creation, not at all like anything seen or heard of before. One might expect, however, that such a uniquely successful document, widely hailed as it has been, had gone on to become the world's standard for nearly all nations—or certainly for nations that have usually been congenial to American policies. But nothing could be farther from the truth. In the Law Library of the Library of Congress, in Washington, D.C., there is a set of metal bookshelves about ten feet wide and rising from floor to ceiling. These are entirely devoted to the current constitutions of virtually every existing sovereign nation. Looking at dozens of constitutions of governments both small and large, there is virtually nothing reminiscent of the American Constitution.

This might be seen as a sign that America's size and wealth have not made others feel impelled to align themselves with it. Surely there has been no unwanted imposition of influence on the subject. American diplomats, presidents, or secretaries of state have not pressed foreign nations (other than small new nations that have actually asked for advice of this kind) to mimic the Philadelphia product as they draw up their own constitutions. But the disinterest in America's example seems to be on two levels: First, other countries have a stylistic feeling very different from Americans. What we think of as brevity or simplicity apparently seems curt and inadequate to them. They want to spell things out at much greater length.

Perhaps more to the point, they feel that the chance to write a constitution presents an important opportunity as a way of continuing to govern. They write several times as many pages and between one hundred fifty and two hundred articles. They are inclined to do as the modern Greeks do—to give the exact wording of what must be said and done on each occasion. For example, although the Greek constitution assures everyone of total religious freedom, it carefully spells out the exact wording of the oath to be taken by members of Parliament, which must include the words, "in the name of the Holy Consubstantial and Indivisible Trinity," regardless of the individual's religion. After this, however, it is stipulated that the parliamentarians enjoy unrestricted freedom of opinion and right to vote according to their conscience.

But to make sure this freedom is not misused, their constitution says they may not "be a partner or administrator of any enterprise that owns or manages a radio or TV station or publishes a newspaper with country-wide circulation in Greece."

Albania, typical of small countries, has a constitution three times as long as America's, with 183 articles. It not only delineates in great detail how prosecutors and judges are to be selected, but also touches on points that might disqualify a high court judge. His term ends when he:

- is convicted of a crime
- reaches the age of sixty-five

or

- does not appear for duty without reason for more than six months

Canada's constitution seems longer than it is because of the need to include both English and French versions, as well as to explain the Constitution Act of 1867, which united Canada, Nova Scotia, and New Brunswick. And the constitution of the Peoples Republic of China has to explain the fact that it is not intended to be an enduring document, but rather a temporary, programmatic instrument to serve the purposes of the state during its progress toward the ultimate goal of communism. (For example, it states, "The Agrarian Reform Law of 1950 was aimed at the eventual collectivization of agriculture.")

If all these other countries want to spell things out so minutely, it is their affair. But it is hard for an American to keep from being somewhat proud that even in the brevity of our Constitution, we signal a willingness to grant the maximum latitude and freedom of choice by using bare instructions and allowing the people of all future generations to interpret them liberally.

If we call it heartwarming that others have their own ways of writing "the soul of their nations" and we Americans have our own, the greater question is whether America's Constitution is such a faithful written expression that it deserves to be regarded as the soul of the nation itself. There is little doubt that it really has a form of life, a spark that seems to make mere words on paper act like living things, capable of imparting confidence and hope.

Most astonishing, however, is what made Madison different from any other thinker or innovator. In the end he copied no one, but defied everyone. For Madison's creation came largely from negative findings in his study of the ancients, as something born from nothing. Those negatives he sought were merely the background for an entirely original thought: everything he encountered in studies of the past failed in the end. Only the Roman example went on long enough to be called a great success, but that clearly was based on a degree of militarism that was not to be attempted in America.

Just as a scientific experimenter, having discarded many substances that would not work, feels that something unheard of has a better chance of succeeding, Madison must have imagined that an approach the ancients never tried was the strongest candidate for success. Let all the people vote—not only property owners or any other select group—and the more people, the better. All those warnings about America's excessive size had it exactly backward; when the Union stretched all the way to the Pacific, it would be even more stable, he said, for with that many voices, a threatening minority would not be able to dominate. Madison could not have felt as certain as he sometimes sounded, for he was a realist. He knew that some of these voters would be evil and some stupid. But he thought greater numbers would move the odds in his favor. Madison invented the notion that a large body politic—composed of all the people and not just certain classes—were likely to reach the best decisions for the political future of the nation.

On one occasion after another, we have seen this "particular life that America elected to live" in 1788 go sadly wrong, with presidents misusing their privileges or misjudging the way to climb out of a hole—personal, economic, or diplomatic—and making their people feel ashamed or briefly un-American. Yet the mass of the people have seemed, on those occasions, to be wiser than their leaders, which is exactly what Madison expected of them. They were able to regain their footing and to show a balanced judgment that gave the onlooking world new confidence in America's future.

Few if any inventors have ever been forced to make their first experiment on such a grand scale. There was no way to rig a smaller test of this new idea about the wisdom of common voters. So James Madison gambled to see whether his experiment would work in practice. It must have been a day-to-day adventure for this inventor to watch the growing joys and pains of his brainchild. In his last days, forty-nine years later, he saw that it was still vibrantly alive.

Alexander Hamilton can also be seen as an inventor. As a young officer in Washington's army, he imagined how management of the country's financial affairs under his tutelage could create a federal government powerful enough to shape a nation and make it great. And it is no exaggeration to say that his Treasury Department accomplished exactly that.

Madison and Hamilton, the two young patriots who invented a new kind of nation: "Such men do not superabound."

The Constitution of the United States

We the People of the United States, in Order to form a more perfect Union, establish Justice, insure domestic Tranquility, provide for the common defence, promote the general Welfare, and secure the Blessings of Liberty to ourselves and our Posterity, do ordain and establish this Constitution for the United States of America.

ARTICLE I

Section 1

All legislative Powers herein granted shall be vested in a Congress of the United States, which shall consist of a Senate and House of Representatives.

Section 2

The House of Representatives shall be composed of Members chosen every second Year by the People of the several States, and the Electors in each State shall have the Qualifications requisite for Electors of the most numerous Branch of the State Legislature.

No Person shall be a Representative who shall not have attained to the Age of twenty five Years, and been seven Years a Citizen of the United States, and who shall not, when elected, be an Inhabitant of that State in which he shall be chosen.

Representatives and direct Taxes shall be apportioned among the several States which may be included within this Union, according to their respective Numbers, which shall be determined by adding to the whole Number of free Persons, including those bound to Service for a Term of Years, and excluding Indians not taxed, three fifths of all other Persons. The actual Enumeration shall be made within three Years after the first Meeting of the Congress of the United States, and within every subsequent Term of ten Years, in such Manner as they shall by Law direct. The Number of Representatives shall not exceed one for every thirty Thousand, but each State shall have at Least one Representative; and until such enumeration shall be made, the State of New Hampshire shall be entitled to chuse three, Massachusetts eight, Rhode-Island and Providence Plantations one, Connecticut five, New-York six, New Jersey four, Pennsylvania eight, Delaware one, Maryland six, Virginia ten, North Carolina five, South Carolina five, and Georgia three.

When vacancies happen in the Representation from any State, the Executive Authority thereof shall issue Writs of Election to fill such Vacancies.

The House of Representatives shall chuse their Speaker and other Officers; and shall have the sole Power of Impeachment.

Section 3

The Senate of the United States shall be composed of two Senators from each State, chosen by the Legislature thereof, for six Years; and each Senator shall have one Vote.

Immediately after they shall be assembled in Consequence of the first Election, they shall be divided as equally as may be into three Classes. The Seats of the Senators of the first Class shall be vacated at the Expiration of the second Year, of the second Class at the Expiration of the fourth Year, and of the third Class at the Expiration of the sixth Year, so that one third may be chosen every second Year; and if Vacancies happen by Resignation, or otherwise, during the Recess of the Legislature of any State, the Executive thereof may make temporary Appointments until the next Meeting of the Legislature, which shall then fill such Vacancies.

No Person shall be a Senator who shall not have attained to the Age of thirty Years, and been nine Years a Citizen of the United States, and who shall not, when elected, be an Inhabitant of that State for which he shall be chosen.

The Vice President of the United States shall be President of the Senate, but shall have no Vote, unless they be equally divided.

The Senate shall chuse their other Officers, and also a President pro tempore, in the Absence of the Vice President, or when he shall exercise the Office of President of the United States.

The Senate shall have the sole Power to try all Impeachments. When sitting for that Purpose, they shall be on Oath or Affirmation. When the President of the United States is tried, the Chief Justice shall preside: And no Person shall be convicted without the Concurrence of two thirds of the Members present.

Judgment in Cases of Impeachment shall not extend further than to removal from Office, and disqualification to hold and enjoy any Office of honor, Trust or Profit under the United States: but the Party convicted shall nevertheless be liable and subject to Indictment, Trial, Judgment and Punishment, according to Law.

Section 4

The Times, Places and Manner of holding Elections for Senators and Representatives, shall be prescribed in each State by the Legislature thereof; but the Congress may at any time by Law make or alter such Regulations, except as to the Places of chusing Senators.

The Congress shall assemble at least once in every Year, and such Meeting shall be on the first Monday in December, unless they shall by Law appoint a different Day.

Section 5

Each House shall be the Judge of the Elections, Returns and Qualifications of its own Members, and a Majority of each shall constitute a Quorum to do Business; but a smaller Number may adjourn from day to day, and may be authorized to compel the Attendance of absent

Members, in such Manner, and under such Penalties as each House may provide.

Each House may determine the Rules of its Proceedings, punish its Members for disorderly Behaviour, and, with the Concurrence of two thirds, expel a Member.

Each House shall keep a Journal of its Proceedings, and from time to time publish the same, excepting such Parts as may in their Judgment require Secrecy; and the Yeas and Nays of the Members of either House on any question shall, at the Desire of one fifth of those Present, be entered on the Journal.

Neither House, during the Session of Congress, shall, without the Consent of the other, adjourn for more than three days, nor to any other Place than that in which the two Houses shall be sitting.

Section 6

The Senators and Representatives shall receive a Compensation for their Services, to be ascertained by Law, and paid out of the Treasury of the United States. They shall in all Cases, except Treason, Felony and Breach of the Peace, be privileged from Arrest during their Attendance at the Session of their respective Houses, and in going to and returning from the same; and for any Speech or Debate in either House, they shall not be questioned in any other Place.

No Senator or Representative shall, during the Time for which he was elected, be appointed to any civil Office under the Authority of the United States, which shall have been created, or the Emoluments whereof shall have been encreased during such time; and no Person holding any Office under the United States, shall be a Member of either House during his Continuance in Office.

Section 7

All Bills for raising Revenue shall originate in the House of Representatives; but the Senate may propose orconcur with Amendments as on other Bills.

Every Bill which shall have passed the House of Representatives and the Senate, shall, before it become a Law, be presented to the President of the United States; If he approve he shall sign it, but if not he shall return it, with his Objections to that House in which it shall have originated, who shall enter the Objections at large on their Journal, and proceed to reconsider it. If after such Reconsideration two thirds of that House shall agree to pass the Bill, it shall be sent, together with the Objections, to the other House, by which it shall likewise be reconsidered, and if approved by two thirds of that House, it shall become a Law. But in all such Cases the Votes of both Houses shall be determined by yeas and Nays, and the Names of the Persons voting for and against the Bill shall be entered on the Journal of each House respectively. If any Bill shall not be returned by the President within ten Days (Sundays excepted) after it shall have been presented to him, the Same shall be a Law, in like Manner as if he had signed it, unless the Congress by their Adjournment prevent its Return, in which Case it shall not be a Law.

Every Order, Resolution, or Vote to which the Concurrence of the Senate and House of Representatives may be necessary (except on a question of Adjournment) shall be presented to the President of the United States; and before the Same shall take Effect, shall be approved by him, or being disapproved by him, shall be repassed by two thirds of the Senate and House of Representatives, according to the Rules and Limitations prescribed in the Case of a Bill.

Section 8
The Congress shall have Power To lay and collect Taxes, Duties, Imposts and Excises, to pay the Debts and provide for the common Defence and general Welfare of the United States; but all Duties, Imposts and Excises shall be uniform throughout the United States;

To borrow Money on the credit of the United States;

To regulate Commerce with foreign Nations, and among the several States, and with the Indian Tribes;

To establish an uniform Rule of Naturalization, and uniform Laws on the subject of Bankruptcies throughout the United States;

To coin Money, regulate the Value thereof, and of foreign Coin, and fix the Standard of Weights and Measures;

To provide for the Punishment of counterfeiting the Securities and current Coin of the United States;

To establish Post Offices and post Roads;

To promote the Progress of Science and useful Arts, by securing for limited Times to Authors and Inventors the exclusive Right to their respective Writings and Discoveries;

To constitute Tribunals inferior to the supreme Court;

To define and punish Piracies and Felonies committed on the high Seas, and Offences against the Law of Nations;

To declare War, grant Letters of Marque and Reprisal, and make Rules concerning Captures on Land and Water;

To raise and support Armies, but no Appropriation of Money to that Use shall be for a longer Term than two Years;

To provide and maintain a Navy;

To make Rules for the Government and Regulation of the land and naval Forces;

To provide for calling forth the Militia to execute the Laws of the Union, suppress Insurrections and repel Invasions;

To provide for organizing, arming, and disciplining, the Militia, and for governing such Part of them as may be employed in the Service of the United States, reserving to the States respectively, the Appointment of the Officers, and the Authority of training the Militia according to the discipline prescribed by Congress;

To exercise exclusive Legislation in all Cases whatsoever, over such District (not exceeding ten Miles square) as may, by Cession of particular States, and the Acceptance of Congress, become the Seat of the Government of the United States, and to exercise like Authority over all Places purchased by the Consent of the Legislature of the State in which the Same shall be, for the Erection of Forts, Magazines, Arsenals, dock-Yards, and other needful Buildings;—And

To make all Laws which shall be necessary and proper for carrying into Execution the foregoing Powers, and all other Powers vested by this Constitution in the Government of the United States, or in any Department or Officer thereof.

Section 9

The Migration or Importation of such Persons as any of the States now existing shall think proper to admit, shall not be prohibited by the Congress prior to the Year one thousand eight hundred and eight, but a Tax or duty may be imposed on such Importation, not exceeding ten dollars for each Person.

The Privilege of the Writ of Habeas Corpus shall not be suspended, unless when in Cases of Rebellion or Invasion the public Safety may require it.

No Bill of Attainder or ex post facto Law shall be passed.

No Capitation, or other direct, Tax shall be laid, unless in Proportion to the Census or Enumeration herein before directed to be taken.

No Tax or Duty shall be laid on Articles exported from any State.

No Preference shall be given by any Regulation of Commerce or Revenue to the Ports of one State over those of another: nor shall Vessels bound to, or from, one State, be obliged to enter, clear, or pay Duties in another.

No Money shall be drawn from the Treasury, but in Consequence of Appropriations made by Law; and a regular Statement and Account of the Receipts and Expenditures of all public Money shall be published from time to time.

No Title of Nobility shall be granted by the United States: And no Person holding any Office of Profit or Trust under them, shall, without the Consent of the Congress, accept of any present, Emolument, Office, or Title, of any kind whatever, from any King, Prince, or foreign State.

Section 10

No State shall enter into any Treaty, Alliance, or Confederation; grant Letters of Marque and Reprisal; coin Money; emit Bills of Credit; make any Thing but gold and silver Coin a Tender in Payment of Debts; pass any Bill of Attainder, ex post facto Law, or Law impairing the Obligation of Contracts, or grant any Title of Nobility.

No State shall, without the Consent of the Congress, lay any Imposts or Duties on Imports or Exports, except what may be absolutely necessary for executing it's inspection Laws: and the net Produce of all Duties and Imposts, laid by any State on Imports or Exports, shall be for the Use of the Treasury of the United States; and all such Laws shall be subject to the Revision and Controul of the Congress.

No State shall, without the Consent of Congress, lay any Duty of Tonnage, keep Troops, or Ships of War in time of Peace, enter into any Agreement or Compact with another State, or with a foreign Power, or engage in War, unless actually invaded, or in such imminent Danger as will not admit of delay.

ARTICLE II

Section 1

The executive Power shall be vested in a President of the United States of America. He shall hold his Office during the Term of four Years, and, together with the Vice President, chosen for the same Term, be elected, as follows

Each State shall appoint, in such Manner as the Legislature thereof may direct, a Number of Electors, equal to the whole Number of Senators and Representatives to which the State may be entitled in the Congress: but no Senator or Representative, or Person holding an Office of Trust or Profit under the United States, shall be appointed an Elector.

The Electors shall meet in their respective States, and vote by Ballot for two Persons, of whom one at least shall not be an Inhabitant of the same State with themselves. And they shall make a List of all the Persons voted for, and of the Number of Votes for each; which List they shall sign and certify, and transmit sealed to the Seat of the Government of the United States, directed to the President of the Senate. The President of the Senate shall, in the Presence of the Senate and House of Representatives, open all the Certificates, and the Votes shall then be counted. The Person having the greatest Number of Votes shall be the President, if such Number be a Majority of the whole Number of Electors appointed; and if there be more than one who have such Majority, and have an equal Number of Votes, then the House of Representatives shall immediately chuse by Ballot one of them for President; and if no Person have a

Majority, then from the five highest on the List the said House shall in like Manner chuse the President. But in chusing the President, the Votes shall be taken by States, the Representation from each State having one Vote; A quorum for this Purpose shall consist of a Member or Members from two thirds of the States, and a Majority of all the States shall be necessary to a Choice. In every Case, after the Choice of the President, the Person having the greatest Number of Votes of the Electors shall be the Vice President. But if there should remain two or more who have equal Votes, the Senate shall chuse from them by Ballot the Vice President.

The Congress may determine the Time of chusing the Electors, and the Day on which they shall give their Votes; which Day shall be the same throughout the United States.

No Person except a natural born Citizen, or a Citizen of the United States, at the time of the Adoption of this Constitution, shall be eligible to the Office of President; neither shall any Person be eligible to that Office who shall not have attained to the Age of thirty five Years, and been fourteen Years a Resident within the United States.

In Case of the Removal of the President from Office, or of his Death, Resignation, or Inability to discharge the Powers and Duties of the said Office, the Same shall devolve on the VicePresident, and the Congress may by Law provide for the Case of Removal, Death, Resignation or Inability, both of the President and Vice President, declaring what Officer shall then act as President, and such Officer shall act accordingly, until the Disability be removed, or a President shall be elected.

The President shall, at stated Times, receive for his Services, a Compensation, which shall neither be encreased nor diminished during the Period for which he shall have been elected, and he shall not receive within that Period any other Emolument from the United States, or any of them.

Before he enter on the Execution of his Office, he shall take the following Oath or Affirmation:—"I do solemnly swear (or affirm) that I will faithfully execute the Office of President of the United States, and will to the best of my Ability, preserve, protect and defend the Constitution of the United States."

Section 2

The President shall be Commander in Chief of the Army and Navy of the United States, and of the Militia of the several States, when called into the actual Service of the United States; he may require the Opinion, in writing, of the principal Officer in each of the executive Departments, upon any Subject relating to the Duties of their respective Offices, and he shall have Power to grant Reprieves and Pardons for Offences against the United States, except in Cases of Impeachment.

He shall have Power, by and with the Advice and Consent of the Senate, to make Treaties, provided two thirds of the Senators present concur; and he shall nominate, and by and with the Advice and Consent of the Senate, shall appoint Ambassadors, other public Ministers and Consuls, Judges of the supreme Court, and all other Officers of the United States, whose Appointments are not herein otherwise provided for, and which shall be established by Law: but the Congress may by Law vest the Appointment of such inferior Officers, as they think proper, in the President alone, in the Courts of Law, or in the Heads of Departments.

The President shall have Power to fill up all Vacancies that may happen during the Recess of the Senate, by granting Commissions which shall expire at the End of their next Session.

Section 3

He shall from time to time give to the Congress Information of the State of the Union, and recommend to their Consideration such Measures as he shall judge necessary and expedient; he may, on extraordinary Occasions, convene both Houses, or either of them, and in Case of Disagreement between them, with Respect to the Time of Adjournment, he may adjourn them to such Time as he shall think proper; he shall receive Ambassadors and other public Ministers; he shall take Care that the Laws be faithfully executed, and shall Commission all the Officers of the United States.

Section 4

The President, Vice President and all civil Officers of the United States, shall be removed from Office on Impeachment for, and Conviction of, Treason,

Bribery, or other high Crimes and Misdemeanors.

ARTICLE III
Section 1
The judicial Power of the United States, shall be vested in one supreme Court, and in such inferior Courts as the Congress may from time to time ordain and establish. The Judges, both of the supreme and inferior Courts, shall hold their Offices during good Behaviour, and shall, at stated Times, receive for their Services, a Compensation, which shall not be diminished during their Continuance in Office.

Section 2
The judicial Power shall extend to all Cases, in Law and Equity, arising under this Constitution, the Laws of the United States, and Treaties made, or which shall be made, under their Authority;—to all Cases affecting Ambassadors, other public Ministers and Consuls;—to all Cases of admiralty and maritime Jurisdiction;—to Controversies to which the United States shall be a Party;—to Controversies between two or more States;—between a State and Citizens of another State;—between Citizens of different States,—between Citizens of the same State claiming Lands under Grants of different States, and between a State, or the Citizens thereof, and foreign States, Citizens or Subjects.

In all Cases affecting Ambassadors, other public Ministers and Consuls, and those in which a State shall be Party, the supreme Court shall have original Jurisdiction. In all the other Cases before mentioned, the supreme Court shall have appellate Jurisdiction, both as to Law and Fact, with such Exceptions, and under such Regulations as the Congress shall make.

The Trial of all Crimes, except in Cases of Impeachment, shall be by Jury; and such Trial shall be held in the State where the said Crimes shall have been committed; but when not committed within any State, the Trial shall be at such Place or Places as the Congress may by Law have directed.

Section 3

Treason against the United States, shall consist only in levying War against them, or in adhering to their Enemies, giving them Aid and Comfort. No Person shall be convicted of Treason unless on the Testimony of two Witnesses to the same overt Act, or on Confession in open Court.

The Congress shall have Power to declare the Punishment of Treason, but no Attainder of Treason shall work Corruption of Blood, or Forfeiture except during the Life of the Person attainted.

ARTICLE IV

Section 1

Full Faith and Credit shall be given in each State to the public Acts, Records, and judicial Proceedings of every other State. And the Congress may by general Laws prescribe the Manner in which such Acts, Records and Proceedings shall be proved, and the Effect thereof.

Section 2

The Citizens of each State shall be entitled to all Privileges and Immunities of Citizens in the several States.

A Person charged in any State with Treason, Felony, or other Crime, who shall flee from Justice, and be found in another State, shall on Demand of the executive Authority of the State from which he fled, be delivered up, to be removed to the State having Jurisdiction of the Crime.

No Person held to Service or Labour in one State, under the Laws thereof, escaping into another, shall, in Consequence of any Law or Regulation therein, be discharged from such Service or Labour, but shall be delivered up on Claim of the Party to whom such Service or Labour may be due.

Section 3

New States may be admitted by the Congress into this Union; but no new State shall be formed or erected within the Jurisdiction of any other State; nor any State be formed by the Junction of two or more States, or Parts of States, without the Consent of the Legislatures of the

States concerned as well as of the Congress.

The Congress shall have Power to dispose of and make all needful Rules and Regulations respecting the Territory or other Property belonging to the United States; and nothing in this Constitution shall be so construed as to Prejudice any Claims of the United States, or of any particular State.

Section 4
The United States shall guarantee to every State in this Union a Republican Form of Government, and shall protect each of them against Invasion; and on Application of the Legislature, or of the Executive (when the Legislature cannot be convened) against domestic Violence.

ARTICLE V
The Congress, whenever two thirds of both Houses shall deem it necessary, shall propose Amendments to this Constitution, or, on the Application of the Legislatures of two thirds of the several States, shall call a Convention for proposing Amendments, which, in either Case, shall be valid to all Intents and Purposes, as Part of this Constitution, when ratified by the Legislatures of three fourths of the several States, or by Conventions in three fourths thereof, as the one or the other Mode of Ratification may be proposed by the Congress; Provided that no Amendment which may be made prior to the Year One thousand eight hundred and eight shall in any Manner affect the first and fourth Clauses in the Ninth Section of the first Article; and that no State, without its Consent, shall be deprived of its equal Suffrage in the Senate.

ARTICLE VI
All Debts contracted and Engagements entered into, before the Adoption of this Constitution, shall be as valid against the United States under this Constitution, as under the Confederation.

This Constitution, and the Laws of the United States which shall be made in Pursuance thereof; and all Treaties made, or which shall be made, under the Authority of the United States, shall be the supreme

Law of the Land; and the Judges in every State shall be bound thereby, any Thing in the Constitution or Laws of any State to the Contrary notwithstanding.

The Senators and Representatives before mentioned, and the Members of the several State Legislatures, and all executive and judicial Officers, both of the United States and of the several States, shall be bound by Oath or Affirmation, to support this Constitution; but no religious Test shall ever be required as a Qualification to any Office or public Trust under the United States.

ARTICLE VII

The Ratification of the Conventions of nine States, shall be sufficient for the Establishment of this Constitution between the States so ratifying the Same.

Done in Convention by the Unanimous Consent of the States present the Seventeenth Day of September in the Year of our Lord one thousand seven hundred and Eighty seven and of the Independence of the United States of America the Twelfth In witness whereof We have hereunto subscribed our Names,

GEORGE WASHINGTON—President and deputy from Virginia
Attest WILLIAM JACKSON *Secretary*

Delaware
GEO: READ
GUNNING BEDFORD JUN
JOHN DICKINSON
RICHARD BASSETT
JACO: BROOM

Maryland
JAMES MCHENRY
DAN OF ST THOS. JENIFER
DANL CARROLL.

Virginia
JOHN BLAIR
JAMES MADISON JR.

North Carolina
WM BLOUNT
RICHD. DOBBS SPAIGHT.
HU WILLIAMSON

South Carolina
J. RUTLEDGE
CHARLES COTESWORTH PINCKNEY
CHARLES PINCKNEY
PIERCE BUTLER

Georgia
WILLIAM FEW
ABR BALDWIN

New Hampshire
JOHN LANGDON
NICHOLAS GILMAN

Massachusetts
NATHANIEL GORHAM
RUFUS KING

Connecticut
WM. SAML. JOHNSON
ROGER SHERMAN

New York
ALEXANDER HAMILTON

New Jersey
WIL: LIVINGSTON
DAVID BREARLEY.
WM. PATERSON.
JONA: DAYTON

Pennsylvania
B FRANKLIN
THOMAS MIFFLIN
ROBT MORRIS
GEO. CLYMER
THOS. FITZSIMONS
JARED INGERSOLL
JAMES WILSON.
GOUV MORRIS

Source Notes

AUTHOR TO READER

vii   *Constitution of the United States of America,* 1938.

viii   *incapable of self-government:* Dudley, *Creation of the Constitution.*

viii   *"not for me to decide":* Randall, *George Washington,* 395.

ix   *"Because I expect no better":* Franklin, Benjamin. *Writings.*

CHAPTER 1

1   *"If we are not a happy people":* Langguth, *Patriots,* 551.

2   *total population from Georgia to Maine:* Sheehan, *Making of American History,* 18, 43.

2   *sent one of its members, Silas Deane:* Bailey, *A Diplomatic History,* 10.

3   *"This Deane must be the most silent man":* Langguth, *Patriots,* 549.

3   *"Figure me in your mind":* Franklin, Benjamin, *Writings,* Vol. VII, 56.

3   *made apparent by a shipment:* Franklin, Benjamin, *Autobiography,* 381.

3   *"The two greatest countries":* Fiske, *Critical Period of American History,* 97.

4   *"Relations between nations should never":* Langguth, *Patriots,* 549.

4   *Historians have differed:* Vandermoortele, *Financial Times,* August 13, 2003.

4   *"crime was rising as population soared":* Reader's Companion to American History, 2.

5   *"General Washington has the Potomac much at heart":* Randall, *George Washington,* 420.

5   *the small-mindedness of local leaders:* Randall, *George Washington,* 421.

5   *"From the present juvenile state of the country":* Randall, *George Washington,* 422–23.

5   *Marquis de Lafayette came to visit:* Randall, *George Washington,* 418.

6   *The reunion with Lafayette:* Thane, *Washington's Lady,* 250.

6   *"My Dear Marquis":* Randall, *George Washington,* 420.

7   *two hundred thousand residents were classified:* Historical Statistics of the United States, Vol.1, 11-12.

8   *City folk were also purchasing:* Larkin, *Reshaping of Everyday Life,* 119.

8   *Clothing too, which had mostly been:* Larkin, *Reshaping of Everyday Life,* 24–25.

8   *people could find the time to read:* Larkin, *Reshaping of Everyday Life,* 35–36.

8   *Some of the newcomers:* Larkin, *Reshaping of Everyday Life,* 113.

8   *The Ellicotts, a great Maryland family:* Cerami, *Benjamin Banneker,* 82–83.

9   *Livingston, President Jefferson's somewhat unruly ambassador:* Cerami, *Jefferson's Great Gamble,* 76–77.

9   *But the booming industry:* Larkin, *Reshaping of Everyday Life,* 204–225.

11   *The leaders were all men of property:* Azimov, *Birth of the United States,* 130.

CHAPTER 2

13   *James was a normal freshman:* Brant, *Fourth President,* Vol 1. Dr. Witherspoon told Jefferson that Madison never took part in frivolous fun, embarrassing the Secretary of State. There is proof to the contrary.

14   *"Everything costs more":* Madison to his father, *Madison Papers,* Vol. I.

14   *"We have a very great scarcity":* Madison to Billey Bradford, *Madison Papers,* Vol. I, 93–106.

14   *taking a lusty interest in the ferocious combat:* Ketcham, *James Madison,* 35–36.

15   *The young men all had telescopes:* Gerson, *Light-Horse Harry,* 36.

15   *"I was on the point":* Madison to Bradford, *Madison Papers,* Vol. I, 97.

16   *It quoted Samuel Butler:* Bradford to Madison, March 1774, *Madison Papers,* Vol. I, 110.

16   *"I am afraid an insurrection":* Madison to Bradford, Brant, *The Fourth President,* 93–106.

16   *His training soon qualified him:* Brant, *The Fourth President,* 120.

17   *"Previous to the Revolution":* *Madison Papers,* Vol. V, xvi.

17   *It is amusing to find:* Brant, *The Fourth President,* 110.

18   *Madison was small in stature:* Brant, *The Fourth President,* 210.

19   *carried separate little notebooks:* Rutland, *James Madison,* 11. Mee, *Genius of the People,* 30–31.

19   *"Hamilton had incited":* Madison to Congress, June 16, 1779, *Madison Papers,* Vol. II, 460.

19   *A voracious book reader:* Rutland, *James Madison,* 12–13.

20   *He was frequently resorting:* Brant, *The Fourth President,* 99.

20   *"Haym Solomon obstinately":* Brant, *The Fourth President,* 99.

21   *despite what he must have been suffering:* Brant, *The Fourth President.*

21   *Madison ran excitedly down the street:* Brant, *The Fourth President,* 286.

22   *"I have know him from 1779":* Brant, *The Fourth President,* 44.

22   *"The true interest of these states":* Brant, *The Fourth President,* 130.

22   *very closely related to a series:* Brant, *The Fourth President,* 139.

22   *"for the gradual extinction":* Brant, *The Fourth President,* 113–114.

23   *With hardly any schooling:* Broadus, *Alexander Hamilton,* Vol. 1, 64–88. Schachner, *Alexander Hamilton,* 9–12.

23   *Only a little taller than Madison:* Berkin, *A Brilliant Solution,* 42.

24   *literate enough to become a clerk:* Chernow, *Alexander Hamilton,* 31.

24   *"I'm no philosopher":* Chernow, *Alexander Hamilton,* 83.

25   *aiming toward a full course of study:* Chernow, *Alexander Hamilton,* 42–43.

25   *"shrewdness and persistence":* Fiske, *Critical Period of American History.*

25   *After barely surviving:* Chernow, *Alexander Hamilton,* 36–37.

26   *imparted by a garrulous new friend:* Chernow, *Alexander Hamilton,* 42.

27   *Looking even younger:* Chernow, *Alexander Hamilton,* 84.

27   *Breaking off his studies:* Chernow, *Alexander Hamilton,* 85.

28   *"But Sir, if we did succeed":* Chernow, *Alexander Hamilton,* 112.

28   *dared to think of improvements:* Chernow, *Alexander Hamilton,* 90.

29   *Some who knew Hamilton:* Chernow, *Alexander Hamilton,* 94–97.

30   *Colonel Hamilton was a firsthand observer:* Chernow, *Alexander Hamilton,* 140–142.

31 " *Why, at an era so awful":* *Pennsylvania Journal,* Oct. 8, 1783.

CHAPTER 3

34   *Over 90 percent of all workers were simple farmers: Encyclopedia of American Political History.*

35   *Grenville had massive problems:* Azimov, *Birth of the United States,* 14.

37   *The reason for the delay in ratification:* Azimov, *Birth of the United States,* 116.

37   *"freemen of each state":* Fiske, *Critical Period of American History,* 50.

38   *No state was to be:* Fiske, *Critical Period of American History.*

40   *nine of the states:* Van Doren, *The Great Rehearsal,* 4.

40   *Washington's wish to be freed:* Brant, *Fourth President,* 126.

41   *set up a "Society of Cincinnati":* Brant, *Fourth President,* 126.

41   *With good humor:* Langguth, *Patriots,* 462, 480.

42   *"Your society, monsieur":* Langguth, *Patriots,* 462, 480.

43   *He was a poor parson's son:* Thane, *Washington's Lady,* 183.

43   *he called those men his "sans-culottes":* Thane, *Washington's Lady,* 182.

43   *Washington himself wrote to the governors:* Randall, *George Washington,* 54.

44   *He remembered with embarrassment:* Randall, *George Washington,* 445.

45   *"The discerning part of the community":* Washington to Henry Knox, May 1786, Van Doren, *The Great Rehearsal,* 6.

45   *"It is not my business to embark":* Washington to John Jay, August 1, 1786, Van Doren, *The Great Rehearsal,* 6.

45   *"As to the future grandeur":* Van Doren, *The Great Rehearsal,* 57–58.

46   *"The times that try men's souls":* Fiske, *Critical Period of American History,* 236.

CHAPTER 4

49   *The terrible acts of the Barbary Pirates:* Azimov, *Birth of the United States, 190–91.* Van Doren, *The Great Rehersal,* 158.

49   *"I am in no doubt":* Dudley, *Creation of the Constitution,* 162.

50   *he voiced agreement with Samuel Chase:* Cerami, *Benjamin Banneker,* 115–118.

50   *confirming the new economic theory:* Dudley, *Creation of the Constitution,* 134–35.

51   *Madison and eleven other representatives:* Charleton, et al., *Framers of the Constitution,* 20.

51   *Hamilton refused to talk of success:* Berkin, *A Brilliant Solution,* 52.

52   *propose this meeting to the Continental Congress:* Fiske, *Critical Period of American History,* 219–221.

52   *"Your Commissioners":* Berkin, *A Brilliant Solution.*

55   *"I am impatient to learn":* Jefferson to Madison, January 30, 1787, *Jefferson Letters.*

55   *"I feel very differently":* Jefferson to Madison, *Jefferson Letters.*

57   *"Let us look to our national character":* Washington to Madison, November 5, 1786, "Letters," Vol. VII.

57   *Madison already planned the role:* Brandt, *The Fourth President.*

59   *George Mason, a brilliant Virginian:* Fiske, *Critical Period of American History.*

CHAPTER 5

61   *Henry offered a loosely worded resolution:* Brant, *The Fourth President,* 89.
62   *North Carolina had ruled explicitly:* Ganyard, *Emergence of North Carolina's Revolutionary State Government.*
64   *Hamilton's problem in his home state:* Chernow, *Alexander Hamilton,* 244–45.
65   *"I believe it would be in general":* Chernow, *Alexander Hamilton,* 197.
65   *In one unusual case:* Chernow, *Alexander Hamilton,* 197–99.
67   *On February 15, 1787:* Fiske, *Critical Period of American History,* 220.
69   *Immigration was now building:* Azimov, *Birth of the United States,* 135.
69   *In July, at a committee session:* Langguth, *Patriots.*
70   *The Congress gave its astonishingly:* Charleton, et al., *Framers of the Constitution.*
70   *And so it was decided:* Brandt, *The Fourth President.*
71   *"My Dear Sir":* Van Doren, *The Great Rehersal,* 6.
71   *The two vastly different personalities:* Langguth, *Patriots.*

CHAPTER 6

75   *Her comfortable rooms:* Peterson, *Madison Biography,* 50.
75   *It was at Mrs. House's:* Brant, *The Fourth President,* Vol 1, 110–11, 281.
76   *"it would be improper":* Peterson, *Madison Biography,* 79.
77   *He arrived in the first week:* Westcott, *History of Philadelphia,* 87.
77   *"Philadelphia was enlightened":* Madison Papers.
78   *"On the banks of the Schuylkill":* Westcott, *History of Philadelphia,* Vol. 5, 1,280.
78   *The completely urban impression:* Carr, *The Oldest Delegate.*
79   *"If there exists an atheist":* Carr, *The Oldest Delegate.*
79   *Franklin's grandson, Benjamin Franklin Bache:* Westcott, *History of Philadelphia,* 340.
80   *The Society of Friends:* Westcott, *History of Philadelphia,* 654.
81   *The city's press was flourishing:* Westcott, *History of Philadelphia,* 340.
81   *told of artists and sculptors:* Westcott, *History of Philadelphia,* 340.
83   *firefighting became a major preoccupation:* Westcott, *History of Philadelphia,* 371.
85   *In 1787 he encouraged:* Westcott, *History of Philadelphia,* 579.
85   *It led them to ask:* Westcott, *History of Philadelphia,* 579.
86   *"I cannot conceive a government":* Bowen, *Miracle at Philadelphia,* 40.
86   *No single ethnic group:* Randall, *George Washington,* 341.
86   *remarkable defenses that Philadephians erected:* Randall, *George Washington,* 342.
88   *financier Robert Morris:* Asimov, *Birth of the United States,* 114. Berkin, *A Brilliant Solution,* 68.
88   *James Wilson, a Pennsylvania delegate:* Charleton, et al., *Framers of the Constitution,* 210.
89   *The treatment of Tories:* Ousterhout, *A State Divided,* 185, 187.
90   *All these South Carolinians were staying:* Carr, *The Oldest Delegate.*
91   *would be forced to leave and take:* Ferling, *Setting the World Ablaze.*
91   *it was seen as a most impressive:* Van Doren, *The Great Rehersal,* 103.

CHAPTER 7

93   *Then George's mother, a chronic complainer:* Langguth, *Patriots.*
94   *But on Thursday, April 26:* Thane, *Washington's Lady,* 269.
94   *The reason for his better spirits:* Langguth, *Patriots.*
95   *Washington finally left for Philadelphia:* Washington, *Diaries,* 210–216.
98   *This time, of course, it was spring:* Van Doren, *The Great Rehersal,* 59.
99   *note that he "waited on the President":* Van Doren, *The Great Rehersal,* 6.

99   *"The history of our Revolution":* Carr, *The Oldest Delegate,* 16.

100   *Item #38, which read:* Schott, *Schott's Original Miscellany,* 136.

100   *He saved at least two lives:* Schott, *Schott's Original Miscellany,* 136.

100   *He had written to a French friend:* Van Doren, *The Great Rehersal,* 3.

101   *a principle he had of "never forcing":* Van Doren, *The Great Rehersal.*

102   *But Franklin was undoubtedly too courteous:* Levy, *Essays on the Making of the Constitution,* 49.

CHAPTER 8

103   *"such members as were in town":* Washington, May 14, 1787, *Diaries,* 216–20.

103   *"Monday last was the day":* Madison to Jefferson, May 15, 1787, *Madison Papers,* Vol. X.

104   *Madison was eagerly waiting:* Van Doren, *The Great Rehersal.*

104   *In his independent way:* Van Doren, *The Great Rehersal,* 20.

105   *"It is too probable that no plan":* Van Doren, *The Great Rehersal,* 14.

105   *Much of the early talk:* Van Doren, *The Great Rehersal.*

105   *A few had been born:* Van Doren, *The Great Rehersal.*

107   *"The delays sour the tempers":* Washington, *Writings.*

107   *"The length of the Convention":* Kammen, *Origins of the American Constitution.*

109   *"after dining at a club":* Washington, *Diaries,* 216–220.

109   *Otto, the major domo:* Dos Passos, *The Men Who Made the Nation.*

110   *he was the son of Lucy Grimes Lee:* Gerson, *Light-Horse Harry,* 9.

110   *admiration for Harry's unequalled daring:* Gerson, *Light-Horse Harry,* 48.

110   *Harry's troop had just brought:* Gerson, *Light-Horse Harry,* 57.

111   *Although these men were always:* Irving, *Life of George Washington.*

114   *"A little flurry has been kicked up":* Grayson to Madison, May 24, 1787, *Madison Papers,* Vol. X.

115   *Mason had the mind:* Van Doren, *The Great Rehersal,* 107.

115   *"how the superior":* Langguth, *Patriots.*

116   *"It is a matter of simple":* Langguth, *Patriots.*

117   *The deliberations under way:* Westcott, *History of Philadelphia.*

118   *Madison had put his finger:* Koch, *Life and Selected Writings of Thomas Jefferson.*

CHAPTER 9

121   *The fifteen tables:* Randall, *George Washington,* 436.

121   *Pennsylvania delegate Robert Morris:* Asimov, *Birth of the United States,* 138–40. Asimov discusses the opening formalities, presentation of the Virginia Plan, and the following debate.

122   *"Do you know that there exists":* Jefferson to Adams, 1815, Bowen, *Miracle at Philadelphia,* 30.

123   *The other candidate was Temple:* Carr, *The Oldest Delegate,* 86–87.

124   *To have secured a majority's approval:* Bowen, *Miracle at Philadelphia.* Azimov, *Birth of the United States,* 139.

125   *It was Tuesday, May 29:* Fiske, *Critical Period of American History,* 231–38.

125   *Madison struck early:* Brant, *The Fourth President,* 147.

126   *The plan that Randolph first laid out:* Fiske, *Critical Period of American History,* 232.

127   *"The Confederation was made":* Langguth, *Patriots.*

129   *during the presidency of Andrew Jackson:* James, *Andrew Jackson,* 213–37.

131   *Wilson spoke incisively:* Kammen, *Origins of the American Constitution.*

131   *"As I see it":* Bowen, *Miracle at Philadelphia,* 107.

131 *"Under the original Virginia":* Fiske, *Critical Period of American History*, 244.

133 *Amazingly, in view of what:* Fiske, *Critical Period of American History*, 244–48.

133 *It was like a well-rehearsed performance:* Mitchell, *Alexander Hamilton*.

CHAPTER 10

136 *William Paterson, leader:* Brant, *The Fourth President*.

136 *But Governor Randolph, gathering fire:* Fiske, *Critical Period of American History*. Fiske discusses the extended debate of New Jersey Plan.

137 *"Throw everything into a hotchpot":* Langguth, *Patriots*.

138 *"The great danger":* Brant, *The Fourth President*.

138 *But that view only roused:* Brant, *The Fourth President*.

139 *At that dramatic point on June 27:* Brant, *The Fourth President*.

140 *"The small progress we have made":* Carr, *The Oldest Delegate*.

141 *It was Sherman who:* Brant, *The Fourth President*.

142 *But when a vote was organized:* Brant, *The Fourth President*.

142 *a young man named Abraham Baldwin: National Cyclopedia of American Biography*, Vol. 9, 178.

145 *Congressional terms of office did not:* Fiske, *Critical Period of American History*.

145 *Madison's single greatest objective:* Fiske, *Critical Period of American History*.

CHAPTER 11

148 *Madison's brief new attempt:* Brant, *The Fourth President*, 148.

149 *Madison was seriously crushed: Madison Papers*, Vol. X.

149 *His studies of history:* Greenidge, *Greek Constitutional History*.

149 *The two sons of Massachusetts laid out a plan:* Fiske, *Critical Period of American History*, 256.

150 *Madison's assertiveness in these days:* Ferling, *Setting the World Ablaze*.

150 *there would be no harm done:* Brant, *The Fourth President*, 162.

150 *Madison was so anxious to scuttle:* Brant, *The Fourth President*, 166.

151 *This issue brought an unusual clash:* Brant, *The Fourth President*, 171–72.

151 *Madison's answer had an unaccustomed:* Levy, *Essays*.

152 *As Professor John Fiske wrote:* Fiske, *Critical Period of American History*.

153 *The southerners claimed that slaves:* Brant, *The Fourth President*, Vol. 1, 388.

154 *"If Negroes are not":* Brant, *The Fourth President*.

154 *"I would sooner submit":* Brant, *The Fourth President*.

156 *"You cannot have it both ways":* Brant, *The Fourth President*.

156 *Table—The slave population…1790:* Levy, *Essays*, 156.

157 *"Every master of slaves":* Brant, *The Fourth President*.

158 *"Such was the aspect":* Brant, *The Fourth President*.

CHAPTER 12

159 *Alexander Hamilton took the floor:* Dudley, *Creation of the Constitution*, 268–71.

159 *Just how many hours:* Padover, *The Mind of Alexander Hamilton*.

160 *This event began when John Dickinson:* Mitchell, *Alexander Hamilton*.

160 *"any general sovereignty":* Padover, *The Mind of Alexander Hamilton*. Quotations from Hamilton's speech of June 18, 1787, from this source.

161 *"The people are turbulent":* Chernow, *Alexander Hamilton*, 232–35.

161 *He considered the British constitution:* Chernow, *Alexander Hamilton*.

161 *"Hamilton's proposals have been praised":* Chernow, *Alexander Hamilton*.

162 *"All communities divide":* Chernow, *Alexander Hamilton*.

163 *"Let us examine the federal":* Chernow, *Alexander Hamilton*.

166 *It should be recognized:* National Cyclopedia of American Biography. John Lansing: Vol. IV, 254. Robert Yates: Vol. V, 260.

167 *"In a word, I almost despair":* Washington, *Writings*, Vol. 29, 245–46.

168 *Very late in his life he spoke:* Brant, *The Fourth President*, 168.

169 *"Why does not Gouverneur Morris":* Brant, *The Fourth President*, 169.

CHAPTER 13

172 *Washington also had the rare gift:* Anderson, "What Would George Celebrate," *New York Times*, July 4, 2004.

172 *"He is too illiterate":* Washington *Post Magazine*, Dec. 15, 2004, 26.

173 *stomp around his office:* Van Doren, *The Great Rehearsal*.

173 *There was one lady:* Randall, *George Washington*, 445–46.

174 *"The weight of General Washington":* Grayson to Monroe, May 29, 1787, Van Doren, *The Great Rehearsal*, 82.

174 *"I find the wisdom and magnanimity":* Van Doren, *The Great Rehearsal*, 82.

175 *there is an anecdote:* Van Doren, *The Great Rehearsal*, 72.

175 *"I think I knew":* Langguth, *Patriots*.

177 *One description of Washington:* Dohla, *A Hessian Diary*.

178 *Washington's reaction at that time:* Van Doren, *The Great Rehearsal*, 178.

CHAPTER 14

182 *One of the great surprises:* National Cyclopedia of American Biography, Vol. VII, 96.

182 *Savannah, at the moment:* Bowen, *Miracle at Philadelphia*, 31.

182 *Mainly, he turned out to have:* Carr, *The Oldest Delegate*, 55–54. Dos Passos, *The Men Who Made the Nation*. Van Doren, *The Great Rehearsal*, 37–39. Pierce's comments (183–86) about several delegates come from these sources.

185 *"I flatter myself I came here":* Van Doren, *The Great Rehearsal*.

187 *Late in life, Madison told:* Carr, *The Oldest Delegate*.

189 *This easy quality was at least:* Charleton et al., *Framers of the Constitution*, 58. Source provides statistics on age of the delegates, from which the author has drawn new conclusions.

189 *Five were aged thirty or less:* Ketcham, *James Madison*.

190 *The first time he assembled:* Palmer, *General von Steuben*.

CHAPTER 15

193 *The method of selecting a chief:* Fiske, *Critical Period of American History*, 277.

195 *feared this choice would incline:* Azimov, *Birth of the United States*, 141.

195 *John Rutledge, an experienced:* Langguth, *Patriots*.

197 *Gouverneur Morris's wish to have:* Azimov, *Birth of the United States*, 141.

197 *Wilson rose to disabuse:* Carr, *The Oldest Delegate*.

198 *At one point, in desperation:* Carr, *The Oldest Delegate*.

200 *All the delegates who had studied:* Ferling, *Setting the World Ablaze*.

201 *"Studying with Mr. E. Shippen":* Madison Papers, Vol. I.

CHAPTER 16

204 *consisted of paper bills that were not backed:* Fiske, *Critical Period of American History*, 163–69.

206 *he was forced to leave:* Charleton, et al., *Framers of the Constitution*, 189.

208 *John Francis Mercer of Maryland had been:* Dudley, *Creation of the Constitution*, 268–71. Fiske, *Critical Period of American History*, 274.

209 *"All debt contracted and engagements":* Charleton et al., *Framers of the Constitution,* 58.

212 *The bargain was this:* Berkin, *A Brilliant Solution,* 112.

213 *Benjamin Franklin disagreed with Morris's:* Van Doren, *The Great Rehearsal,* 114.

CHAPTER 17

215 *"It was a bargain":* Fiske, *Critical Period of American History,* 262–65.

216 *Sherman and Morris thought:* Berkin, *A Brilliant Solution,* 114.

216 *The Convention was stunned:* Fiske, *Critical Period in American History,* 266–71.

217 *It was one of several times:* Bowen, *Miracle at Philadelphia,* 202.

217 *"agreed to the new government":* Bowen, *Miracle at Philadelphia.*

219 *"an African sanctuary":* Rutland, *James Madison,* 70.

220 *the nation planned to create:* Fowler, *Rebels Under Sail,* 97.

220 *One of the most resistant subjects:* Brant, *The Fourth President,* 221.

221 *Despite this, Trenton had:* Brant, *The Fourth President.*

222 *Interwoven with these semi-finished:* Charleton, et al., *Framers of the Constitution,* 57, 99, 101, 102–3, 153, 885. Newmyer, *John Marshall,* 148–52. Details of the founding of the Supreme Court and the multi-tiered judiciary.

223 *loathing of Jefferson:* Brant, *The Fourth President,* Vol. 3, 53.

223 *This regard lingered:* Brant, *The Fourth President,* Vol. 3, 205.

CHAPTER 18

228 *a daily weather log:* Carr, *The Oldest Delegate.*

229 *after another month had passed:* Charleton, et al., *Framers of the Constitution.*

229 *One of those days, July 31:* Von Doren, *The Great Rehearsal.*

230 *But lately, after Morris:* Dos Passos, *The Men Who Made the Nation.*

230 *They transformed the broad general authority:* Brant, *The Fourth President,* 240.

231 *The committee dared to change:* Brant, *The Fourth President.*

232 *Only since the Twenty-second Amendment:* Austin, *Political Facts.*

233 *Forty-one men were in the room:* Bowen, *Miracle at Philadelphia.*

233 *George Washington's proposal:* Berkin, *A Brilliant Solution,* 295.

CHAPTER 19

236 *Jefferson's comments about the end:* McCullogh, David, *John Adams,* 444.

237 *But most of all:* Jefferson to James Madison, various letters, Koch and Peden, *Writings of Thomas Jefferson.* Foner, *Basic Writings of Thomas Jefferson.*

237 *One letter written on July 31, 1788:* Foner, *Basic Writings of Thomas Jefferson.*

239 *"We have now lands":* Jefferson to John Jay, Aug. 23, 1785, Foner, *Basic Writings of Thomas Jefferson.*

240 *"I received this summer":* Jefferson to Madison, Sept. 20, 1785, Koch and Peden, *Writings of Thomas Jefferson.*

242 *"If all sovereigns of Europe":* Jefferson to George Wyeth, Aug. 13, 1786, Koch and Peden, *Writings of Thomas Jefferson.* Foner, *Basic Writings of Thomas Jefferson.*

243 *"I am deeply sensible":* Jefferson to Jean Pierre Brissot de Warville, Feb. 11, 1788, Foner, *Basic Writings of Thomas Jefferson.*

244 *He employed the unoriginal:* Jefferson to Maria Cosway, Foner, *Basic Writings of Thomas Jefferson.* Koch and Peden, *Writings of Thomas Jefferson.*

245 *"Dear Madam—":* Jefferson to Mrs. William Bingham, May 11, 1788, Foner, *Basic Writings of Thomas Jefferson.*

246 *"How do you like our new Constitution":* Jefferson to John Adams, Nov. 13, 1787, Koch and Peden, *Writings of Thomas Jefferson.* Foner, *Basic Writings of Thomas Jefferson.*

247 *Also from Paris:* Jefferson to George Washington, May 2, 1788, Foner, *Basic Writings of Thomas Jefferson.*

248 *By December 4, 1788:* Jefferson to Washington, Dec. 4, 1788, Foner, *Basic Writings of Thomas Jefferson.*

CHAPTER 20

250 *Europe at the time:* Berlin, *Roots of Romanticism,* 34.

252 *As Nye writes:* Nye, *Cultural Life of the New Nation,* 9–15.

252 *Another view of nature's effect:* Geldard, *Boston Globe,* Sept. 20, 2003.

253 *"No common interests or passion":* Brant, *The Fourth President.*

CHAPTER 21

261 *One of the amazing things:* Chernow, *Alexander Hamilton.*

261 *Broadus Mitchell, one of Hamilton's:* Mitchell, *Alexander Hamilton.*

262 *One opponent who wrote:* Kammen, *Origins of the American Constitution.*

263 *In 1803, Chief Justice John Marshall:* Newmyer, *John Marshal,* 481.

265 *The fact that the Supreme Court:* Fiske, *Critical Period of American History,* 300.

267 *But ratification still had to be:* Fiske, *Critical Period of American History,* 332.

268 *The absence of a bill:* Wills, *James Madison,* 39.

CHAPTER 22

271 *Reaching for reasons to oppose:* Kammen, *Origins of the American Constitution,* xix.

274 *A more serious complaint:* Nye, *Cultural Life of the New Nation,* 202–208.

277 *"Such a test would have been":* Fiske, *Critical Period of American History,* 322.

278 *As Professor Fiske describes:* Fiske, *Critical Period of American History,* 340.

279 *"I mentioned that the question":* Hamilton to Madison, May 10, 1788, *Writings* Vol. 9, 431.

280 *Hamilton went back into:* Mitchell, *Alexander Hamilton,* Vol. 1, 417–63.

280 *It should be noted:* Berkin, *A Brilliant Solution.*

281 *But at one point:* Newmyer, *John Marshall,* 127–31.

282 *Henry said that if:* Fiske, *Critical Period of American History,* 336.

CHAPTER 23

286 *the greater happiness:* Randall, *George Washington.*

287 *The old Constitutional Congress was:* Jensen, et al, *Documentary History.*

288 *But of the 138 electoral votes:* Papers of George Washington.

288 *an unaccustomed fear:* Randall, *George Washington,* 442.

288 *"My movement to the chair":* Randall, *George Washington,* 437.

289 *Madison, at this time:* Brant, *The Fourth President,* 238–40.

289 *"I am very troublesome":* Randall, *George Washington.*

291 *An open break between Hamilton:* Azimov, *Birth of the United States,* 151–54.

CHAPTER 24

296 *thirteen individuals signed a letter:* Fiske, *Critical Period of American History,* 359.

CHAPTER 25

299 *The new members would not:* Rutland, *James Madison,* 53.

300 *Madison would have run:* Rutland, *James Madison,* 44.

300 *It seemed that Madison was one:* Brant, *The Fourth President.*

300 *Alexander Hamilton, in writing:* Chernow, *Alexander Hamilton,* 260.

301 *Jefferson, on the contrary:* Chernow, *Alexander Hamilton,* 552.

301 *he had clearly been preparing:* Brant, *The Fourth President,* 231–36.

301 *By June 8 Madison was ready:* Azimov, *Birth of the United States,* 210–12.

306 *Hamilton was genuine in his wish:* Chernow, *Alexander Hamilton,* 298–303.

307 *The nation, too, was different:* Azimov, *Birth of the United States,* 210–12.

308 *In these feverish moments:* Fiske, *Critical Period of American History,* 60.

308 *At the time of the first census:* Austin, *Political Facts of the United States,* Table 7.1. *Encyclopedias Brittanica and American.*

308 *Madison looked ahead:* Rutland, *James Madison,* 251.

309 *Among all the leaders:* Rutland, *James Madison,* 18–19.

309 *"Thou must come to me":* Brant, *The Fourth President.*

310 *letters they exchanged have been:* Brant, *The Fourth President,* 247.

310 *"If his theory of government":* Mitchell, *Alexander Hamilton,* Vol. 1, 412.

311 *"On this subject":* Kammen, *Origins of the American Constitution,* 99.

EPILOGUE

313 *"The Constitution is the soul":* Greenidge, *Greek Constitutional History.*

314 *Some of the fascinating:* Renfrew, *The Emergence of Civilization.*

314 *Athenians began keeping:* Gorman and Robinson, *Studies in Constitutions.*

316 *And since he was:* Madison's ties to Freemasonry are confirmed by Mr. Dustin Smith, Librarian of the Masonic Temple, Alexandria, Va. (703-683-2007, ext. 17).

316 *rules that working masons:* *Anderson's Constitutions,* May 1998, www.fm-fr.org.

316 *the admired Constitution of the Masons:* Rivista di Massonedria, *The Conventions of the Masons of Strasbourg,* 1459.

NOTE:

During his life, Madison gave numerous papers to his kin as mementos. After his death, Mrs. Dolley Payne Madison sold many of his papers to the federal government and made a longtime loan of some others to William Cabell Rivers, Madison's first biographer. Only a part of this loan was returned.

Separately, Mrs. Madison's son, John Payne Todd, withdrew many papers (probably without his mother's knowledge) and later turned them over to a Washington man, James C. McGuire. After McGuire's death, they were widely dispersed when his collection was sold in a series of public auctions. The Library of Congress has reassembled a good many, but not nearly all, of the papers that were in James Madison's possession at the time of his death.

Bibliography

Austin, Eric W. *Political Facts of the United States Since 1789*. Columbia U. Press.

Azimov, Isaac. *The Birth of the United States: 1763–1816*. Boston: Houghton Mifflin, 1974.

Bailey, Thomas A. *A Diplomatic History of the American People*. New York: F.S. Crofts & Co., 1941.

Berkin, Carol. *A Brilliant Solution*. New York: Harcourt, 2002.

Bowen, Catherine Drinker. *Miracle at Philadelphia*. Boston: LittleBrown & Co., 1966.

Brant, Irving. *The Fourth President: A Life of James Madison*. Indianapolis: Bobbs Merrill Co, 1970.

Carr, William G. *The Oldest Delegate*. Newark: University of Delaware Press, 1990.

Charleton, Ferris, and Ryan, eds. *Framers of the Constitution*. Washington, D.C.: National Archives and Records Administration, 1986.

Chernow, Ron. *Alexander Hamilton*. New York City: Penguin Press, 2004.

Cochran, Thomas C. *Pennsylvania: A History*. New York: W.W. Norton & Co., 1978.

Constitution of the United States of America (Annotated). Washington, D.C.: U.S. Government Printing Office, 1938.

Dohla, Johann Conrad. *A Herssian Diary of the American Revolution*. University of Oklahoma Press, 1990.

Dos Passos, John. *The Men Who Made the Nation*. New York: Doubleday, 1957.

Dudley, William, ed. *The Creation of the Constitution*. San Diego: Greenhaven Press, 1995.

Dumont, Dwight Lowell. *Antislavery: The Crusade for Freedom in America*. Ann Arbor: University of Michigan Press, 1961.

Encyclopedias Britannica and Americana.

Encyclopedia of American Political History. New York: Charles Scribner's Sons.

Ferling, John. *Setting the World Ablaze*. Oxford, NY: Oxford University Press, 2000.

Fiske, John. *The Critical Period of American History: 1783–1789*. Boston: Houghton Mifflin, 1888.

Foner, Philip S. *Basic Writings of Thomas Jefferson*. New York: Willey Book Company, 1944.

Foster, Theodore. *Minutes of the Convention Held at South Kingston, R.I. in March 1790*. Freeport, N.Y.: Book for Libraries Press, 1929.

Fowler, William. M. Jr., *Rebels Under Sail*. New York: Charles Scribner's Son, 1976.

Franklin, Benjamin. *Autobiography*.

Franklin, Benjamin. *Writings*, Vol. VII.

Ganyard, Robert L. *Emergence of North Carolina's Revolutionary State Government*. Raleigh, N.C: N. C. Department of Cultural Resources, August 2003.

Gerson, Noel B. *Light-Horse Harry*. Garden City, N.Y.: Doubleday & Co., 1966.

Greenidge, A.H.J. *Greek Constitutional History.* London: Macmillan & Co., Ltd, 1911.

Hamilton, Alexander. *Writings.* Vol. 9. New York: G.P. Putnam's Sons, 1904.

Irving, Washington. *Life of George Washington.* Tarrytown, N.Y: Sleepy Hollow Restoration, 1975.

James, Marquis. *Andrew Jackson: Portrait of a President.* New York: Garden City Publishing Co., 1837.

Jensen, Merrill et al., eds. *The Documentary History of the First Federal Elections: 1788–1790.* Four volumes. Madison, Wisconsin. 1976–1989.

Kammen, Michael. *The Origins of the American Constitution.* New York City: Viking Penguin, 1986.

Kane, Joseph Nathan. *Facts about the Presidents.* New York: H.W. Wilson Co., 1993.

Ketcham, Ralph. *James Madison.* Charlottesville: University of Virginia Press, 1990.

Koch and Peden. *The Life and Selected Writings of Thomas Jefferson.* New York: Random House, 1944.

Langguth, A. J. *Patriots.* New York: Simon & Schuster, 1988.

Larkin, Jack. *The Reshaping of Everyday Life.* New York: Harper & Row, 1988.

Levy, Leonard W. *Essays on the Making of the Constitution.* New York: Oxford University Press, 1987

Madison Papers. University of Chicago Press, 1962.

McCullogh, David. *John Adams.* New York: Simon & Schuster, 2000.

Mee, Charles L. *The Genius of the People.* New York: Harper & Row, 1987.

Mitchell, Broadus. *Alexander Hamilton: Youth to Maturity.* Vol. 1. New York: The Macmillan Company.

National Cyclopedia of American Biography. New York: James T. White & Co., 1899.

Newmyer, R. Kent. *John Marshall and the Heroic Age of the Supreme Court.* Baton Rouge: Louisiana State University Press, 2001.

Nye, Russell Blaine. *The Cultural Life of the New Nation: 1775–1830.* New York: Harper & Row, 1960.

Ousterhout. Anne M. *A State Divided.* New York: Greenwood Press, 1987.

Padover, Saul K. *The Mind of Alexander Hamilton,* New York: Harper & Bros., 1958.

Palmer, John McAuley. *General Von Steuben.* New Haven: Yale University Press, 1937.

Peters, William. *A More Perfect Union.* New York: Crown Publishers, 1987.

Peterson, Merrill D. *Madison Biography in His Own Words.* New York: Newsweek Books, 1974.

Historical Statistics of the United States: Colonial Times to 1970; Vol . 1, 1975.

Purcell, Sarah J. *The Early National Period.* Facts on File, 2004.

Randall, William Sterne. *George Washington.* New York: Henry Holt & Co., 1997.

Reader's Companion to American History. Boston: Houghton Mifflin Internet Program.

Renfrew, Colin. *The Emergence of Civilization.* London: Methuen & Co., Ltd., 1972.

Rivista di Massoneria. *The Conventions of the Masons of Strasbourg.* 1459.

Rutland, Robert A. *James Madison: The Founding Father.* New York: Macmillan, 1987.

Schachner, Nathan. *Alexander Hamilton: Nation Builder.*

Schott, Ben. *Schott's Original Miscellany.* New York: Bloomsbury, 2003.

Sheehan, Donald, ed. *The Making of American History.* New York: Dryden Press, 1954.

Sparks, Jared. *Writings of George Washington.* New York: Harper & Brothers, 1847.

St. John, Jeffrey. *Constitutional Journal.* Ottawa, Illinois: Jameson Books, Inc., 1987.

Thane, Elswyth. *Washington's Lady.* New York: Dodd Mead and Company, 1960.

Turpin, Colin. *British Government and Constitution.* London: Weidenfeld & Nicolson, 1985.

Van Doren, Carl. *The Great Rehearsal.* New York: The Viking Press, 1946.

Washington, George. *Diaries.* Boston: Mount Vernon Ladies with Houghton Mifflin.

Washington, George. *Writings.* Ed. Jared Sparks. New York: Harper & Bros., 1847.

Westcott, Thompson. *History of Philadelphia.* Brinton Coxe, 1886.

Wills, Garry. *James Madison.* New York: Henry Holt and Co.

Wirt, William. *Life of Patrick Henry.* Freeport, New York: Books for Libraries, 1970.

Zall, P.M. *Ben Franklin Laughing.* Los Angeles: University of California Press, 1991.

Index

Reader's Discussion Guide

We make the acquaintance of the two unlikeliest "revolutionaries" in world history, James Madison and Alexander Hamilton. The first is a small, pale, young man with an unimpressive voice and a shy manner. The second is an even younger immigrant orphan whose way to America was paid by benefactors, but whose lightning-fast mind first captivates New York then promotes him to a colonel's rank as General Washington's favorite aide. When the Revolutionary War ends, Madison and Hamilton discover each other and find that, with all their differences, they are firmly together in their opposition to the flimsy and bankrupt Confederate government. That government is barely holding the thirteen states together, but the strategies of Madison and Hamilton break the entrenched power of the states and make the people supreme.

1. You will notice that the author has done something quite different from any previous account of the Constitutional Convention. He wants the reader to sense the inner life of these young men who set out to overturn the existing government. And he wants you to weigh their personal qualities—good and bad—as the basis for their political success.

2. As you meet some of the leaders in their early years, what do you notice about them that might make you think them capable of being "revolutionaries" who would try to overturn the old government and create a new one?

3. After reading the first few chapters, which character did you think of as likeliest to control the Convention's great test of brains and wills?

4. Compare the early training and careers of Madison, Gouverneur Morris, James Wilson, and Abraham Baldwin. Do you agree that their accomplishments point to a fine education as an absolute necessity for success in that era? If so, what are your thoughts about Hamilton, who was mostly self-taught?

5. You have read that in the first months of the Revolutionary War, the British suddenly were willing to drop most of their demands and offer the colonies much more self-government. Do you think Americans should have given this idea consideration, or would such a compromise have led to a huge disappointment?

6. Some of the Tories who preferred to remain with the British Empire were people who simply believed in loyalty to their king. Do you feel it was right for them to lose virtually all their property for having chosen the losing side?

7. Do you think most of the Convention delegates were wrong in believing that Americans were unprepared for the responsibilities of true self government? Or is it possible that the Constitution itself gave the people a feeling of responsibility that lifted their performance?

8. How important do you believe George Washington was in bringing about the final result? Was he, in his quiet way, more a shaper of events than he let anyone see? Or had he become essentially a figurehead, allowing the younger men to use his prestige for their own purposes?